A Man of Letters

A Man of Letters

SELECTED ESSAYS

V. S. PRITCHETT

CHATTO & WINDUS
LONDON

First published in 1985 by
Chatto & Windus . The Hogarth Press
40 William IV Street
London WC2N 4DF

British Library Cataloguing in Publication Data
Pritchett, V.S.
A man of letters: selected essays.
I. Title
082   PR6031.R7
ISBN 0 7011 3971 4

Printed in Great Britain by
Redwood Burn Ltd,
Trowbridge, Wiltshire

For My Wife

CONTENTS

PREFACE

If, as they say, I am a Man of Letters I come, like my fellows, at the tail-end of a long and once esteemed tradition in English and American writing. We have no captive audience. We do not teach. We are rarely academics though we owe a great debt to scholars. We earn our bread and butter by writing for the periodicals that have survived. If we have one foot in Grub Street we write to be readable and to engage the interest of what Virginia Woolf called 'the common reader'. We do not lay down the law, but we do make a stand for the reflective values of a humane culture. We care for the printed word in a world that nowadays is dominated by the camera and by scientific, technological, sociological doctrine. We still believe, with Dostoevsky, that 'without art a man might well feel that his life was not worth living'. We ourselves have written novels, short stories, biographies, works of travel. Some of us are poets. And we know that literature is rooted in the daily life of any society but that it also springs out of literature itself. The difference between the traditional Man of Letters and us survivors today is that what we have to say must be done in a couple of columns whereas the Victorians – look at Henry James – could go on in the Monthlies and Quarterlys for dozens of pages. When, at the beginning of World War II I was asked to write a page under the title of Books in General, for the *New Statesman*, paper was rationed in Great Britain and I was soon cut down from 1850 to 1800 words. It was a training in the allusive and laconic style that has remained with me for the fifty years I have given to writing essays such as these in this book.

This selection is taken from pages I have contributed to the *New Statesman*, the *New Yorker*, and the *New York Review of Books* and some from my first book of essays during the War, now out of print. It is strange to look back at the early ones and to remember reading, say, the four volumes of *Clarissa* in one week or perhaps *Gil Blas*,

Balzac or Turgenev the next, as I travelled by slow trains packed with troops (and from air-raid warning to air-raid warning), to shipyards and factories in the North to report about 'the war effort' and to write between the hours of my comic duties with the local militia and fire-watching. Why was I asked to write on these authors? Contemporary writing had stopped. We were left with the major and the minor masters of the past. Air-raid shelters for the mind? Not at all. These authors, we found – to use a phrase common at the time – had also lived in 'times of transition', in or 'between wars'. They were embalmed in their genius but had lived, as we did, in a changing society. Look back and we could see the rogue turning into the Puritan and the Puritan revealing a hidden and even exuberant imagination. We could see Scott evoking a splitting society. We saw literature growing out of life and the common experience. I had fortunately read such books when I was a youth. I had also earned my living in trades that had brought me close to people more diverse than the literary. I was not a product of Eng.Lit. I had never been taught and, even now, I am shocked to hear that literature is 'taught'. I found myself less a critic than an imaginative traveller or explorer – a slow reader too – moving from sentence to sentence, pausing to see the view and the writer arriving at the clinching detail. I had a double contact with human nature, first as a writer crossing frontiers in Ireland, France, Spain and the Americas and as a traveller in the use of writing in these countries. I was travelling in literature.

V. S. PRITCHETT

HENRY FIELDING

An Anatomy of Greatness

There are two books which are the perfect medicine for the present time: Voltaire's *Candide* and Fielding's *Jonathan Wild*. They deal with our kind of news but with this advantage over contemporary literature: the news is already absorbed, assumed and digested. We see our situation at a manageable remove. This is an important consolation and, on the whole, *Jonathan Wild* is the more specific because the narrower and more trenchant book. Who, if not ourselves, are the victims of what are called 'Great Men'? Who can better jump to the hint that the prig or cut-purse of Newgate and the swashbuckler of Berchtesgaden are the same kind of man and that Cæsar and Alexander were morally indistinguishable from the gang leaders, sharpers, murderers, pickpockets from whom Mr Justice Fielding, in later years, was to free the City of London? Europe has been in the hands of megalomaniacs for two decades. Tyranny abroad, corruption at home – that recurrent theme of the eighteenth-century satirists who were confronted by absolute monarchy and the hunt for places – is our own. Who are we but the good – with a small middle-class 'g' – and who are 'they' but the self-elected 'leaders' and 'the Great'? And *Jonathan Wild* has the attraction of a great *tour de force* which does not shatter us because it remains, for all its realism, on the intellectual plane. Where Swift, in contempt, sweeps us out of the very stables; where Voltaire advises us not to look beyond our allotments upon the wilderness humanity has left everywhere on a once festive earth, Fielding is ruthless only to the brain. Our heads are scalped by him but soul and body are left alive. He is arbitrary but not destructive. His argument that there is an incompatibility between greatness and goodness is an impossible one, but of the eighteenth century's three scourgers of mankind he is the least egotistical and the most moral. He has not destroyed the world; he has merely turned it upside down as a polished dramatist will force a play out of a paradox:

... contradicting the obsolete doctrines of a Set of Simple Fellows called, in Derision, Sages or Philosophers, who have endeavoured as much as possible to confound the Ideas of Greatness and Goodness, whereas no two Things can possibly be more distinct from each other. For Greatness consists in bringing all Manner of Mischief on Mankind, and Goodness in removing it from them.

Jonathan Wild is a paradox sustained with, perhaps the strain, but above all, with the decisiveness, flexibility and exhilaration of a scorching trumpet call which does not falter for one moment and even dares very decorative and difficult variations on the way to its assured conclusion. When we first read satire we are aware of reading against the whole current of our beliefs and wishes, and until we have learned that satire is anger laughing at its own futility, we find ourselves protesting and arguing silently against the author. This we do less, I think, in reading *Jonathan Wild* than with *Candide* or *Gulliver*. If there is any exhaustion in *Jonathan Wild* it does not come from the tussle of our morality with his. There is no moral weariness. If we tire it is because of the intellectual effort of reversing the words 'great' and 'good' as the eye goes over the page. Otherwise it is a young man's book, very vain of its assumptions and driven on with masterly nonchalance.

To the rigidity of his idea Fielding brought not only the liveliness of picaresque literature but, more important, his experience as a playwright. Of its nature satire deals in types and artifices and needs the schooling of the dramatist, who can sweep a scene off the moment the point is made and who can keep his nimble fingers on a complicated plot. Being concerned with types, satire is in continual need of intrigue and movement; it needs tricks up the sleeve and expertness in surprise. We are distracted in *Jonathan Wild* between pleasure in his political references (the pointed one on the quarrels between the gangsters about the style of their hats for example, which Wild settles with the genius of a dictator), and the dexterity of the author. 'Great men are lonely': one of the best scenes in the book, one fit to stand beside Wild's wonderful quarrel with his wife Tishy when he calls her a bitch, sets off the farce of Wild's soliloquy in the boat. Put adrift in an open boat by the Captain who has rescued Heartfree's wife from Wild's attempt at rape, Wild has his 'black Friday' and muses on the loneliness of 'the Great', their fear of death and their unhappiness. Since death is inevitable, Wild cries, why not die now? A man of action, for ever acting to an audience if only an imaginary one, he staggers us by at once throwing himself into the sea. Were we wrong? Was he courageous after all? We knew that a crook lives on gestures, that a show of toughness is all – but were we misreading him? Down comes the curtain, the chapter ends. Its dramatic effect is enormous, quite beyond the reach of the picaresque novelists who depend on the convolutions of intrigue alone. Among the satirists, only Voltaire, another writer for the stage, was capable of Fielding's scene; Swift was always willing to let a situation ease off into ironical discussion. And then, up goes Fielding's curtain again: Wild does not die. He is saved. He is in a boat once more. Saved by one of those disillusioning miracles of fiction? Not at all. He is back in his own boat. *He swam back to it.* Philosophy had told him to die, but Nature, whom he knew had designed him to be Great, told him not to be such a fool. That is a masterstroke.

Such cross-ruffing is the heart of farce and of the ordinary literature of roguery. But as Wild picks the pockets of his accomplices, double-crosses the card-sharping Count, swindles and is swindled in turn, each act shows a further aspect of his character and is a new chapter in the anatomy of Greatness. It has been said that Fielding's common sense and his low opinion that human beings were moved chiefly by self-interest, restricted his imagination. This may be so, though the greater restriction was to his sensibility. In the light of our present painful knowledge of Great Men of action we are not likely to think the portrait of Wild unimaginative simply because Fielding takes an unheroic view. There is the episode of the jewels. The Count who, with Wild, has swindled Heartfree over the casket of jewels, has double-crossed his partner by substituting paste for the stolen treasure. Worse still, Tishy whom Wild intends to seduce by the gift of the casket, has worked in a pawnbroker's and knows paste when she sees it. Wild is left to another soliloquy, to the sadness of Berchtesgaden or neo-Imperial Rome. 'The Great' are always sad:

How vain is human Greatness! . . . How unhappy is the state of Priggism! How impossible for Human Prudence to foresee and guard against each circumvention! . . . In this a Prig is more unhappy than any other: a cautious man may in a crowd, preserve his own Pockets by keeping his hands in them; but while he employs his Hands in another's pockets, how shall he be able to defend his own? Where is his Greatness? I answer in his Mind; 'Tis the inward Glory, the secret Consciousness of doing great and wonderful Actions, which can alone support the truly Great Man, whether he be a

Conqueror, a Tyrant, a Minister or a Prig. These must bear him up against the private Curse and public Imprecation, and while he is hated and detested by all Mankind, must make him inwardly satisfied with himself. For what but some such inward satisfaction as this could inspire Men possessed of Wealth, of Power, of every human Blessing, which Pride, Luxury, or Avarice could desire, to forsake their Homes, abandon Ease and Repose, and, at the Expense of Riches, Pleasures, at the Price of Labour and Hardship, and at the Hazard of all that Fortune hath liberally given them could send them at the Head of a Multitude of *Prigs* called an Army, to molest their Neighbours, to introduce Rape, Rapine, Bloodshed and every kind of Misery on their own Species? What but some such glorious Appetite of Mind. . . .

Intoxicating stuff. The eighteenth century's attack on absolutism, its cry of Liberty, its plea for the rational, the measured, and even the conventional culminated – in what? Napoleon. And then democracy. It is painful to listen to the flying Prigs, to democracy's *Jonathan Wild*. Was the moral view of human nature mistaken? Is the Absolute People as destructive as the Absolute King? Is the evil not in the individual, but in society? We rally to the eighteenth-century cry of 'Liberty'; it is infectious, hotter indeed than it sounds today. We reflect that those good, settled, educated, middle-class men of the time of Queen Anne owed their emancipation to a Tyrant who burned half Ireland, killed his King and went in private hysterical dread of the devil. Under that smooth prose, under that perfect deploying of abstractions, the men of the eighteenth century seem always to be hiding a number of frightening things that are neither smooth nor perfect. There is the madness of Swift, there is the torment of Wesley. Or was Fielding imagining the paradise of the anarchists where our natural goodness enables us to dispense with leaders? Sitting under the wings of the flying Prigs, we observe the common, indeed the commonplace, non-combatant man, behaving with a greatness which appears to require no leader but merely the prompting of sober and decent instincts.

Of course if the Great are wicked, the good are fools. Look at the Heartfrees! What a couple! But here again if you have made your head ache over Fielding's impossible theme, it is cured at once by the felicities to which the Heartfrees drive Fielding's invention. The letters which Heartfree gets from his impecunious or disingenuous debtors are a perfect collection; and Mrs Heartfree's sea adventures in which there is hardly a moment between Holland and Africa when she is not on the point of losing her honour, are not so much padding but give a touch of spirit to her shopkeeping virtues and also serve the purpose of satirising the literature of travel. It is hard on Mrs Heartfree; perhaps Fielding was insensitive. Without that insensibility we would have missed the adventure with the monster who was 'as large as Windsor Castle', an episode which reminds us that the spirit of the nine o'clock news was already born in the seventeenhundreds: 'I take it to be the strangest Instance of that Intrepidity, so justly remarked in our Seamen, which can be found on Record. In a Wood then, one of our Mucketeers coming up to the Beast, as he lay on the Ground and with his Mouth wide open, marched directly down his Throat.'

He had gone down to shoot the Monster in the heart. And we should have missed another entrancing sight. Mrs Heartfree perceived a fire in the desert and thought at first she was approaching human habitation: '. . . but on nearer Approach, we perceived a very Beautiful Bird just expiring in the Flames. This was none other than the celebrated Phœnix.' The sailors threw it back into the Fire so that it 'might follow its own Method of propagating its Species'.

Yes, the Heartfrees would have a lot to talk about afterwards. There is a charm in the artlessness of Mrs Heartfree, if Heartfree is a bit of a stodge; one can understand why she introduced just a shade of suspense in the account of how she always managed to save her virtue at the last minute.

(1941)

SAMUEL RICHARDSON

Clarissa

The modern reader of Richardson's *Clarissa* emerges from his experience exhausted, exalted and bewildered. The book is, I fancy, the longest novel in the English language; it is the one most crowded with circumstantial detail; it is written in the most dilatory of narrative methods, i.e. in the form of letters. It is a novel written through a microscope; it is a monstrosity, a minute and inordinate act of prolonged procrastination. And the author himself is a monster. That a man like Samuel Richardson should write one of the great European novels is one of those humiliating frolics in the incidence of genius. The smug, juicy, pedestrian little printer from Derbyshire, more or less unlettered, sits down at the age of fifty and instructs young girls in the art of managing their virtue to the best advantage. Yet, ridiculous as *Pamela* is, her creator disarms criticism by a totally new ingredient in the novel: he knows how to make the reader weep. And, stung by the taunts of the educated writers of his time, Richardson calmly rises far above *Pamela* when he comes to the story of Clarissa Harlowe; he sets the whole continent weeping. Rousseau and even Goethe bow to him and take out their handkerchiefs; the vogue of sensibility, the first shoots of the Romantic movement, spring from the pool of Richardson's pious tears like the grateful and delicate trees of an oasis. Yet there he is, plump, prosaic, the most middling of middling men, and so domestically fussy that even his gift of weeping hardly guarantees that he will be a major figure. Is there not some other strain in this dull and prodigiously painstaking little man? There is. Samuel Richardson was mad.

I do not mean that Richardson was a lunatic. I do not mean he was mad as Swift was mad. At first sight, an immeasurable smugness, an endlessly pettifogging normality seem to be the outer skin of Richardson's character. We know, as I have already said, that from his youth he was an industrious and timid young man who was, for some reason or other, used by young women who wanted him to write their love letters. Profoundly sentimental, he sat like some pious old cook in her kitchen, giving advice to the kitchen maids, and when he came to write novels he was merely exalting this practical office. He lived vicariously like some sedentary lawyer who has to argue the disasters of other people's lives letter by letter, but who himself never partakes. Genteel, he is, nevertheless, knowing; prim and cosy, he is, nevertheless, the victim of that powerful cult of the will, duty and conscience by which Puritanism turned life and its human relations into an incessant war. There is no love in Puritanism; there is a struggle for power. Who will win the daily battle of scruple and conscience – Pamela or the young squire; Clarissa or Lovelace? And yet what is urging Richardson to this battle of wills? What is it that the Puritan cannot get out of his mind, so that it is a mania and obsession? It is sex. Richardson is mad about sex.

His is the madness of Paul Pry and Peeping Tom. I said just now that *Clarissa* is a novel written under the microscope; really it is a novel written about the world as one sees it through the keyhole. Prurient and obsessed by sex, the prim Richardson creeps on tip-toe nearer and nearer, inch by inch, to that vantage point; he beckons us on, pausing to make every kind of pious protestation, and then nearer and nearer he creeps again, delaying, arguing with us in whispers, working us up until we catch the obsession too. What are we going to see when we get there? The abduction, the seduction, the lawful deflowering of a virgin in marriage are not enough for him. Nothing short of the rape of Clarissa Harlowe by a man determined on destroying her can satisfy Richardson's phenomenal day-dream with its infinite delays.

The principle of procrastinated rape is said to be the ruling one in all the great best-sellers. It was in Richardson's genius that he was able to elevate the inner conflict of the passions and the will to an abstract level, so that the struggle of Clarissa and Lovelace becomes a universal battle-piece; and, in doing this, Richardson was able to paint it with the highly finished realism of the Dutch painters. At the beginning one might simply be reading yet another novel of intrigue, which just goes on and on; and but for the incredible suspense in the narrative I think many readers must have given up *Clarissa* by the end of the first volume. It is not until the third and fourth volumes are reached, when Richardson transposes his intrigue into the sustained and weeping music, the romantic tragedy of Clarissa's rape and long preparation for death, that we get his measure. She dies piously, yet like a Shakespearean waking remorse in all around her by the starkness of her defeat. At the beginning we are not prepared for this greatness in Clarissa; even in that last volume we are often uncertain of her real stature. It is not easy for virginity to become Virtue. Would she be anything without Lovelace? And yet, we know, she is the crown upon Lovelace's head. He too becomes tragic under her judgment as she becomes tragic by his act. These two reflect glory upon each other, like saint and devil. But in the first volume there is no difficulty about deciding who is the greater as a character or as an abstract conception. Lovelace has her beaten hands down. A practical and languid correspondence wakes up when he takes pen in hand. Anna Howe, the 'pert' friend, makes circles round her. Arabella, with her nose out of joint, is livelier comedy. The scheming brother, the gouty father with his paroxysms, the supplicating and fluttering mother, and the endearing uncles with their unendearing family solidarity, make a greater mark on our minds than the all-too-articulate Clarissa does. Our one hope is that witty Miss Howe is right when she teases Clarissa with maidenly self-deception. 'The frost piece,' as Lovelace called her, looks exactly like one of those fascinating prudes whose minds are an alphabet that must be read backwards. But no; though she will enchant us when she is rattled, with cries like 'Oh, my Nancy, what shall I do with this Lovelace?' her course and her motives are clear to her; and we begin the slow and painful discovery of a virtue which finds no exhilaration except in scruple. We face an inexhaustible determination, and this is exhausting to contemplate, for Clarissa is as interested in the organisation of human motives as Richardson himself; and he insinuates himself in her character so thoroughly, niggling away with his 'ifs' and his 'buts', that he overwhelms her, as Flaubert overwhelmed Madame Bovary.

Still this does not take from the drama of Clarissa's situation, and does, in fact, increase the suspense of it. If we skip – and of course we do, looking up the letters in the obliging synopsis – we do not, as in other novels, find ourselves caught out by an overlooked sub-plot; we are back in the main situation. Will the family relent? Will Lovelace abduct, marry, rape or reform? There's hardly a sub-plot worth mentioning in this huge novel. It follows the labyrinth of a single theme. And though we turn to Anna Howe for glimpses of common sense, and for a wit to enliven the glum belligerents of what

Lovelace – always a psychologist and nearly a Freudian – called 'the Harlowe dunghill' with its wills and deeds of settlement, we see in Clarissa's stand something more than a virtuous daughter bullied by her parents. She is a lawyer in family morals, and in Lovelace's too; but she is the first heroine in English fiction to stand against the family. Richardson called them 'the embattled phalanx', and in *Clarissa* he goes to the heart of the middle-class situation; money, accretion of estate, the rise in the world, the desire to found a family, in conflict with the individual soul. She and Lovelace complement each other here. She thinks her family ought not to do evil to her, yet takes their evil upon herself; she is not a rebel but is tricked and driven into becoming an outcast and at last a saint. Like Lovelace, she has asked too much, 'for people who allow nothing will be granted nothing; in other words, those who aim at carrying too many points will not be able to carry any'. Yes, and those who put up their price by the device of reluctance invite the violence of the robber. By setting such a price upon herself, Clarissa represents that extreme of puritanism which desires to be raped. Like Lovelace's, her sexuality is really violent, insatiable in its wish for destruction.

Lovelace is Richardson's extravagant triumph. How did such a burning and tormented human being come out of that tedious little printer's mind? In the English novel Lovelace is one of the few men of intellect who display an intellect which is their own and not patently an abstract of their author's intellectual interests. He is half-villain, half-god, a male drawn to the full, and he dominates English fiction. He is all the more male for the feminine strains in his character: his hatred of women, his love of intrigue, his personal vanity, his captiousness and lack of real humility. A very masculine novelist and moralist like Fielding is too much a sanguine man of the world to catch a strain like that. And how Lovelace can write! When Clarissa's letters drag, like sighing Sunday hymns, or nag at us in their blameless prose, like the Collect for the day, the letters of Lovelace crackle and blaze with both the fire and the inconsequence of life. His words fly back and forth, throwing out anecdotes and the characters of his friends, with wonderful transitions of mood. In one paragraph he is writing a set apostrophe to Clarissa, full of longing and half-way to repentance. He shakes the mood off like a man who is drunk with grief and throws off this description of his gouty old kinsman:

And here (pox of his fondness for me; it happens at a very bad time) he makes me sit hours together entertaining him with my rogueries (a pretty amusement for a sick man!) and yet, whenever he has the gout, he prays night and morning with his chaplain. But what must *his* notions of religion be, who, after he has nosed and mumbled over his responses, can give a sigh or groan of satisfaction, as if he thought he had made up with Heaven; and return with a new appetite to my stories? – encouraging them, by shaking his sides with laughing at them, and calling me a sad fellow, in such an accent as shows he takes no small delight in his kinsman.

The old peer has been a sinner in his day, and suffers for it now; a sneaking sinner, *sliding*, rather than *rushing* into vices, for fear of his reputation; or rather, for fear of detection, and positive proof; for this sort of fellow, Jack, has no real regard for reputation. Paying for what he never had, and never daring to rise to the joy of an enterprise at first hand, which bring him within view of a tilting or the honour of being considered as the principal man in a court of justice.

To see such a Trojan as this just dropping into the grave which I hoped ere this would have been dug, and filled up with him; crying out with pain and grunting with weakness; yet in the same moment crack his leathern face into a horrible laugh, and call a young sinner charming varlet, encoring him as formerly he used to do the Italian eunuchs; what a preposterous, what an unnatural adherence to old habits.

Or there is the awful description of that old procuress, Mrs Sinclair, a horror out of Rowlandson, who advances upon Clarissa on the night of the rape, when all Richardson's fascination with carnal horror breaks out. There is a double terror in it, because Lovelace himself is writing as if trying to drive evil out of his mind by a picture of evils still greater:

The old dragon straddled up to her, with her arms kemboed again, her eyebrows erect like the bristles upon a hog's back, and, scowling over her shortened nose, more than half hid her ferret eyes. Her mouth was distorted. She pouted out her blubber-lips, as if to bellow up wind and sputter into her horse-nostrils, and her chin was curdled, and more than usually prominent with passion.

The temperate, lawyer-like mind of Richardson does not prepare one for passages like this. When there is matter-of-factness in the eighteenth century, one expects it to be as regular as Pope's couplets were. But Richardson is not consistent. In the sheer variety of their styles the letters in this novel are astonishing. The bovine uncles, the teasing parenthetical Miss Howe, the admonitory Belford, the curt Colonel Morden, heading for his duel, the climbing neurotic brother whose descendants were no doubt in the British Union of Fascists, all have their styles, and they are as distinctive as Lovelace's or Clarissa's. Richardson is the least flat, the most stereoscopic novelist of an age which ran the plain or formal statement to death in the end.

Another point: he is a master of indirect narrative. We are shown scenes at second hand, for the epistolary method requires it so; and we become used to a sort of memoranda of talk and action which will tire our inward eye because our judgment is called upon at the same time. So there are many reported scenes which are relative failures, for example, the early and rather confusing ones between Clarissa and her mother. One has a muddled impression of two hens flying up in the air at each other and scattering their feathers. Yet even in this kind of scene Richardson can, at times, write talk which is direct and put action wonderfully under our eye. The scene of the rape is tremendous in this respect; and so is the awful picture of the brothel when Mrs Sinclair breaks her leg and the harridans come out in their night attire; and there is the comic, savage picture of Lovelace defeating the attempt of his family to try him. But where Richardson shook off the slavery of his own method is shown at its best, I think, in Belford's letter describing the prison scene where the two prostitutes offer to bail Clarissa out:

'We are surprised at your indifference, Miss Harlowe. Will you not write to any of your friends?'
'No.'
'Why, you don't think of tarrying *here* always.'
'I shall not live always.'

Even in those few lines one sees Richardson advancing his inner narrative and, if one continues this conversation, one also sees him patiently and unerringly preserving character. One might almost say that prolix as it was, his method was economical, given his chosen end. The slowness comes from an excess of examination, not an excess of words. No prose has fewer redundancies.

We come to the death scene. The torment of Lovelace pacing his horse past the gate of the house he dare not enter, though Clarissa lies dying within, is not rhetorical. It is defiant as fits a being so saturnine, it is in the mind as becomes a man of intellect, it is the changeable, imploring, raging madness of a clever mind that has met its conqueror. Lovelace is a villain no man hates, because he is a man. He is candid, if he is vain. He can argue like Iago or debate like Hamlet, and in between send a purse of a few guineas to a rogue who has helped him to his present catastrophe. It is strange to think of him – the only Don Juan in English fiction and done to the last Freudian detail. Clarissa dies like a swan amid the formal melody of a prose into which Richardson fell without affectation.

Her breath being very short, she desired another pillow. Having two before, this made her, in a manner, sit up in her bed; and she spoke then with more distinctness; and seeing us greatly concerned, forgot her own stutterings to comfort us; and a charming lecture she gave us, though a brief one, upon the happiness of a timely preparation, and upon the hazards of a late repentance, when the mind, as she observed, was so much weakened, as well as the body, as to render a poor soul hardly able to contend with its natural infirmities.

It is a strong test of the illusion that Richardson has cast upon us, that we think of Lovelace like a shadow cast upon Clarissa as she dies; and of Clarissa rather than of Lovelace when *he* appears. These lives are known by their absences; they are inextricable, tangled in the thousands of words they have spoken about each other, and are swept away at last into other people's words.

(1943)

LAURENCE STERNE

Tristram Shandy

A little of Sterne goes a long way – as long as nearly two hundred years, for his flavour never dies in the English novel. It is true we cannot live on tears, fancy cakes and curry. But, take him out of the English tradition; point out that George Eliot, D. H. Lawrence, Conrad – the assembled moral genius of the English novel – ignore him; explain that he is not Henry James; despise him because he created 'characters', a form of dramatic person out of fashion for a generation or more – and still his insinuating touch of nature comes through. He is obvious in figures as different as Thackeray and Firbank; and *Ulysses* is sometimes thought of as the *Tristram Shandy* of our century. We see the releasing hand of Sterne in those instances where the English comic genius leaves the usual moral territory of satire or the physical world of knockabout, and finds a third region which is neither pure intellect, pure fantasy nor pure imagination and which is indeed an evasion of all three. To call this the eccentric strain explains nothing; it is well known that the English are eccentric. Sterne – it is better to say – is mad, using the word as we commonly do in England to avoid facing and judging people who themselves are engaged in not facing what they are really up to. Eccentricity is, in fact, practical madness. It is resorted to, Henry Adams said in his severe and shrewd New England way, by those who are up to something shameful or stupid or muddleheaded. And, in England, most of us are.

It is possible that the comedy, half artifice and half nature, which we extract from our 'madness' is fundamentally stupid; there is an excessive and stupid streak in Ben Jonson where this comedy abounds. All the same we have sometimes raised stupidity to the level of a fine art. The 'madness' of Sterne, the hostile critic might say, is a practical device for foisting upon the reader a brilliant but shameless egotism, an inexhaustible selfishness and a clever smirking insincerity. Compare his shamelessness with Boswell's: the Scotsman is wanton, transparent and artless, haunted by fear of the Presbyterian devil, whereas we can be sure the devil himself was afraid that the half-Irish Sterne would drag him into bad company. Boswell calculated nothing or, at any rate, nothing right, except his money. Sterne calculated eloquently. Constantly he reckoned up how much he was going to feel before he felt it; even calculated his words so subtly that he made a point of not ending half his sentences and preferred an innuendo to a fact. He relied on the reader's imagination. I notice that in the sympathetic and unprejudiced inquiry that Mr Peter Quennell made into Sterne's character in *Four Portraits* – and this contains the most illuminating study of Sterne that I know of – there is the suggestion that he was the first to use the word 'sentiment' in our imaginative literature and to found the modern meaning of the sentimental. I do not know whether this is so, but it ought to be. For Sterne was a sentimentalist, because his imagination was morbidly quick to impose the idea of a feeling, its image-provoking words and its *ambiance* long before the feeling was evoked. He could talk his heart into beating. He could talk tears into his eyes. Or so we feel as we read him; never sure whether this sociable, good-natured, too impressionable man is sincere or not.

One can see Sterne's temperament at work in the account of the beginnings of the Widow Wadman's love of Uncle Toby. The widow's passion was not born until she had seen him among her things in her own house:

> There is nothing in it out of doors and in broad daylight, where a woman has a power, physically speaking, of viewing a man in more lights than one – but here, for her soul, she can see him in no light without mixing something of her own goods and chattels along with him – till by reiterated acts of such combinations he gets foisted into her inventory –

This may be a universal truth about love, but down to the last *double entendre* – and, above all, because of it – the fancy encases the feeling as it did in the parallel circumstances of Sterne's courtship of his wife. His passion warmed when she let her lodgings to him in her absence.

'One solitary plate,' he wrote, 'one knife, one fork, one glass! I gave a thousand pensive penetrating looks at the chair thou hadst so often graced, in those quiet and sentimental repasts – then laid down my knife and fork, and took out my handkerchief, and clapped it across my face, and wept like a child.' Obviously one who felt so strongly for a chair could live very well alone in the comforts of his own imagination.

Alone: it is that word which rises at last to the mind after it has been dragged for miles at the heels of the bolting, gasping fancies and verbosities of *Tristram Shandy*. The gregarious, egotistical Sterne is alone; garrulously, festively and finally alone. If there is one thing he likes better – again, in literature as in life – than the accident of meeting, it is the agreement to part. One can put this down, at a guess, to his severance from his detested mother. In *Tristram Shandy* it is notable and important that all the characters are solitaries. Mr Shandy and his wife, Dr Slop, Uncle Toby and the Corporal live shut up in the asylum of their own imaginations, oysters itching voluptuously upon the pearl within. Mr Shandy silences his brother with his philosophical systems and his cross-references, never sees a fact but he recedes from it into abstraction, and is determined that the palaverings of the search for Truth shall have one end only: that he gets his own way in his own home. The blameless Uncle Toby sits in his innocence, conducting his imaginary campaigns, short of speech and blinking at the world. Mrs Shandy hurriedly agrees with her husband; nobody knows what is on *her* mind. Dr Slop is shut up in the horror of his pendulous belly and Corporal Trim does what he's told, loves his master, but lives by his memories of his poor brother Tom in Lisbon. Habit rather than communication keeps them all happily together. They are bound by ennui, grey days and indolence. But, read the dialogue: it is a collection of monologues. True, Uncle Toby and the Corporal have occasional awkward interchanges, but the general impression is that no one answers serious questions and that they know one another far too well to listen. In family life there is nothing to do about the hard core of the human ego, but to accept it. The indecencies and the double meanings of Sterne, if anything, intensify the solitude; they provoke private reflection and erect barriers of silent lecherous satisfaction. How can the Widow discover where Uncle Toby was wounded, when he can only answer: 'In the siege of Namur.' Sterne displays the egotist's universe: life is a personal dream.

Those who deny Sterne talent of the highest order and think of him as outside our tradition, must strip away half our tradition and character first. Sterne's discovery of the soliloquising man, the life lived in fantasy, is the source of what is called the 'great character' in the English novel, a kind which only Russian fiction, with its own feeling for 'madness' in the 19th century, has enjoyed. *Tristram Shandy* is the inspiration of the solitaries of Dickens, the idea-ridden people in Peacock and many others in our literature; they are not literary theories but comic abstractions from a faculty of life. It must be admitted that Mr Shandy and Uncle Toby are both very stupid men; they are funny because Sterne is so much cleverer than either. He plays tunes on them. They are also bores – always the richest game for the comic instinct. If we compare them with other great bores, like Bouvard and Pécuchet, the Shandys have the advantage of not riding their hobby-horses to any purpose. They prove nothing either to us or to themselves, but illustrate rather the vegetable inertia of the fanciful life and display the inhabiting of one's temperament as the most sensible thing to be engaged in. Every dog to his basket. Even in the torpor of their domesticity, the imagination can beguile.

The bother was that Sterne was a bore himself, as boring in his way as Mr Shandy is. That Irish loquacity which he got from his mother and his early years in Tipperary had deluded him. He has that terrible, professional, non-stop pedantry of the Irish. One feels, sometimes, that one has been cornered by some brilliant Irish drunk, one whose mind is incurably suggestible. Although we have a hypnotised picture of Uncle Toby's dubious fortifications they take on, in our minds after an hour or two, the heavy appearance of those surly battlements one sees during the migraine. *Tristram Shandy* must be the most put-down book in English literature. One can respond, of course, to the elaborate cunning of its counter-point; there is method in the anarchy. But the book is a collection of fragments in which every fragment sticks: Mr Shandy fallen geometrically with grief in his bed; Uncle Toby dazed by the fire; the pipe stem snapping as the child is born upstairs; the ludicrous discussion about the landboat, with its foreshadowing of Peacock; Bridget putting Mrs Wadman to bed; Mr and Mrs Shandy on the 'bed of justice' with the inevitable chamber pot sticking out from under the valance while they talk of putting young Tristram into breeches; the pretty picture of Brother Tom going into his sausage shop in Lisbon where there was a Negress driving off fleas with a feather.

Sterne has a genius for mosaic; for being any self he has decided to be; for living in the effervescence of his nature. The sentimentalist is a cynic, naturally: 'Love, you see, is not so much a Sentiment as a Situation, into which a man enters, as my brother Toby would do, in a *corps* – no matter whether he loves the service or no – being once in it, he acts as he did. . . .'

Many have wondered at the feverish receptivity of his eye and some have seen the dread of death – for he was a consumptive – in his determination to look at each event through a microscope as if enlarging it would slow the course of time. That Sterne's sensibility to the passage of time was unusual is certain; he seemed to see each minute as it passed, and to be eager to hold it with a word. But others – of whom Mr Quennell is one – see in his minuteness the training of the painter. Every sight, every thought was a physical model. There can be no doubt that he broke into the stream of consciousness and was the first to splash about there – in rather shallow water; there can also be no doubt that he was never going to commit himself to anything deeper. It was enough that one thing led to another and that the sensibility was ready for the change. It was Sterne's wife, a woman heavily committed to housework and a bad temper, who, for a time, went out of her mind.

(1943)

THOMAS DAY

The Crank

If we are to define the spirit of the eighteenth century by its favourite word, I think the word 'man' or 'mankind' even more than words like 'order' or 'reason', is the one we ought to choose. Man dominates the minds and ultimately the hearts of the eighteenth-century writers, where God had dominated the mind of the seventeenth century. After the battles, the factions, the treasons, the private and partisan faiths of the religious wars, the men of the eighteenth century were concerned to impose an order on that chaos, to seek the common denominator, to reassemble the judgment of divided human nature. The warring consciences were to be fused once more into an amenable moral animal with all his greatness and all his folly. The lines of Pope proclaim him:

> Know then thyself, presume not God to scan,
> The proper study of Mankind is Man.
> Plac'd on this isthmus of a middle state,
> A Being darkly wise, and rudely great:
> With too much knowledge for the Sceptic side,
> With too much weakness for the stoic's pride,
> He hangs between; in doubt to act or rest;
> In doubt to deem himself a God, or Beast;
> In doubt his Mind or Body to prefer;
> Born but to die, and reas'ning but to err;
> Alike in ignorance, his reason such,
> Whether he thinks too little or too much:
> Chaos of Thought and Passion, all confus'd;
> Still by himself abus'd or disabus'd;
> Created half to rise, and half to fall;
> Great lord of all things, yet a prey to all;
> Sole judge of Truth, in endless Error hurl'd:
> The glory, jest, and riddle of the world!

And Man is not yet trapped in our later prefixes and qualifications. He is not yet industrial man, economic man, evolutionary man,

civilised man, massman or man in transition. He is simply himself, a
wonder ordained, like a tree watched in a garden. Inconstancy,
levity, cruelty may be his habits; but so are generosity, the noble and
the useful virtues. Even Swift declares that he loves plain John, Peter
and Thomas. The name of Candide is itself a commendation.
However ferocious the satire of the eighteenth century it is always
balanced by a pleasure, sometimes trite and complacent, but always
ingenuous and warm, in the habits of the newly-discovered species;
and we ourselves respond to such a fundamentally sanguine and
well-found conception of human nature, even as we smile at the neat
eighteenth-century labels. The Age of Reason was a revised, replan-
ted and well-tended Eden; the serpent himself did obeisance to the
great landscape gardener; and when we look back upon that world
we cannot but suspect that half our present miseries date from the
dissipation of the common feeling and philosophy that ensured the
apparent sanity of the age.

The notion of the sufficiency of man in himself encouraged the
growth of peculiar character. The century enjoyed its fantastics. It
allowed people to grow as they willed. One delighted in inventing
more and more deformities and vices for one's enemies, more and
more foibles and scandals for one's friends. The eccentrics of the age
grew like cultivated blooms for all to admire; and its cranks could
rely on the affection if not on the support of their circle. Misanthropy
was especially respected, for among people who live well the melancholy man is slipped in by nature as a kind of sport and to restore the
balance; and when the misanthropic man was a crank into the
bargain, he was observed with that delighted eagerness which a
naturalist feels for the smallest hint of a new mutation.

In this period, there is no more suggestive example than the author
of *Sandford and Merton*. Mr Day is the modest and entrancing crank
of the century. He is a crank who is the guide to all cranks, the
pattern of the tribe. In their lives few earnest men have been more
ridiculous. After his death, the growth of his influence indicated the
crank's embarrassing usefulness: if he was ridiculous, we were
dreadful; if he was to be laughed at, we were to be wept over. For the
case of Mr Day perfectly illustrates the point that the crank is one of
the growing points of society. He shows us not indeed what we shall
become, but the direction we are likely to take. The special madness
of Mr Day was the belief that the errors of life were not due to
original sin, but to stupidity and the formation of bad habits. If we

could be caught young enough, in the age of natural innocence, we could be trained to be wiser and better than our stupid fathers. It was the madness of education. We shall see this when we come to *Sandford and Merton*, but before we do so, a glance at Mr Day himself, as he is drawn full length in the *Memoirs* of his friend Richard Edgeworth, is indispensable.

Nature is malicious. She is likely to arrange that those who have revolutionary ideas about the education of children shall have no children of their own; and here we come upon the first flaw in Mr Day's private life. He did not succeed in getting any children of his own; he was without the recklessness of the philoprogenitive. An abnormal caution governed the revolutionary life of Mr Day. He was unable for many years to master the initial difficulty of getting a wife. Women surrounded him, but none came up to his severe requirements. He believed, like any rationalist, in the sufficiency of man; his cross was the insufficiency of woman. The heart of the problem was that Mr Day was a perfectionist; he not only believed in the perfectibility of man which is arguable, but he also believed in the perfectibility of women, and women take unkindly to the notion that they can be improved. The susceptible Mr Day – and he was very susceptible – had either to take what he could get and like what he got, as the common run of men have to do, or – the logic is unanswerable – construct his own wife from blue prints in advance. Admirable mind of the eighteenth century: Mr Day chose the second course.

What were the requirements of Mr Day? Like a planner, he wanted to begin from the beginning, to make a fresh start. The whole invention called woman was in error. First of all one had to persuade women of this fundamental error in creation. Then one isolated them, cured them of silliness, frivolity, caprice, love of clothes, love of flirtation, love of chatter, flattery and society, the tendency to disobedience, lying and deception. One cured them of their slavery to fashion. Into the resulting vacuum, one poured modesty, decorum and the higher mental interests; the sex would learn, not indeed to converse themselves, but to follow a man's conversation and to assimilate his opinions. And they would be the most advanced opinions. Mr Day was sick of the silly women of the eighteenth century, the creatures who were seduced, abducted and swindled, who giggled and fainted, danced and gambled and talked of nothing but clothes. The story is well known. Cautiously he obtained the two famous orphans – two because he realised there might be a failure. Lucretia and Sabrina were immured in the country, and Day waited for them to grow to the point where he could attend to their minds. Alas, the reformer who did not believe in original sin, had not reckoned with invincible dullness! Lucretia turned out to be quarrelsome and trivial. She was married off quickly to a draper. For a time Sabrina seemed more hopeful. But it could not be concealed that she disliked reading. She could not bear science. She could not keep a secret. And she had no control over her emotions. Day established all these points by experiment. For example, to test her self-control he fired pistols close to her ears and her petticoats. She screamed. More serious – she was found secretly to be buying hats and putting lace on her dresses.

The experiment of Mr Day's is notorious. It caused the greatest astonishment in France where he took the two girls on an educational tour; but incredulous Frenchmen were at last convinced that Mr Day was genuinely engaged in an educational exercise, and retired from his party in terror. Mr Day was prepared to fight a duel with anyone who imperilled the curriculum. But the experiment is a mere episode in Mr Day's search for the right partner. He was only twenty-one when he undertook it.

At this point it is important to reveal the existence of another character who had been experimenting also, and who was the close witness and associate in some of Day's adventures. I refer to Richard Edgeworth. Here comedy fills out. Day is the initiator, but Richard Edgeworth is the foil. One man is the making of the other; and it is through the delightful memoirs of Maria Edgeworth's father that we see Mr Day drawn full-length with all the century's love of strange human beings and with its special regard for friendship. The two men are examples of the dyspeptic and the eupeptic schools of experiment. They were both rich. They were both country gentlemen.

On the one hand there is the ingenious Mr Day, the exemplary Mr Day, the Mr Day who talked like a book, who neglected his appearance, who refused to dress like a man of fashion, who despised the polite conventions, who began his addresses to women by denouncing the sex. A clumsy man, greasy haired in the days of wigs, pock-marked and brilliant, Mr Day scowled cautiously all day over his scruples. At a time when a good masculine leg was admired he was painfully knock-kneed. On the other hand there was Richard

Edgeworth, Irish, headstrong, handsome, generous, hot-tempered and gallant, the best dancer in Europe. Like Day he was a man with theories of education – he was bringing up his son on the lines laid down by Rousseau, to the astonishment of his neighbours and the despair of his lamenting wife – like Day he was a man of scruples. But his passions were always growing stronger and his scruples growing less.

And then Day was the theorist and Edgeworth was the man of practice. Day would a thousand times sooner read a book on housing than address a carpenter. His theories about women could be seen as a protective device. Edgeworth's character was the opposite. In the matter of education he got a son and tried his educational theories on him. In the matter of women – Edgeworth married four times, three times very happily. He was an incurable inventor of contraptions – one-wheeled coaches, patent turnip cutters, railway lines, interlocking carriages, telegraphs, patent tips and loading devices, a notable forerunner of the next century's engineers. One can see that a love of mischief was part of his ingenious temperament, and that it must have directed his affection for the prosaic Mr Day.

There is one remarkable episode in their friendship. It happened when Day had reached the point of desperation in his search for a wife. A delightful young woman called Elizabeth Sneyd who was Edgeworth's sister-in-law (years later she was to become Edgeworth's wife) agreed to consider Mr Day if he would improve his appearance and polish his manners. Not a simple decision for a man like Day; for him, polish was the Arch-Enemy, fashion the Pollution of life. To his drastic and puritan mind, the wearing of a wig meant the renunciation of his republican principles. But he was a desperate man. He agreed. He went off to France with Edgeworth, and, in his own mind, sold himself to the devil. Edgeworth describes how they got to Lyons where he had an enormous social success, while Day went through the pitiless school of a French dancing master. They cropped Day's lank Cromwellian locks. They piled a huge horsehair wig on his head. They dressed his ungainly body in the latest Parisian clothes. They taught him to bow and to dance. It was difficult for him to do this gracefully because of his knees and so soon Edgeworth put his legs between boards which were screwed tight so that he could not move. Edgeworth had engineering projects of his own on the Saône, but he took a special and wicked interest in Mr Day's knee-straightening machine. It was no good. The knees still knocked. 'I could not help pitying my philosophic friend,' says Richard Edgeworth, 'pent up in durance vile for hours together, with his feet in the stocks, a book in his hand and contempt in his heart.' Day returned at last to England, but when Elizabeth Sneyd saw the Puritan Malvolio come bowing into the room, she collapsed with laughter, and that was the end of that.

Let us leave Mr Day standing with unbendable rectitude amid the debris of his personal comedy. He did find a wife in the end, exactly the wife he desired, who was delighted to abandon all her personal tastes, including her love of music – an art which distressed him – and to devote her ear to his endless conversation. It was usually about education, and education killed him in the end. Kindness to animals was one of his principles, and Day was killed trying out a new 'natural' method of educating an unbroken horse. The Age of Reason conceived wild nature and the noble savage to be tamer than they were.

When we read *Sandford and Merton* we feel that Day had a delusion about children. He had none of his own. Would they have broken him? Or would he have broken them? The father-prig, endlessly eloquent, mellifluously disposed to draw the ever-recurring moral, always pat with the tendentious anecdote, is a strain on his children. They relieve it at last by laughter. Perhaps Day would have become the ridiculous father as *Sandford and Merton* is the father's ridiculous book.

But not basically ridiculous. I have already suggested that *Sandford and Merton* is the fruit of the eighteenth century's humane belief in the sufficiency of man and the light of reason. The book is not merely a child's book with a purpose; it is a child's book with a coherent philosophy, and that humane philosophy seems to me to have made *Sandford and Merton* far superior to the religious literature prescribed for children up to and, indeed, after that time. In how many biographies do we read of children who were terrified by *Foxe's Book of Martyrs*? How many have been made to snivel in misery over *Sandford and Merton*'s pious rival of the nineteenth century, *The Fairchild Family*? Some undoubtedly enjoyed the terrors, and I am not sure that it is wise to prevent a child from transposing his inheritance of the guilt and crimes of human nature into the pages of imaginative literature. Throughout the nineteenth century Day's book was disliked because it was said to ignore religion. In fact it did not, for it contains a simple account of Christ's morality; but Day certainly was no friend to the idea of original sin, and he did not set out to take the growing mind from a consideration of its responsibilities to the world outside itself, by nagging it continually with morbid images of the world within. If he was going to talk about hell, it was the hell of poverty, the several hells which men make for their fellows, not the hell invented by sadistic servants. One of the important aims of Day – and also of Edgeworth, who has some claim to be called the father of modern education – was to free the children of the well-to-do from the corrupting influence of nurses, chambermaids and butlers. But Day's philosophy must be judged by the kind of interests it encouraged. No doubt, as Edgeworth at last came to see, we are not certain to choose virtue just because our reason tells us that vice leads to misery and unhappiness; no doubt authority and discipline are required. But what new fields the freedom of philosophy opened to the curious mind! While the fearful and pious child was sobbing over the catastrophes of sin and was enclosed in the dank cloisters of self-pity, the prim little rationalists of *Sandford and Merton* were seeing the world. They were exploring South America, studying elephants and tigers, conducting experiments with the sun and the moon, and learning about the society they lived in.

It is strange that such an uninspiring man as Day, a man so full of crotchets and so devoid of instinct, so poor in response to everything except a generality, should have written a book as limpid and alive as *Sandford and Merton*. He hits one or two tastes of children with nicety: the complacency of children, their priggish and fierce delight in codes of conduct and honour; their love of a crude argument in black and white; their cocky moments of discovery; their passion for being heroes. Day understands the elementary principle that children are human beings who are growing taller and more powerful every day. 'We are but little children strong' – not weak. It is true that the tears and the piety of the awful little Harry Sandford mark a stage in the 'too noble by half' tradition; but I imagine that the child reader identifies himself with the wilful Tommy Merton, and attends only to Harry Sandford's remarkable practical capabilities – he knows how to deal with snakes, for example, and can take a thrashing without turning a hair – without being much perturbed by his virtues. Even the sentimentality about the honest poor, with its underhand appeal to childish pity, catches the child's love of showing off and making himself important. Day's Mr Barlow, to do him justice, has an inkling of this.

But the important charm of *Sandford and Merton* is extraneous to these matters. Day succeeds because he has created a kind of travelling zoo, an elegant and orderly zoo whose head keeper maintains a lively and picaresque running commentary. Now he is telling the visitor about the elephant, about elephants he has seen, elephants in the wild, elephants he has tamed, how you ought to handle them, and what happened to a tailor who made the mistake of playing a trick on one. The jungle, the native village, the regal procession are thrown in; and the whole stream of pictures flows smoothly by. They flick away before boredom starts. We have the pleasure of listening to someone talking to himself. This musical and vivid manner comes straight out of Day's own character. He was a man who never stopped talking. The ladies found this suffocating. But a child would listen for ever, for Day was so delightfully unreal. 'Is not that the country, Sir, where the cruel animal, the crocodile, is found?' asks Harry Sandford, when Mr Barlow shows the human weakness of stopping for breath. The invitation is not to be resisted. 'It is an animal,' says the invincible Mr Barlow, off again for another couple of pages, 'that lives sometimes upon the land, sometimes in the water. It comes originally from an egg. . . .' Little Harry Sandford, so liable to be infected by every germ of virtue blowing casually on the air, catches this manner in his talks with Tom Merton. Harry has just been thrashed by the wicked Squire for refusing to tell him which way the hare went, and Tom is sympathising:

H.   Oh! It's nothing to what the young Spartans used to suffer.
T.   Who were they?
H.   Why, you must know they were a brave set of people that lived a great while ago; and as they were but few in numbers and were surrounded by enemies . . .

And so, by yet another happy dislocation of the narrative, the babbling stream of information resumes its cheerful flow.

Sandford and Merton is one of those books which are rich because they have taken a long time to mature and have outgrown their original plan. Day's first notion was to rewrite a number of well-known stories and fables for children; but he gradually saw that the stories could lead to Socratic dialogues and the arguments to still more stories.

Mr B.   But when a person is not good to him, or endeavours to hurt him, it is natural for an animal to run away from him, is it not?
T.   Yes.

Mr B.   And then you say he is wild, do you not?

T.   Yes, Sir.

Mr B.   Why, then, it is probable that animals are only wild because they are afraid of being hurt, and that they only run away from the fear of danger. I believe you would do the same from a lion or a tiger.

T.   Indeed I would, Sir.

Mr B.   And yet you do not call yourself a wild animal?

Tommy laughed heartily at this and said No.   Therefore, said Mr Barlow, if you want to tame animals, you must be good to them, and treat them kindly, and then they will no longer fear you, but come to you and love you.   Indeed, said Harry, that is very true; for I knew a little boy that took a great fancy to a snake that lived in his father's garden; and, when he had milk for breakfast, he used to sit under a nut tree and whistle, and the snake would come to him, and eat out of his bowl.

T.   And did it not bite him?

H.   No; he sometimes used to give it a pat with his spoon if it ate too fast; but it never hurt him.

The aim of Day was to give a tendentious education. He loathed all that was meant by a man of fashion. He loathed everything that Lord Chesterfield stood for, almost as much as Lord Chesterfield's son came to do. He loathed idleness, profligacy, the self-indulgence of the rich. He loathed the man of fashion's attitude to children. He was a plain Republican who believed that no one should eat who did not work. He was one of the earliest Abolitionists. All these views are directed at Tommy Merton, whose father is a rich slaveowner:

And what right have the people who sold the poor negroes to your father to sell them, or what right has your father to buy them? Here Tommy seemed a good deal puzzled, but at length he said: They are brought from a country that is a great way off, in ships, and so become slaves. Then, said Mr Barlow, if I take you to another country in a ship I shall have a right to sell you?— T.   No, but you won't, sir, because I was born a gentleman. – Mr B. What do you mean by that, Tommy? – Why (said Tommy a little confounded) to have a fine house and fine clothes, and a coach, and a great deal of money, as my papa has. – Mr B. Then if you were no longer to have a fine house, nor fine clothes, nor a great deal of money, somebody that had all these things might make you a slave, and use you ill, and beat you, and insult you, and do whatever he liked with you? – T. No, Sir, that would not be right, neither, that anybody should use me ill. – Mr B. Then one person should not use another ill? – T. No, Sir. – Mr B. To make a slave of anybody is to use him ill, is it not? – T. I think so. – Mr B. Then no one ought to make a slave of you? – T. No, indeed, Sir. – Mr B. But if no one should use another ill, and making a slave is using him ill, neither ought you to make a slave of anyone else. – T. Indeed, Sir, I think not.

If Day's instruction was tendentious and was written on the revolutionary impulse of the eighteenth century, his methods were

also new. Lord Chesterfield's son was intended to be a miniature
Lord Chesterfield, an awed and suitably diminished reflection of his
father. Day's notion was that a child is a new and independent life.
His education in fact and morality was to be gained in the course of
living; he was not to inherit a convention. If father's gluttony leads to
gout, if father's wealth leads to restlessness, cruelty and guilt, if
mother's spoiling leads to ill-health, the child's rational faculty must
be strengthened until he sees that other courses are better. Education
is a guidance in the choice of good habits and the cultivation of a
humane disposition.

This was revolutionary. So revolutionary that old Edgeworth was
obliged to disinherit his own son who had taken the bit of freedom
between his teeth. Reason, alas, could not control him; neither a
parent's reason nor his own. Edgeworth hastened to warn parents
that he and his friends had been labouring under an appalling error.
This was years later; and there is no doubt that Tommy Merton was
drawn from Edgeworth's dashing and wilful eldest son. And then
there was another aspect to the revolution. The coddled manikin of
the eighteenth-century portraits was given a healthier life. He was
given lither, freer clothes and was sent to harden himself to sun and
cold. The Spartan ideal was established. But, excellent as a revolution and adventure, the Spartan ideal itself became a kind of grim,
vested interest, a terrifying convention in the English public schools
of the nineteenth century. The cult of nature became the cult of
neglect. The gentleman of fashion was succeeded by the gentleman
tough.

(1945)

WALTER SCOTT

The Heart of Midlothian

'No one reads Scott now': how often one has heard these words! I have no doubt they are true, at any rate true of English readers. At some time in the last thirty years feeling against dialect and especially the Scottish dialect has hardened into a final dislike. It is troublesome to the eye, it is a language which nags and clatters; one would as soon read phonetics. And then dialect suggests the overweening conceit of local virtue, and if anything has died in the last thirty years, it is regionalism. Our society – why pretend? – has made war on regionalism and has destroyed it. We may question whether, under any disguise, it can be reborn in the modern world. That is the first difficulty when we look at the long brown row of the Waverley novels that have stood high out of reach on our shelves, unopened since our childhood. And here the second difficulty arises. We read Scott in our childhood and he is not suitable reading for children; few of the great novelists are. Why should a man, writing in his maturity, scarred by life, marked by the evils of the world, its passions and its experience in his blood, be consigned to the young who know nothing of themselves or the world? The fault is partly Scott's: this great man, the single Shakespearean talent of the English novel, drew far too often the heroes and heroines which have always appealed to the adolescent and gently reared reader – wooden idealisations, projections of our more refined, sixteen-year-old wishes. At sixteen we are in love with those sexless heroines with their awful school-mistressy speeches. We are in love with those stick-in-the-mud heroes whose disinterestedness and honour pervert the minds of boys with a tedious and delusive idealism. One grows up in the day-dream that Scott has generated to discover it is a swindle; and one never forgives him.

Yet, if we except this serious criticism for the moment, and measure Scott in the light of the full noon of life, we see that he belongs to that very small group of our novelists – Fielding and Jane Austen are the chief of them – who face life squarely. They are grown up. They do not cry for the moon. I do not mean that to be grown up is the first requirement of genius. To be grown up may be fatal to it. But short of the great illuminating madness, there is a power to sustain, assure and enlarge us in those novelists who are not driven back by life, who are not shattered by the discovery that it is a thing bounded by unsought limits, by interests as well as by hopes, and that it ripens under restriction. Such writers accept. They think that acceptance is the duty of a man.

An error of our boyhood reading of Scott is, I fancy, the easy assumption that Scott is primarily an historical novelist. There is more reason to think of him as a comic writer. We would make a similar kind of error about Defoe, Fielding or Richardson if we took them at their word and believed that their only aim was to reform morals. The historical passion of Scott or the moral passion of these other novelists was the engine of their impulse. Where that engine took them is another matter. Hazlitt saw this when, in his too drastic way, he said that Scott was interested in half of life only: in the past of man and not in what he might become; and Hazlitt went to the length of thinking Godwin's *Falkland* fit to be compared with *Waverley*. But Scott's history meant simply his preoccupation with what is settled – and, after all, a great deal *is* settled for better or worse, in human life and character. One might even see in Scott's history the lame man's determination to impose and ennoble normality. The feuds of the clans are done with, the bloody wars of the Border are over, Jacobitism is a mere sentiment notable for its ironical inconsistencies as well as its heroic gestures. A period has ended and, for a novelist, there is no more favourable moment. Now he can survey. Scott gazes upon it all like a citizen who has dressed up. Now, vicariously, he can be physically heroic; but the real result of the historical impulse is not history but an immense collection of small *genre* pieces, a huge gallery of town and country faces in their inns, their kitchens, their hovels, their farms and their rambling houses. And the painting of them is as circumstantial, as middle-class – in the anti-romantic sense – and as non-aristocratic as anything of Hogarth's. Scott does not revive the past or escape into it; he assimilates it for his own time and for his own prejudices. He writes like a citizen. He asserts the normal man, the man who has learned to live with his evil; what his evil might have done with him if he had not

learned to live with it can be guessed from the grotesque decla-
mations of *The Black Dwarf*, the creature who cuts himself off from
mankind.

The Black Dwarf is not a good novel. There are awkward lumps
of unreality in it. The bad thing is the central drama, and this points
to Scott's obvious fault as a novelist. He has an immense memory
and the necessary taste for improving on memory. He has the power
to present the outside of a character and to work from the outside to
the inside. But once inside, he discovers only what is generic. That is
the fault. He has, I would say, no power to work from the inside to
the outer man. There is nothing feminine in him. So the black dwarf
is excellent when he is seen as local recollection, a piece of Border
hearsay, and no one could surpass Scott in portraying that tortured
head, with its deep-sunken pin-point eyes, the almost legless and
hairy little body with its huge feet, and the enormous voice that issues
from the abortion. But when we come to the mind of this tortured
creature, when he speaks, what we get is not horror but a dreary,
savage Calvinist lecture. The black dwarf's misanthropy is a mere
exercise, a sermon turned inside out. There is a complete breakdown
of the imagination: compare this story with Turgenev's *Lear of the
Steppes*. I suspect that as we continue our rediscovery of Scott we
shall often find that the chief drama of the novels breaks down in this
way, for the great protagonists of fiction begin from the inside of a
writer. One is inclined to divide the Scott characters into two classes:
the secondary and minor ones who are real and are truly recollected,
the children of his wonderful memory; and the major ones who are
the awkward, stage figures of an imagination that is cut off from the
sap of life. To go back to Hazlitt: Scott lacked a vital sense, the sense
of what people may become. His history was not real history. It was
the settled, the collectable, the antique.

I turn to *The Chronicles of the Canongate*, the tales of the second
series, to see whether my last sentence is too sweeping. There is *The
Highland Widow*. Here is real history – but you notice at once –
history without costume. History in the rags of the people. The
widow's husband has been a bandit, the Robin Hood of a clan that
has almost died out. Her son perceives that times have changed; he
enlists in the army which was once his father's enemy. The mother is
appalled by the disgrace and plots to restore her son to a life of crime.
The tragedy which is enacted springs from the clash of two orders of
virtue, and the virtue of one age has become the vice of the age that

succeeds it. There is no dialect in this story. It is heroic and not Hogarthian. It is the kind of thing that Mérimée and Pushkin took from Scott. And here, better than in his more elaborate compositions, we see the mark of Scott's genius as a storyteller. I say nothing of the suspense of which he is always a master; I am thinking of his power of suggesting the ominous, the footsteps of fate coming to meet one on the road. Frequently Scott used the supernatural and the hints of second sight to get this effect, and they are all the more effective for being explained as the domestic beliefs of his characters which the author himself hesitates to accept. But in *The Highland Widow* we come upon one of those real omens, one of those chance remarks made by a stranger which have a different meaning to the one who hears. It is a device much used by Hardy. In Scott's story the young soldier has been drugged by his fanatical mother so that he shall not return to his regiment. The boy wakes up and rushes out to find what day of the week it is, for he fears more than anything else the degradation of his honour. The first person he meets is a minister, who replies: 'Had you been where you should have been yesterday, young man, you would have known that it was God's Sabbath.' The two meanings of those words mark the crisis of the tale, and after looking back upon it one realises how ingenious and masterly has been the construction of a simple story. The end we could foresee; the means we could not, and it is in the means that Scott always shows the power of a master.

It is less the business of the novelist to tell us what happened than to show how it happened. The best things in Scott arise out of the characters. He especially understands, as I said before, the generic differences between people. He understands the difference between the fisherman and the farmer, the shepherd and the drover, and so on. He understands, in other words, what all ordinary, simple, observant men know about one another: the marks of their trade, their town, their family. (His view of women is that of the simple man: he knows them by their habits in the house. In love he does not know them at all.) The tale called *The Two Drovers* is a fine example of Scott's watchfulness of male character. The honour of Robin, the Highland drover, seems to be quaint silliness to Wakefield, the stolid Yorkshireman; the sense and fair play of Wakefield, who cannot believe that enmity will survive a little amateur boxing, are meaningless to the Highlander. Each is reasonable – but in a different way. The clash when it comes is tragic; again two kinds of virtue are

irreconcilable. The scene in the inn is wonderfully true to the men
there, and the talk slips naturally off their clumsy tongues. Wakefield
has challenged Robin to fight with his fists. Robin can't see how this
will mend a quarrel.

Harry Wakefield dropped the hand of his friend or rather threw it from
him.

'I did not think I had been keeping company for three years with a
coward.'

'Coward pelongs to none of my name,' said Robin, whose eyes began to
kindle, but keeping the command of his temper. 'It was no coward's legs or
hands, Harry Waakfelt, that drew you out of the fords of Frew, when you
was drifting ower the plack rock, and every eel in the river expected his share
of you.'

'And that is true enough, too,' said the Englishman, struck by the appeal.

'Adzooks!' exclaimed the bailiff – 'sure Harry Wakefield, the nattiest lad
at Whitson Tryste, Wooler Fair, Carlisle Sands, or Stagshaw Bank, is not
going to show the white feather? Ah, this comes of living so long with kilts
and bonnets – men forget the use of their daddles.'

'I may teach you, Master Fleecebumpkin, that I have not lost the use of
mine,' said Wakefield, and then went on. 'This will never do, Robin. We
must have a turn-up or we shall be the talk of the countryside. I'll be d——d
if I hurt thee – I'll put on the gloves gin thou like. Come, stand forward like a
man!'

'To be peaten like a dog,' said Robin, 'is there any reason in that? If you
think I have done you wrong, I'll go before your shudge, though I neither
know his law nor his language.'

A general cry of 'No, no – no law, no lawyer, a bellyful and be friends' was
echoed by the bystanders.

'But,' continued Robin, 'if I am to fight, I have no skill to fight like a
jackanapes, with hands and nails.'

And here once more the agent of tragedy is moving slowly down
the road towards the two friends – the drover who is carrying
Robin's dirk for him, to keep him out of trouble and to circumvent
the fate that was foretold at the beginning of the story.

Except in the outbursts of *The Black Dwarf*, Scott appears to see
evil as a fatality that ensues from the nature of the times. The civil
wars have made men narrow and ruthless, and he writes at the end of
an era, surveying the broken scene and pleading for tolerance. The
crimes in *The Chronicles of the Canongate* are 'errors of the
understanding', not examples of absolute wickedness. When we turn
to *The Antiquary* we meet another side of his talent; his humour. I
wonder how many of those who, like myself, had not read Scott since
their schooldays will recall that Scott is one of the great comic

writers? It is not purely Scottish humour, depending on the canniness of the speaker or on a continuous sly, nervous snigger, or on the grotesque and pawky asides of dialect. Scott's humour, like his best prose, is cross-bred with the English eighteenth century. Sterne and Fielding have put red blood into it. A character like Jonathan Oldbuck does not make thin jokes down his nose, but stands solidly and aglow beside all the well-found comics of our literature. The secret is that Scott's animal spirits are high, as Fielding's were. I have always enjoyed that strange scene in the early pages of *The Antiquary* in which Oldbuck supervises the rescue of the foolish, snobbish, bankrupt, treasure-hunting Sir Arthur, and his stick of a daughter, from the rising tide. Jonathan Oldbuck who has only an hour before been snubbed by the angry baronet, now watches the men heave the scarcely conscious gentleman up the rock:

'Right, right, that's right, too – I should like to see the son of Sir Gamelyn de Guardover on dry land myself – I have a notion he would sign the abjuration oath, and the Ragman-roll to boot, and acknowledge Queen Mary to be nothing better than she should be, to get alongside my bottle of old port that he ran away from, and left scarce begun. But he's safe now, and here a' comes – (for the chair was again lowered, and Sir Arthur made fast in it, without much consciousness on his own part) – Here a' comes – bowse away, my boys! – canny wi' a tenpenny tow – the whole barony of Knockwinnock depends on three plies of hemp – respice finem, respice funem – look to your end – look to the rope's end.'

I can read about half of *The Antiquary* and enjoy the flavours of what I read. After that I skip through the preposterous plot and willingly leave the wooden Lovel and the disdainful Miss Wardour to the pleasure of talking like public statues to each other. In one respect it must be admitted they do surpass modern lovers. Severely regulated by their families and by circumstance, these antique couples are obliged to know their subject. The obstacles to love ensure that the lovers shall concentrate.

The criticism that Scott cannot draw a heroine has to be modified after we have read *The Heart of Midlothian*. To judge by this book Scott could not draw a hero. For neither the pious, pettifogging Butler nor the wicked George Staunton can be called human beings of anything but conventional interest. Effie and Jeanie Deans are quite another matter. They are peasants and Scott condescends to them with the gentlemanliness of his time, but they are alive as his peasants always are. Scott's inability to draw women life-size seems to be due to the fact that he can think of them only as creatures high above him, or safely below him; and the ones below are drawn better than the ones above. The maid is more interesting than the mistress. We owe this romantic and pedestalled conception of women partly to the lame man's feeling of inferiority. He idealised what he could not approach. But these idealisations also arise from that curious split in the puritan middle-class mind which had begun to unsex itself so that it might devote all its will to the adventure of getting on in the world of money or honour, leaving the warmer passions to the lower orders. But unlike the early Victorian novelists, Scott is not a prude. Miss Bellendon's maid, in *Old Mortality*, nudges, winks and uses all her enticements on the soldiery; speech is very free in the farms and the inns; only Miss Bellendon in her castle stands like a statue and talks like an epitaph. Once Scott is free of these inhibitions – and in the main they are fixed by considerations of class – Scott describes women as well as they can be described from the point of view of a man in the house; that is as scolding, fussing, gossiping, pestering, weeping, wilful and mercenary adjuncts of domestic life. They can always answer back. They never forgive a slight, they can always be persuaded to condone a crime. Expressed without satire but with sense and geniality this view has inspired many robust minor portraits of womanhood in Scott. The loveliness and attraction of Di Vernon in *Rob Roy* is due, I fancy, to the fact that she has a good deal of male in her. What is missing from all these portraits is the vitalising element: the sense a woman has of herself, the sense of what she may become – that sense of our fate which alone gives meaning to our character. And as I have said before, Scott's direct intuitive sense of that fate seems to have been weak; he grasps the importance of it only through the labours of the historian and the documentary artist. His researches, not his instinct, gave us his remarkable portrait of the passionate mother in *The Highland Widow*, and his researches also revealed to him, in the same way, the larger meaning of Jeanie Deans' character in *The Heart of Midlothian*.

A modern novelist who rewrote *The Heart of Midlothian* would certainly stress the unconscious jealousy which Jeanie must have felt towards her younger sister by her father's second marriage. We would say that Jeanie's refusal to tell the lie that would save Effie from the scaffold was not a stern moral act, but an animal retaliation; for psychology has altered for us the nature of many ethical dilemmas. Scott ignores the evident jealousy. And though Effie, in a remarkable prison scene, flies out at her sister, we are left with the impression that Jeanie is either too stupid or too conceited in her conscience to be endured. But Scott's strength in the handling of the situation between the two women comes from his knowledge of the effect of history upon them. They are children of history. And the one part of history Scott knew inside out was its effect upon the conscience. Jeanie's refusal to tell a lie had generations of Calvinistic quarrelling behind it, the vituperations of the sectaries who had changed the sword of the clan wars and the civil wars for the logic-chopping of theology. Instead of splitting skulls, they had taken to splitting hairs. The comedies, the tragedies, the fantastic eloquence and tedious reiteration of these scruples of conscience are always brilliantly described by Scott, who has them in his blood. And so Jeanie's refusal to lie and her journey to London on foot to seek her sister's pardon are not the result of conceit, heartlessness or even literalness of mind: they are the fruit of history.

And a history which produces not only plump, dumb, resolute figures like hers, but men of roystering violence like the bloody Porteous, tortured believers in predestination like Staunton, fanatics like old Deans, cranks like Saddlebright, lunatic harlots like Madge Wildfire, adventuresses like Effie, wonderful sea-lawyers of the criminal world of old Edinburgh, like Ratcliffe, the thief, and wonderful fools like the gaping old laird of Dumbiedikes. There is none of the sentimentality which Dickens spread like a bad fog over the suffocated bastards, baby-farmers, harlots and criminals of his novels; none of the melodrama. Scott's realism belongs to the time when gentlemen knew the mob because they were not yet afraid of the mob. There is only one false episode in *The Heart of Midlothian*; and that is the wildly improbable meeting between Jeanie and George Staunton at his father's vicarage in England, and we owe that to the influence of the theatre on the English novel. For that matter, none of the English scenes is really good and the final third of the novel is a failure. Here Jeanie is diminished as a character by the condescension of the author. But when she is in Scotland, we feel the force of her country and her fate in her, and these make her into a woman. One sees her even more clearly and fully late in the book when it is she, the rescuer, who has to pay tribute to Effie, the adventuress, who has, after all, got away with it. Scott was too much the man of the world to prevent Effie getting away with a good deal more than Dickens or even Thackeray were later on to allow their giddy-pated or wicked women. Scott recorded wilfulness in women with an appreciative eye; and an ear cocked for the back answer.

It has often been said that the decay of our interest in problems of conscience is a major cause of the feebleness of the modern novel; but there have been many poor novels stuffed tight with conscience. Might we not say more justly that the problems of conscience have changed? Our habit is to weigh man against society, civilisation against man or nature; individuals against groups. The greatness of *The Heart of Midlothian* arises, first of all, in the scope that the problem of conscience gave to Scott's imagination. He was not arguing in a void. His argument was creating real people and attracting real people to it. He made the story of Effie's murdered baby a national story. And then how wide his range is! The scenes in the Tolbooth are remarkable, and especially those that are built about the figure of Ratcliffe when the governor is working to turn him into an informer. Scott had the eighteenth-century taste for rogues, and their talk is straight from nature.

'Why, I suppose you know you are under sentence of death, Mr Ratcliffe?' replied Mr Sharpitlaw.

'Ay, so are a', as that worthy minister said in the Tolbooth Kirk the day Robertson wan off; but naebody kens when it will be executed. Gude faith, he had better reason to say than he dreamed of, before the play was played out that morning!'

'This Robertson,' said Sharpitlaw, in a lower and something like a confidential tone, 'd'ye ken, Rat – that is, can ye gie us ony onkling where he is to be heard tell o'?'

'Troth, Mr Sharpitlaw, I'll be frank wi' ye: Robertson is rather a cut abune me – a wild deevil he was, and mony a daft prank he played; but except the Collector's job that Wilson led him into, and some tuilzies about run goods wi' the guagers and the waiters, he never did ony thing that came near our line o' business.'

'Umph! that's singular, considering the company he kept.'

'Fact, upon my honour and credit,' said Ratcliffe, gravely. 'He keepit out o' our little bits of affairs, and that's mair than Wilson did; I hae dune business wi' Wilson afore now. But the lad will come on in time; there's nae fear o' him; naebody will live the life he has led, but what he'll come to sooner or later.'

'Who or what is he, Ratcliffe? You know, I suppose?' said Sharpitlaw.

'He's better born, I judge, than he cares to let on; he's been a soldier, and he has been a playactor, and I watna what he has been or hasna been, for as young as he is, sae that it had daffing and nonsense about it.'

'Pretty pranks he has played in his time, I suppose?'

'Ye may say that,' said Ratcliffe, with a sardonic smile, 'and' (touching his nose) 'a deevil amang the lasses.'

'Like enough,' said Sharpitlaw. 'Weel, Ratcliffe, I'll no stand niffering wi' ye; ye ken the way that favour's gotten in my office; ye maun be usefu'.'

'Certainly, sir, to the best of my power – naething for naething – I ken the rule of the office,' said the ex-depredator.

Then there is Scott's power of describing a crowded scene. I am thinking of the long narrative about the crowd's storming of the Tolbooth and the killing of Porteous. Scott has looked it all up, but his own version is so alive, so effortless, so fast moving. Every detail tells; the very pedantry of it is pedantry washed down by the rough wine of life. Everything is carried off with the authority of a robust and educated style, the style of a man fit to understand, master and govern, a man endlessly fair and excitingly patient in his taste for human nature. He understands popular clamour. He understands the mysteries of loyalty – all the diverse loyalties of a man's life and trade.

And after that Scott has the story-teller's ability to build a great scene and to make a natural use of it. 'I'm thinking of the search in the dark on Salisbury Crag when the police have persuaded Ratcliffe to help them catch Robertson, and Ratcliffe has brought Madge Wildfire with him to show them all the way. Madge is semi-lunatic, and Ratcliffe has to use all his guile to keep her to the job. He knows her mind is stuffed full of old wives' tales, and he reminds her of a notorious murder that was done on the Crag years before – a story the reader has already been prepared for: Scott's antiquarian asides ought never to be skipped – but Ratcliffe's cunning is turned against him at the moment of its success by the madness of the woman. She accuses him of being as bad as the murderer.

'I never shed blood,' he protested.

'But ye hae sauld it, Ratton – ye hae sauld blood mony a time.'

That chance shaft hits Ratcliffe's conscience and wrecks the expedition. In a short chapter Scott has ingeniously extracted every kind of surprise and apprehension; and without any frivolity or artifice. This adventure could have happened; indeed, we say, if we had had eyes at the back of our heads, we would have known that it *must* have happened so, fabulous as it is. Scott's knowledge gives a sense of necessity to his picture of life, and his freedom in mixing the comic with the serious, even at the most dramatic moments, adds to this pleasant sense. He is not overdriven by his imagination, whereas a writer like Dickens was. Scott, like Fielding, has both feet firmly on the ground.

Rob Roy is admired – but for one or two scenes only when we examine the matter, and it is really a poor novel. At first sight the claims of *Old Mortality* are less emphatic upon the reader's attention, and since Scott repeated himself so often one is tempted to neglect this novel. It should not be neglected. Into this book Scott put all his tolerance and civilisation, his hatred of fanaticism, and illuminated the subject of the religious wars in Scotland with all his irony, humour, all his wiriness of intellect and all his human sympathy. In Burley he drew the rise and the corruption of the fanatical character, and I do not know any other in Scott whose character grows and changes so convincingly. There is real movement here; elsewhere the sense of movement in his characters is more the result of Scott's habit of dissertation than a real enacting of change. The portrait of Claverhouse is debonair, and the battle scene when the insurgents rout him is almost Tolstoyan; how much Scott owes to a sincere pleasure, even a joy, in the accoutrement of life. One can see how the Russians, like Tolstoy, Gogol and Pushkin first of all, must have been caught by Scott's wonderful pictures of the eccentric lairds. The miser in *Old Mortality,* or the ridiculous, gaping laird in *The Heart of Midlothian* must have fathered many a landlord in *Dead Souls* and other Russian stories. Where the Russians were to succeed and where Scott failed was in conveying the sense of an abiding destiny going on beyond the characters described. For Scott life is a book that one closes; to the Russians it is a book that one opens. And although one feels his animal zest for life, one feels it as a delightful recollection of hours that are ended, not as the perturbation or languor of the hour which has still to go by on the clock as we read.

One looks up the critics. What did Scott add to the English novel? Is he just another Fielding, but planted in Scottish history? Has he simply added a change of scene and material? It looks like that at first glance: he is a writer from the outside looking in. But I think there is something else. I would like to argue that Scott is a complement to Richardson – an analytical and psychological novelist who describes to us the part of our motives formed by public events. He is certainly the first novelist to describe the political influence of religion and the peculiar significance of superstitions and legend in the mind; and he uses them to illustrate the promptings of unconscious guilt and fear.

One sees this in the character of Ratcliffe in *The Heart of Midlothian* and in innumerable instances elsewhere; Scott does not use his apparitions and legends merely for the purpose of putting a shiver or a laugh in his story. They are there to convey hidden processes of mind. No English novelist has added to that sense of a general or public mind, and certainly no great novelist – Hardy is the atheistical exception – has used religion as Scott used it.

AMELIA OPIE

The Quaker Coquette

If there is not a novel in every man and woman we meet, there is at
any rate a cautionary tale. 'That ridiculous and excellent person, Mrs
Opie,' said Miss Mitford. 'What a miserable hash she has made of
her existence.' Somewhere in the world – so we may console
ourselves when we feel ignored and forgotten – there is bound to be a
Miss Mitford holding us up as an awful warning, using us as a
frightful example of what can happen to a human being when he or
she strays from the Mitford path. We have, of course, our bad
moments and it must be agreed that Miss Mitford had caught the
widow of Opie, the painter, at that point in middle age where so
many women are clumsy with their cues and seem not to know in
what play they are acting. After a life of triumphant gaiety in London
and Paris, after writing a number of gaudy, guilty and improper
books, the tantalising and beautiful widow had suddenly rejoined
the Quaker circle in Norwich where she had passed her youth. She
had put on the Quaker gown and bonnet, she had started writing
very boring, didactic tales and went about thee-ing and thou-ing her
embarrassed acquaintances with all the gush of a convert and all the
bounce of a reformed sinner. Norwich raised its eyebrows. The good
may cry Hallelujah when the lost soul repents and returns to the fold,
but there is often a touch of disappointment not to mention suspicion
in the cry, for where would the good be if there were no sinners left to
hearten them on their hard pilgrimage? At Earlham, the home of
Elizabeth Fry and the Gurney family who thought they knew their
Amelia so well, such doubts could not be concealed. A Quaker – but
wasn't Mrs Opie still a friend of Lady Cork's? Hadn't she still got in
her drawer the manuscript of an unfortunate novel? Could one credit
the champion of Mary Wollstonecraft and Godwin with a change of
heart? What prospect was there of 'the inner light' shining for long in
a mind bedizened with the memories of fashionable society, of 'pink'

parties for the gay and 'blue' parties for the highbrow? Wasn't Amelia Opie congenitally 'shallow'? Her conversion might even be a leg pull, for she did seem to have what George Fox would have called (in the century before Quakerism became mellow), a 'light and chaffy' nature. But neither the Quakers nor Miss Mitford could take the severe view of Mrs Opie's vivacious character for long. They loved her too well to regard her finally as the awful warning against worldliness. And the truth is that Amelia Opie had not so much the awfulness of a warning as the piquancy of a recurrent type. Born in 1769 and dying in 1853, she had fed on ideologies. She had lived through a revolution and a European war, and then had repented. Today her kind of character and repentance has become common if not yet modish. Mrs Opie is a kind of heroine of our time.

What is the type? Amelia was a flirt, a highbrow flirt. She was the adored and adoring daughter of a Norwich doctor. Her mother had been an invalid for years and when she died the girl was still in her teens. She became her father's hostess. When one goes into the question of her coquetry one comes immediately upon that so common decision of Nature that girls who have an inordinate devotion to their fathers shall deal coolly and indecisively with other men or shall prefer those who are much younger or much older than themselves. Add to this the intellectual tastes of Amelia's father and one finds a young lady who coquettes with literature, politics and religion and calls them in to aid her in the more important business of catching men. Her susceptible nature – it was susceptible rather than passionate – made her into one of those women who, when they come into a room, shine with the certainty that they will succeed and the lightness of their feeling makes them do so. Later she was to harden into the vivacious snob and to fatten into the determined celebrity hunter who bosomed her way into the limelight with the infallible flair of the woman who knew her geniuses.

Being irresistible was not only an instinct but a business with Amelia Opie. She wrote frightful novels which made Sir Walter Scott weep, and awful verses which Sydney Smith quoted in his lectures – the bad taste of great men has a long history – but she had taken care, it might be observed, to get to know the great first. She asked Southey once to say a word to the reviewers. She was one of those women who, having addled a man's judgment by making herself physically desirable, like an ice on a hot day, then change about and insist on being admired for their minds. She was quite candid about this technique in her last novel. She was irresistible, she says, because she was herself unable to resist – at first; she began resisting only when, by flattering them, she had made others think they had become irresistible themselves. No grand passions for her, she said, no durable affections. 'My object is to amuse life away and *a little love*, just enough to give interest to scenes and places, is delightful. . . . My attachments are like gentle squeezes of the hand.' A great passion would destroy her 'peace of mind'. No wonder the Norwich Quakers, plump, benevolent but trimly literal in matters of virtue, were a little dubious when the chatty best seller who knew all the celebrities of London and Paris, put on the Quaker bonnet. Was the accomplished actress just putting on another act? Of course she was. And yet, of course, she was not. Amelia had some of that stupidity in her nature which some call ingenuousness. It is the price a woman has to pay for being vain of her unconventionality. But Amelia is a delightful argument for the charm of an ill-adjusted life, for the attraction of being a bit of a fraud and for a dash of the prude in a wanton female character.

During the many years of her mother's illness, Amelia's childhood had been one of solitude and constraint. She was shut away, silenced, ignored. Imagination awakened. She quickly picked up a love of the sensational, the guilty and the morbid. The effect of the death of her mother was to release Amelia suddenly from a world of dark, dramatic and lugubrious brooding into a world of sociability and light. The late eighteenth century was made for escapades of the mind, and many of the English provincial towns had the intellectual liveliness of little capitals. In Norwich, Crome was painting. Holcroft, Godwin and the Radical leaders dined with the doctor. The ideas of the French Revolution were in the air and, as she listened to her father's praise of Lafayette, the young hostess became a republican at a bound. Alone in her room, she began to write plays and poetry and when she had done a few pages she found that great men liked to be asked for their criticisms. At least, with young ingenuity, she *thought* that this was what interested them. Her mind (she was to tell Godwin and Holcroft as they looked with desire upon her person) was her chief preoccupation. It is a weakness of intellectuals to be interested in minds and Amelia's fervid talk about hers was the ideal bait; ideal because it hooked the listener and yet kept him threshing away unavailingly at a safe distance, at the end of the line. With Godwin hooked, with Godwin jealous of her friends, begging her to rule her emotions by the light of Reason while he himself fell into an irrational condition because she would not kiss him, Amelia's technique was established. Now she could deal with anyone, indeed preferably with several at a time. She sat down to write an anonymous book called *The Dangers of Coquetry*.

In the meantime she had made another conquest, one which lasted her lifetime and which did not spring from her engaging vanity but was directed by a warmer need of her nature. As a child Amelia had not known the geniality of normal family life. She needed a family and she conquered one. The Gurneys of Earlham were Quakers, a large family of children younger than herself and glad to admire and love the literary belle with her poems and her song. Quakerism had softened; music, painting and dancing were permitted to the younger Gurneys who turned to Amelia with all the love which the prim feel for the worldly. The young Gurneys were in revolt against their traditions, its politics, its culture. Where was there not revolt in that generation? There were Corresponding Societies – the English equivalent of the Jacobin Clubs – in Norwich, respectable 'pinks' were being spied on and even tried for sedition, treason and revolutionary activity; even the religious faith of the younger Gurneys was lapsing. To Amelia who was 'in the movement' and who had run into scandal because of her passion for Mary Wollstonecraft and her defence of Godwin's marriage, they turned as to a goddess. The fact that she was known by now to be in love with a married man brought even brighter confidence to the agony of the young atheists. They were to get their own back later when time brought their repentance, and Amelia, the converter was to be reconverted by them. Elizabeth Fry was one of those children and Amelia, at her gayest and most 'worldly', in the midst of writing her 'immoral' novels about seduced heroines, mad fathers and women ruined by 'a false step', always responded uncomfortably to criticism from Earlham.

But this quaint fruit of Amelia's deep affection for the Gurneys was to ripen slowly. By the time she was twenty-eight and still unmarried Norwich had begun to shake its head. It was all very well to be clever, beautiful, mysterious, the skilful heartbreaker (Norwich said), but the coquette who turns down one proposal too many ends on the shelf. And Amelia was in her first mess. 'Mr B', the married man, was only too well married and there was no way of getting him. It was a crisis of the heart; it was, even more, a crisis for her vanity with all Norwich watching, the Gurneys above all. The solution was

– and how true to her type she was – to drown a scandal in a sensation. She did so. The elegant young provincial married Opie. Opie was a peasant with a strong Cornish accent, shocking table manners, a divorced wife. Amelia did not love him. But he was a fashionable painter and thoroughly in the limelight. His table manners made her hesitate – odd things made her hesitate in her life: after Opie's death she went all out for a peer with the idea of reforming him and turned him down in the end because 'they both had enough to live on' – but in the end she plunged. She married Opie. She pushed him into society, saw to it that he got commissions. Now it was that she wrote. When her husband's work went temporarily out of fashion she buckled to and wrote a bestseller. And when he died – for the marriage was a short interlude in her life – she fought to get him buried in St Paul's Cathedral and grieved so extravagantly, in so many poems, panegyrics, memoirs, and so loudly that her friends had to remind her that she was enjoying herself more than the onlookers.

The Gurneys were worried. They enjoyed being stirred up by the celebrity, though by this time Amelia's claim to have a mind was mocked by reviewers. The Gurneys were older. They had returned to respectable opinions and even to their old religion. A reconquest of the Gurneys was necessary, a new disturbing of their godliness. To this period belongs her characteristic affair with Joseph John Gurney, a strict young Quaker, and with Haydon, the elderly reprobate of Bognor, who had had a notorious *ménage à trois* with his wife and his servant. To Joseph John she talked and wrote about 'the world', a subject which shocked and fascinated him; to Haydon, she talked about religion, which shocked and fascinated *him*. Haydon was old, Joseph John was young. He listened, he reproved, he lectured. Amelia loved it. She was delighted that he did not despair of bringing her back into the fold. It would have dismayed her to know that the prudent Quaker would succeed in recapturing her for the Lord, but would be careful to marry someone else.

The second mess, 'the miserable hash' in fact, was the direct cause of her conversion. Sooner or later that amusing vanity, that too clever susceptibility, was certain to be snubbed. One does not suppose she loved Tom Alderson, her knowing young cousin, very deeply, but she was humiliated when he turned her down. The answer again was a new sensation: the Quaker bonnet. We need not agitate ourselves, as the Quakers did, about the sincerity of that conversion. At sixty when she broke out again and went to Paris on a celebrity hunt after Lafayette and to renew her revolutionary enthusiasms, D'Angers the sculptor called her a Janus, a two-faced siren who instinctively showed you the profile you did not ask for. Her misleading Puritanism, so perfectly chaste but with delusive promise of wantonness, delighted the Frenchman. But Miss Mitford cattily noted that Amelia ordered the silk for her Quaker gown from Paris; and Paris was astonished and enchanted by a celebrity who arrived in the disguise of the Meeting House. It was all in character. In her youth she had stood in court watching the trial of Holcroft for treason and had cried, Liberty in the streets; but she had insisted on meeting the aristocratic *émigrés* too.

And how misleading she is even in her portraits. The plump, soft, wistful wench with the murmuring eyes and sensual mouth, in Opie's painting, does not look like the dazzler of the great. The humorous, blunt-faced, double-chinned sexagenarian of D'Angers' medallion does not look like the spiritualised creature which his ecstatic letters describe. What was it that got them all? Was it the famous technique, the flattery of the perpetual promise? Or the most flattering of all flatteries, the most active and subtle of the social arts (as indeed the last of her 'unredeemed' novels suggested), the art of listening? For one cannot, one must not, believe that the title of the first book, written after her redemption, offers the clue. It was a didactic work entitled *Lying, In all its Branches*.

(1942)

LORD BYRON

Letters

Byron's letters are among the most spirited in the English language, and are irresistible. They amount to an autobiography of the duelling kind. Byron is a good letter writer because whether he is scoffing, arguing, or even conducting his business affairs, he has a half-laughing eye on his correspondent; although he can turn icily formal, he has mainly a talking style of worldly elegance and is spontaneously the half self of the moment, for not only he but everyone else knew the duality of his nature. The whole person can be deduced from what he dashingly offers. His character is a springboard from which he takes a dive into what he has to say about himself for the moment, bringing other people to half life in the splash. In saying that his style is conversational, one means that he was at his best when talking *tête-à-tête* – when he could be free with asides, sudden images, ironical glimpses of confession. He plays with his masks. He enjoyed scandal – not for its mean side but for its flashes of satirical fantasy and because it is 'a sort of cayenne to the mind'. In letters, as in talk, 'all subjects are good in their way providing they are sufficiently diversified.' As a passionate extremist and opponent, he easily dropped into the anticlimax of affectionate good humour. He was, as many have said, an opportunist where the passions were concerned; yet he had a plodding care in daily life for routine and regular habits. According to Lady Blessington, he said in one of their platonic chats, 'People take for gospel all I say, and go away continually with false impressions ... Now, if I know myself, I should say, that I have no character at all. . . [This also was Balzac's view of himself and of artists in general.] I am so changeable, being every thing by turns and nothing long, – I am such a strange *mélange* of good and evil, that it would be difficult to describe me. There are but two sentiments to which I am constant, – a strong love of liberty, and a detestation of cant, and neither is calculated to gain me friends.'

The meetings with Lady Blessington occurred in 1823 in Genoa, where she arrived with her husband and her necessary dandy, the Count D'Orsay. Byron was well settled with the Countess Guiccioli and her father in their common exile in the nine months that preceded the poet's fatal departure for Greece. Leslie A. Marchand's *A Heart for Every Fate* is the tenth, and penultimate, volume of the excellent unexpurgated edition of all known Byron letters, and covers this period. The letters of the new volume are discernibly less vivacious than those in which Byron was seen, at the age of thirty-one, falling in love with the nineteen-year-old Countess and causing alarm among the Austrian secret police. After four years, the liaison is in the pleasant doldrums of something like a marriage. If, as Byron wrote, 'the great object of life is sensation – to feel that we exist,' the sensational is now in abeyance. He is even dieting to keep down the threat of corpulence; there is no pursuit of other women, though the pretty Countess is often jealous. But there are signs of another restlessness: the political. The sight of the sea at Genoa – the port of so many adventurers – perhaps revived temptation. If there are signs of conjugal 'settling down', there are also rather secretive indications of 'clearing up' and putting his money affairs in order for a bolder purpose. He knows he is risking his life. There is a rush, canto by canto, to finish *Don Juan*, as if the poem were an investment; this leads to the quarrels with John Murray, his publisher, who is tiring of *Don Juan* and wants him to get back to the manner of *Childe Harold*. A canto of this period opens with a comic attack on the metaphysics of Berkeley. The poet says he has moved from the 'metaphysical' to the 'phthisical', because 'ever and anon comes Indigestion', not to mention inflammations and chilblains.

> I don't know what the reason is – the air
> Perhaps; but as I suffer from the shocks
> Of illness, I grow much more orthodox.

To the extent of going back to his early Old Testament Calvinist terrors and writing the play *Cain* in language that has lost its tune.

So his restless mind turns to Greece, in order to escape his buried despairs. He is happy with the Countess; nevertheless, he schemes to go, torn between guilt about her and his new desire. She fights back and wants to go with him – 'of course the idea is ridiculous.' She must be kept out of harm's way:

> If she makes a scene – (and she has a turn that way) we shall have another romance – and tale of ill usage and abandonment – and Lady Caroling – and Lady Byroning – and Glenarvoning – all cut and dry; there never was a man who gave up so much to women – and all I have gained by it – has been the character of treating them harshly. . . When a man merely wishes to go on a great duty for a good cause – this selfishness on the part of the 'feminie' – is rather too much.

Before this, there is the professional annoyance: Murray delays publishing the new cantos of *Don Juan* and pretends to have mislaid the manuscripts. He gets many blasts from the poet, who eventually hands his work to Leigh Hunt's brother and the banker Kinnaird.

To Murray:

> I have received and answered through Mr Kinnaird your enigma of a note to him – which riddle as expounded by Œdipus – means nothing more than an evasion to get out of what you thought perhaps a bad business – either for fear of the Parsondom – or your Admiralty patrons – or your Quarter*lyers* – or some other exquisite reason – but why not be sincere & manly for once – and say so? . . . The truth is that you never know your own mind – and what between this opinion and that – and sundry high & mighty notions of your own extreme importance in the planetary system – you act like the philosopher in Rasselas who took the direction of the Winds under his auspices – take care – that one of them don't blow you down some morning.

But he goes on to say that he believes, or at least hopes, that after all Murray 'may be a good fellow at bottom', and then makes a plea on behalf of one of Murray's authors, who is on her beam-ends, and who, instead of applying to the Bishop or Mr Wilberforce, 'hath recourse to that proscribed – Atheistical – syllogistical – phlogistical person – *mysen* – as they say in Notts.' The raillery and rancour often glide away like this, and turn into a half-Scottish peer's teasing of a Scottish tradesman. And there are other touchy domestic matters, such as Byron's famous loathing of Leigh Hunt's 'six little blackguards', who are 'dirtier and more mischievous than Yahoos' ('what they can't destroy with their filth they will with their fingers'). There is his charity to their father – Byron calls him 'a bore' but won't let this unworldly and childish man starve. After all, he *is* a combative liberal enemy of established society – a Radical – even though trying to help him 'is like pulling a man out of a river who directly throws himself in again.'

This comedy is very well known to literary history. There are tender, playful letters to his sister Augusta – letters that have a touch of the guilty 'little language' he and his sister had in common. He supposes that a Pimlico lady who has fallen in love with him for having written *Don Juan* is either mad or 'nau' (i.e., naughty), like Constantia, Echo, and La Swissesse – old loves Augusta will giggle about. There is a grotesque account of a flood in Genoa, where a preaching friar who prophesied the immediate date of the Day of Judgement had persuaded the population to send him 'presents' to avert it. The Genoese, true to their traditions, asked for their money back when the Judgement did not occur, and then had a fiesta. And there is news of new London scandals, such as the strange transformation of Lord Portsmouth after his marriage to a lawyer's daughter who horsewhipped him, seemingly because he was impotent and a lunatic, whereas he had appeared to be a man 'who had been allowed to walk about the world five and forty years as Compos – of voting – franking – marrying – convicting thieves on his own evidence – and similar pastimes which are the privileges of Sanity.' There is a pleasant friendship with a cousin of some sort, Lady Hardy, who is being pursued vainly by a coxcomb – 'now conceited into a knight (but of no order – a regular Address and City knight)' – who swears that his black wig is the 'flaxen poodle furniture with which Nature had decorated his head ten years ago.' Byron tries to make this ass return to his wife in Lausanne and utters the moral that lovers cannot be friends, 'because there must always be a spice of jealousy – and a something of Self in all their speculations.' Indeed, love is 'a sort of hostile transaction.' (He said the same of bargains in general, especially with Murray.) The reflection went into two lines of the continuing *Don Juan*. His own 'Love perils are – I believe pretty well over,' he tells Lady Hardy, and hers, 'by all accounts are never to begin.' However, '*la mia Dama*' (the Countess Guiccioli) was having 'a furious fit of Italian jealousy' because he went riding with Lady Blessington (of whom Lawrence had painted a portrait 'that set all London raving') and her supposed lover the Count D'Orsay. In later years, the Guiccioli said of one of Byron's own early jealous letters to her that it had a '*jalousie magnifique – passionné – sublime mais très injuste*'. In another letter to his sister Augusta, he once said that the Countess was indeed pretty but 'a great Coquette – extremely vain – excessively affected – clever enough – without the smallest principle – with a good deal of imagination and some passion.' But a bore as an equestrian: 'Can't guide her horse – and . . . begins screaming.'

Byron admires the Count D'Orsay, because he

penetrated *not* the *fact* – but the *mystery* of the English Ennui at two and
twenty. – I was about the same age when I made the same discovery in almost
precisely the same circles . . . but I never could have described it so well. . . .
He ought to have seen the Gentlemen after dinner – (on the hunting days) . . .
and the women looking as if they have had [sic] hunted – or rather been
hunted – too. . . . [Dessert] was hardly on the table – when out of 12 of the
masculine gender – I counted *five asleep*.

Byron admired D'Orsay's 'Journal' and showed it to Teresa Guiccioli, who found it gave her a much better notion of English society
than 'all Madame de Stael's metaphysical dissertations.' We doubt if
she had ever read those philosophical writings.

In all the 'clearing up' letters, in which he is obliged to look after
the legal complications of his estate and his separation from 'Lady B'
and is at pains to cause no trouble, one detects a desire to get rid of
encumbrance for good and to make a bid for another romance –
fame in the Greek cause. At the same time, one is struck by his skill in
making the fuss of financial and organisational detail lively. As a
libertine, he was a pedant. Byron was stirred by every intrigue,
however mundane, that human nature is up to. The poet was very
much a man of the world, the expatriate had a lot of time on his
hands: the tedium had to be dispelled. He was more calculating than
erratic. The play *Cain* brings his haunting private despair to the
surface, but the letters contain nothing of it. The bravura is still there,
and the amateur Satan's careless good nature is a kind of noblesse
oblige.

(1980)

THOMAS LOVE PEACOCK

The Proximity of Wine

The desire for settlement comes with peculiar force to stockbrokers; but the wish of Mr Crotchet, the retired City man of Weybridge, is common to us all:

'The sentimental against the rational,' said Mr Crotchet, 'the intuitive against the inductive, the ornamental against the useful, the intense against the tranquil, the romantic against the classical: these are the great and interesting controversies which I should like, before I die, to see satisfactorily settled.'

Even those of us who have not the disputatious, metaphysical Scottish blood which Peacock had slyly infused into the veins of Mr Crotchet, may join in his unhopeful sigh. What is the good of inviting intellectuals down for the week end unless they settle matters like these once and for all? Alas, the habit of the intellectual is to be unsettling and in both senses of the word. There is a chronic Mr Firedamp in every *posse* of the brainy; even when final order seems to have been achieved, there is always one bat left in the belfries:

'There is another great question,' said Mr Firedamp, 'greater than those, seeing that it is necessary to be alive in order to settle any question and this is the question of water against human woe. Wherever there is water, there is *malaria*, and wherever there is malaria there are the elements of death. The great object of a wise man should be to live on a gravelly hill, without so much as a duckpond within 10 miles of him, eschewing cisterns and water butts. . . .'

Dr Folliott, a Tory and a practical man, had at any rate, the answer in his cellar. 'The proximity of wine', he said, was of more importance 'than the longuinquity of water.' After sufficient Burgundy the endless and cantankerous algebra of life appears lucid and limited. Wine has the triple merit of enriching the vocabulary, cheering the heart, and narrowing the mind, and the sooner one cuts the cackle of the intellectuals with some good food and drink the sooner comes peace on earth.

The food and drink question is fundamental in Peacock. On
Samuel Butler's theory that all Radicals have bad digestions, it is
clear that from the wine and food test Peacock comes out true-blue
Tory. There is no stab of that sublimated bellyache which drives the
rest of us into progressive politics. Of course we know that Peacock
called himself a Liberal and wrote for the Liberal reviews; but the
enemies of the Utilitarians considered him a joke and Hazlitt teased
him for 'warbling' on the wrong side of the fence.

The game Peacock played was a dangerous one, and in a man less
original and gifted it would have been disastrous. Peacock's virtue
was that he had no political opinions in a very political age; or rather,
that he had all the opinions, as a dog has fleas in order to keep his
mind off being a dog. Peacock's mind kept open house and ruled the
table; too often that leads, in literary circles, to banging the table.
One can see this in the Rev Dr Folliott. A great character, perhaps the
greatest of the Peacock characters, but how close the guzzling
clergyman comes to being one of those vinous boors, one of those
bottled, no-nonsense dogmatists who tyrannise the table and bully
the world of letters with comic bluster about their common sense:

MR MACQUEDY.   Then, sir, I presume you set no value on the right
    principles of rent, profit, wages and currency.
REVD DR FOLLIOTT.   My principles, sir, in these things are to take as
    much as I can get and to pay no more than I can help. These are everyman's
    principles, whether they be the right principles or no. There, sir, is political
    economy in a nutshell.

There is too great a finality in the well-fed; and though Dr Folliott
redresses a balance and is a brilliant and mature device for winding
the theorists back to the earth – very necessary in the novel of ideas –
one's mind does wander to 'poor Mrs Folliott' who, having combed
her husband's wig, is firmly left at home. One remembers other poor
Mrs Folliotts pecking a timid and hen-like way behind their boozy,
commonsensical cockalorums. And while we have still got political
economy in a nutshell it is interesting to note how strong a respect for
money is ingrained in the crackling, phlegmatic temper of our
satirical writers. It is strong in Iago, it is strong in Swift (the Drapier
letters), Shaw is an enthusiastic accountant and Peacock's principles
regarding paper money amount to mania. On that subject he was a
Firedamp. We may imagine his reactions when, having invited
Shelley to live in Marlow, he heard that the poet was giving away his
clothes and his money to the indigent inhabitants. It is always

surprising when poetic justice is benevolent, and most critics have gasped with incredulous satisfaction at Peacock's luck in hooking a job worth £2,000 a year or more out of the East India Company; what is significant and even more poetically fitting is that Peacock was a success at the job. He it was who organised the building and dispatch of the flat-bottomed gunboats used by the company in the East. There blossomed the Utilitarian. One doubts whether Wordsworth was as efficient at the Excise.

The life of Peacock covers a period of enormous differences. One of Peacock's modern critics, Mr John Mair, has pointed out how fantastic is the range of his life.

He lived through the French Revolution and the Great Exhibition; he could have read his first books to Nelson and his last to Bernard Shaw [who would not have understood it], Dr Johnson died a year before his birth and Yeats was born a year before his death. He both preceded and survived Byron, Shelley, Keats and Macaulay; he was contemporary with Rowlandson and with Landseer.

For a satirical mind this was the perfect feast; history at its most conflicting and indigestible. For a temperament liable to be infected by all schools of thought in turn and unable to resist cocking snooks at them, here was wealth. Peacock dined off his disabilities and one can almost hear his unholy highbrow cackle when he finds himself not only pre-dating but surviving his victims. Some annoyance has been felt because he became a kind of reactionary by default; you ought not to pull the leg of your own party. But could there have been a more delightful occupation for one whose baptismal water had a drop of the acid of perversity in it? A Grub Street hack in his time, and one who (according to Hazlitt anyway) overpraised as wildly as any of our commercial reviewers, he sneers at the puffs of Grub Street. A hater of Scotsmen, he was a theoretical Scotsman for, as Professor Saintsbury discovered, Peacock was baptised at the Scottish kirk. He scarifies Miss Philomel Poppyseed for saying true love is impossible on less than £1,000 a year but is as acute about the marriage settlements of his own characters as Jane Austen herself. Everywhere the satirist is reacting against his own wishes and disappointments. There is little doubt that an erratic education fostered his originality as it also failed to provide some strong stamp which would have made up his mind; there would have been no Peacock if he had gone to the University. But those sneers at the University which always crop up in his books are prolonged; and when the debates between the deteriorationists, the progressives, the transcendentalists and rational economists bore us, we cannot reject the suspicion that Peacock spent a good deal of his literary life training to be an undergraduate.

If Peacock's mind was not made up, if he snapped at his opponents and his friends, it would be a mistake to think of him as a complete *farceur*. When the effervescence has died down there is a deposit of belief which is not party belief but is rather his century's habit of mind. The eighteenth century had formed him; he belonged to that middleman and professional class which did not share – at least, did not directly share – in the rewards of the industrial revolution. When Mr Escot speaks against the mills in *Headlong Hall*, he is not putting a party view; he is pleading like a merchant philosopher for the content of living in a world that was violently altering its form in the optimistic delusion that the content would look after itself. If Mr Peacock-Escot is a reactionary, then one can only reply that it is the rôle of reactionaries, once they have given up obstruction, to remind us that the Sabbath was made for man. Their function is to preserve amenities and that private humanity which revolutionaries care for so little. Here is Mr Escot with his everything-is-as-bad-as-it-can-be-in-the-worst-of-possible-worlds:

> You present to me a complicated picture of artificial life, and require me to admire it. Seas covered with vessels; every one of which contains two or three tyrants, and from fifty to a thousand slaves, ignorant, gross, perverted and active only in mischief. Ports resounding with life: in other words with noise and drunkenness, the mingled din of avarice, intemperance and prostitution. Profound researches, scientific inventions: to what end? To contract the sum of human wants? to teach the art of living on a little? to disseminate independence, liberty and health? No; to multiply factitious desires, to stimulate depraved appetites, to invent irrational wants, to heap up incense on the shrine of luxury, and accumulate expedients of selfish and ruinous profusion.

He goes on to a description of children in the cotton mills, a true piece of Dickensian phantasmagoria – 'observe their pale and ghastly features, more ghastly in that baleful and malignant light and tell me if you do not fancy yourself on the threshold of Virgil's Hell. . . .' Did that passage have any effect on the more ruthless of Peacock's readers? One doubts it. The voice of the Age of Reason was reactionary and decadent from the point of view of the nineteenth-century liberals, and most of us were born into the nineteenth century's belief that a period is decadent which has arrived at the civilised stillness of detached self-criticism. Peacock said the wise thing in the wrong way, i.e. the detached way. It was the attached people, more vulgar, more sentimental, more theatrically subject to the illusions of the new period, who could and did attack child labour and the mills with some effect.

For a man as mercurial and unseizable as Peacock was, what really counted was the farce. Detached, isolated, hiding caution behind a fantasticating brain, silent about the private urges of his heart, unimaginative, timid of 'acrimonious dispute' (as the scathing so often are), he enjoyed the irresponsibilities of an intellect which cannot define its responsibilities. His cruelty to his victims is merely the brain's. There he can display an extravagance which elsewhere a prudent nature denies him. His satire was not resented, as far as one knows, by the victims. Shelley laughed at Scythrop in *Nightmare Abbey*. No doubt Shelley's own irresponsibility responded to Peacock's distorted picture of him torn between Harriet and Mary Godwin, 'like a shuttlecock between two battledores, changing its direction as rapidly as the oscillations of a pendulum receiving many a hard knock on the cork' – the cork! – 'of a sensitive heart and flying from point to point in the feathers of a super-sublimated head'.

As they come fragmentarily into focus, the Peacock novels have the farcical dream-atmosphere of the surrealists' dreams. Their slapstick and their unexpected transitions, their burlesque discussions, and their fancy lead through *Alice in Wonderland* to the present. It is amusing to find present parallels for the deteriorationist and the rational economist. Peacock chose permanent types; but without the knock-about and the romance, that amusement would soon become bookish and musty. Scythrop concealing his lady in the tower and lying about the movable bookcase, Mr Toobad jumping out of the window at the sight of the 'ghost' and being fished out of the moat by the dreary scientists who are down there with their nets fishing for mermaids, Squire Headlong's experiments with explosives, Dr Folliott's adventures with the highwaymen – this picaresque horseplay is the true stuff of the English comic tradition from Sterne and Fielding, a new gloss on the doings of the Pickwick Club. And Peacock can alternate the perfunctory with the heroic manner, which our tradition especially requires. Gradually, as he perfected his genre, progressing from the Hall to the Abbey, from the Abbey to the Castle, Peacock balanced his extremes. Romantic love plays its part, not the wild meadowy stuff of course, but a romance which secretes an artificial sweetness, the *faux naturel* of the eighteenth century, which at once suggests the formal and untutored. In this heady world the women alone – if one excepts the highbrow Poppyseed and the awful Mrs Glowry – have the sense and sensibility. Peacock cuts short the sighs; marriages are arranged, not made in Heaven, dowries are not forgotten; but what a delightful convention (the India clerk reminds us) marriage is.

One might expect more broadness in so keen a reader of Rabelais, but Peacock (unless my memory is bad or my ear for *double entendre* dull) appears to share the primness of Dr Folliott, a primness one often finds among the drinkers. There is only one smoke-room remark in *Crotchet Castle* – and a very good one it is. It occurs after the cook has set her room on fire when she has fallen asleep over a treatise on hydrostatics in cookery:

LORD BOSSNOWL.   But, sir, by the bye, how came your footman to be going into your cook's room? It was very providential, to be sure but . . .

REVD DR FOLLIOTT.   Sir, as good came of it, I shut my eyes and ask no questions. I suppose he was going to study hydrostatics and he found himself under the necessity of practising hydraulics.

I suppose it should be argued that Dr Folliott's anger about the exhibition of an undraped female figure on the stockbroker's mantelpiece was grounded less in the prudery of the bibulous than in the general Peacockian dislike of popular education. He was against putting ideas into his footman's head. An act of benevolence, for no one knew so well as Peacock how funny a man with an idea in his head can be.

(1944)

A Rough English Diamond

One impression of ordinary English life from the mid-eighteenth century to the middle of the nineteenth is that it is thronged by an ever-increasing crowd of grotesque bodies, sprawling in their energetic vulgarity or skinny in their dramatic misery. The over-whelming impression is of a crowd bursting with involuntary imaginative and moral life, in the pathos, absurdity, and animality of the flesh. I refer not only to what we have had from novelists but, of course, to the caricaturists especially and masterly graphic artists, like Hogarth, Rowlandson, Gillray, and finally Cruikshank. In the last, the sense of the crowd becomes at times mythical and animistic; Napoleon is seen early in Cruikshank's career standing on a vast pyramid of crowded skulls; in the 'Hungry Forties' a giant mincer is seen turning thousands of sewing girls into the coins of the Capitalist's profits; as London expands crowds of steel spades looking like devilish Martians are tearing up the countryside without human aid; at the Great Exhibition, England pours its whole population – so that a city like Manchester is left empty – into Piccadilly; the tender triumph of Cupid packs the drawing with clouds of babies.

But after the Great Exhibition the free-for-all calms down, the country turns from its disaffections to self-satisfaction and gentility, and now Cruikshank's reign as the leading humorist and caricaturist of the time begins to decline. The middle-class respectability of *Punch*, for which he refused to draw, is established; low life is 'out' or is seen as 'a problem'. Cruikshank's *genius* did not decline, but he was less prolific, narrowed his field to propaganda against the evils of drink, and indeed changed his style.

Now Richard A. Vogler gives us a scholarly selection of 279 of Cruikshank's etchings and drawings taken from the five or six thousand he is known to have done. Each of them has a short and expert commentary and there is a long introduction expounding the techniques, changes of process, and other influences of his trade on his genius. There also is a serious defence of popular comic art, which has been neglected by art historians, and indeed of the essentially anarchic nature of comedy. Vogler protests against regarding Cruikshank in a belittling way purely as an illustrator of books.

Little is known about his daily life beyond the fact that he was a perpetual worker who liked jolly and Bohemian company and avoided High Society when he rapidly became famous. In person he was celebrated for the originality of his fantastically designed whiskers and for the ingenious pattern of his hair style: the strands were artfully held into place by concealed elastic bands. He could be said to have etched his hair.

Born in 1792 he was the son of a graphic artist who had migrated from Scotland to London and settled in the jungle of poor streets that lie between Pentonville and Camden Town – the deeply Dickensian maze. He and his brother and sister took up the father's craft, working for newspapers and booksellers, i.e. publishers, as caricaturists and illustrators. Cruikshank rarely left London or his district in the eighty-five years of his life though he once did a Cockney trip to Boulogne for a few days and (because he was something of a singer and actor) appeared in one of Dickens's amateur theatrical ventures in the North.

Ainsworth, Dickens, and others found him delightful company but distinctly quirky and stubborn in working arrangements. (In old age he claimed that these novelists owed many of their best touches to him, a matter which is hotly disputed: one trouble is that his work was copied and recopied without further pay from the booksellers and he strongly resented this.) Still, he did pretty well, married twice. Though it is thought he had no children, there is a suspicion that he had a secret family of nine or ten to whose mother he left a substantial legacy. Some of his impish illustrations of children's books suggest that he had strong philoprogenitive feelings.

There was one dramatic change in Cruikshank's life. It happened when he was forty-seven. The convivial fellow who had once begged Dickens to walk home with him because he feared what his wife would say about his unsteady condition, suddenly gave up the bottle for good and now spent as much time speaking at temperance meetings as he did at his work. He became a fanatical propagandist and some critics, especially Ruskin, said this had a dulling effect on his work. Mr Vogler does not agree with this conventional view. Cruikshank gave up drink when he reached the age at which his father had died after a drinking bout: the conversion may owe something to superstition.

A more important argument surely is that hard drinking is incompatible with the minute and delicate demands of the etcher's art. Equally important was Cruikshank's long-frustrated ambition to equal the great Hogarth who was his master and to do a series of pictures that would bring Gin Alley up to date. Finally, Cruikshank was a man of strong will with an individualist's social conscience and a professional sense of the topical. The formidable temperance movement had begun.

In a well-known essay Thackeray called Cruikshank 'a fine rough English diamond' and 'diamond' is the sparkling word that sticks in the mind. Baudelaire wrote that his special merit lies 'in his inexhaustible abundance of grotesque. A verve such as his is unimaginable. . . . The grotesque flows inevitably and incessantly from Cruikshank's etching needle, like pluperfect rhymes from the pen of a natural poet.'

The perceptions of the comic genius, even when they are directed to the vulgar or ordinary, are almost always poetic. Vogler speaks of 'the anarchic power of comedy': Cruikshank was neither a radical nor a conservative – he satirised universal suffrage; he did not agree with Dickens that the sole causes of the appalling evils of drink in the Victorian age were poverty and misery. There were others. His object was 'to cleanse by mirth' and strip away 'smugness'. And on his defence of Cruikshank as a popular artist, Vogler says,

an artist like Cruikshank became the nineteenth-century exponent of a visual tradition in European religious and secular art which relates symbols and language in a unique way. Pictorial traditions tend to survive more pervasively in popular art forms like caricature than in almost any other kind of art. . . . The recurrent use of a dunce's hat in Cruikshank goes back to the basic iconology available to artists from the time of the Renaissance. Cruikshank is a late but direct inheritor of a very complex visual language that has steadily lost its power over the modern world.

He is also very literary. These lines are written to stir the art historians. Let us look at Cruikshank's early graphics done during the Regency. One notices at once the bite and grace of ingeniously placed detail. Byron takes his romantic farewell to England in a boat full of luscious adoring ladies, but the comments of the vulgar seamen are rudely offhand; Napoleon's soldiers are not simply stuck in the Russian snow, they are up to their elegant cocked hats in it. The remnants of the Grande Armée are skeletons, their uniforms are in ridiculous rags. As for royalty at home – George IV is a balloon of flesh. A fat couple are stuck in a doorway of a crowded and fashionable drawing room. The appalled eyes, the pursed apologetic little mouth of the lordling who has trodden on a lady's trailing skirt are a subtle composite of the grimace and speechless abuse that will twitch on a polite face for a split second. Notice the man's clawed hand, notice also the young couple having a peaceful chat in this melée of colliding bellies.

In 'Villagers Shooting out the Rubbish' the coarse villagers are pushing out the bewigged clergyman and the gentry in wheelbarrows. In 'Effects of a Heavy Lurch on board an East Indiaman' the artist catches every bizarre angle into which arms and legs can fall, every shape of a shouting mouth, while an undisturbed seaman grunts, 'Hang on by your eyelids.' Note also the Hogarthian variety of detail, down to the upturned dog biting a passenger's leg; and, of course, a stout lady with her legs in the air as the centrepiece. She has just given a whack on the nose to a gentleman who is trying nervously to pull back her leg into decency. There are cracks at illness: gout and the colic are celebrated by gangs of devils – surfeit is a joke. There are the parades of monstrous fashions at Brighton. And if the Radical Reform has a death's head it is leading the scum of the prisons, the sword of constitutional Britannia has buckled and becomes putty. Cruikshank hated revolution; on the other hand, the English boroughmongers are seen pouring out bribes and sinecures from a water mill, while the poor lie dying under the pillars of Parliament.

It pays to use a magnifying glass on many of Cruikshank's smaller graphics and Vogler's notes are enlightening both on Cruikshank's fancy and on his topicality. So the *Sunday in London* series (1833) was undertaken as a humorous protest against an attempt to introduce a Bill in Parliament which would impose strict observation of the Sabbath – Dickens wrote an indignant pamphlet on the same subject. There was an attempt to close Sunday street-trading – a long-standing London liberty – during church services. The bill was an attack on the lower classes: the servants and delivery boys of the wealthy were exempted from restrictions! In 'The Pay Table', a drunken workman comes up for his wages, while a tavern-keeper stands by the employer in order to deduct the man's drinking debts from his pay. One sees the common crowd brawling cheerfully as they are being turned out of gin palaces, at church time, and the series ends with the high order sitting smugly in church. In contrast, in an illustration of Scott's *Heart of Midlothian*, Captain of Knockdunder is seen defying the preacher by smoking a foul pipe in church. Another sketch – an example of Cruikshank's jolly anthropomorphic fancy – shows a preacher in the shape of a weeping crocodile.

Vogler's book includes the pictures relating to 'The Loving Ballad of Lord Bateman' – a popular song which was one of Cruikshank's party turns. Bateman, the 'ruler' of Northumberland, travelled to Turkey, was imprisoned, but was set free by the Sultan's daughter to whom he promised marriage. He got away, was about to marry 'another', but the Turk's daughter rushed over to claim him – a delightful ballet – for Cruikshank was an incurable dancer.

Mr Vogler notes the use of language and punning symbols in his drawings. In 'The Fall of the Leaf' – in which half a dinner party is thrown to the ground when the leaf of the table collapses – there is a dim picture of Niagara Falls on the wall and on the floor there is a copy of Gibbon's *Decline and Fall of the Roman Empire*. Overdoing a joke? No. Echoes and repetitions extend the farce. Whether Cruikshank adds these glosses or is closely following 'things' that are tucked unannounced in a text he is illustrating, we see he is one artist complementing another. I go back to that overwhelming Victorian sense of the crowd: it is a crowd not only of people but of fantasies. They are like the charivari of gargoyles and imps on the Gothic cathedrals, a Gothic revival. Cruikshank's picture of himself in 'Reverie' shows him sitting smoking his pipe and puffing out thousands of passing delineations of people; in his 'Temptation of St Anthony' the saint is surrounded by a primitive bestiary most of which can be traced back to fantasies not unlike those of Bosch.

The best-known illustrations are those done for *Sketches by Boz* and *Oliver Twist*. To the last – except for Nancy – Cruikshank has been the classic guide. (So magical has been the picture of 'Oliver asking for more' and so strong the literary tradition among cartoonists, that an American cartoonist used it in connection with the request of Congress for more tapes in the Watergate scandal.) In the pictures of Fagin and Sikes it is noticeable that a preoccupation with strangulation and hanging slips in; the picture of Sikes's dog, faithfully following him to the roof from which Sikes jumps to hang himself by accident, is as chilling as it is in Dickens.

Yet Cruikshank could move with ease to the theatrical thunder and lightning of Ainsworth's histories. Some readers – and I was among them when I was a boy brought up on late-Victorian conventions – have felt that Cruikshank's fantasies were at disconcerting variance with the realistic images we imposed on the text; but this showed our blindness to the essence of the imagination of both artists. Also we had failed to accept the Gothic self-imagination of that escape from grim work into the dream-life of a riotously inventive and expansive age at grips with its conscience, its conviviality, its crimes, and the contrasts of rich and poor in the streets. Cruikshank was as prolific as the first half of the century was, and his sense of so many public scenes being, at heart, a brawl or a fight, albeit caught with robust laughter or an irony as sharp as the etcher's acid, turning hard times into phantasmagoria.

His anti-drink drawings for *The Bottle* are plain, realistic confrontations: the sober become comely in their domestic virtue, the sinners go step by step downhill as in the plain moralising manner of Hogarth, dragging decency down into the unanswerable pathos of the home destroyed before us. The feverish care of the artist is still there; his wonderful command of details of people in their scene is unabated, though the crowd has gone, and the private moral life and the sinister figures who prey on individuals replace myth. Victorian drinking was indeed ruinous to the poor and Cruikshank's *The Bottle*, like Zola's *L'Assommoir*, was an inescapable social document.

The strange thing is that, in this austere period of his life, Cruikshank made a hero of the great legendary figure of Falstaff who is still a bursting wine-skin but who looks like a benign, rather cleaned up Henry VIII. In this portrait Cruikshank indeed standardised the Falstaff of theatrical productions for several generations. One can account for this only by Cruikshank's love of historical subjects and their clothing and the fantasies of the unreal world of the Victorian theatre. And that brings one back to an essential in his art – his constant, even theatrical eye for staging his scenes, whether they are large or minute, tragic, pathetic, or comic, and for the hundreds of ways the dressed-up body can behave when taken unawares. Human beings are clothed doubles; they stand in a room or the street, yet in their minds they are also standing elsewhere in the passions of the moment. Standing? Not quite – something in them is on the move.

(1980)

R. S. SURTEES

The Brutal Chivalry

Robert Surtees is a sport, in both senses of the term, who flashes in and out of the English novel, excites hope and reduces the critical factions to silence. He has all the dash, all the partiality and all the prospect of an amateur. There is a rush of air, a shower of rain drops from the branches, a burst of thundering mud, a crashing of hazel, the sight of a pink coat and, as far as the English novel is concerned, he has gone. In that brief appearance he has made the genial suggestion that all the other English novelists have been mistaken; they have missed the basic fact in English life – that we are religious, that our religion is violent sport. The unwritten life of a large proportion of the characters in English fiction is passed in playing or watching games in the open air; nature is being worshipped with the senses and the muscles. We are either bemused by fresh air or are daydreaming of some lazy, cunning and exhausting animal life in the open. In that condition, our hourly and sedentary habit of worry as a substitute for thought vanishes and we become people in love. It takes an amateur, like Surtees, to see an obvious thing like this and to exaggerate so that the part becomes the whole of English life. He was a north-country squire, an excellent sporting journalist, but hand-somely innocent of the future of hunting in England. He really believes that the Industrial Revolution would make the sport democratic. His assumption is that English violence can be appeased only by the horse. He is the final authority on our horse civilisation, and Jorrocks is a sort of Don Quixote of the last phase of a brutal chivalry. *Après moi* (he might have said) *le garage*.

It is natural that hunting people should admire Surtees. It is not surprising that serious literary critics should admire him also. He creates a complete world. It is the world which Fielding's and Thackeray's people knew in their off-stage lives. It has no relation with the feeble sub-culture of horse-lovers, pony-worshippers, or

with the gentility of the jodhpur that spread over England as the
coach gave way to the railway, provoking the cult of the New Forest
pony. The natural democrats of England live in the north and,
though Surtees was a Tory squire, he sincerely believed that the horse
was an insurance against the new, snobbish exclusiveness of the
shot-up Victorian middle class. He imagined, as so many have done
before, that class revolutions will not become snobbish and
exclusive. Happy pastoral delusion! Surtees did not foresee either the
hardness or the sentimentality of the coming urban England. Or,
perhaps, he half guessed it. For the point about Jorrocks is that he is
(1) not a horse-lover but a fox-lover, (2) that he rides, buys and sells
horses, (3) that he has not an aitch to his name. He is, boldly,
incontrovertibly, aggressively, in mid-nineteenth century – a grocer.
His fame is that he is not merely a sportsman, but a Cockney
sportsman. He has all the trading sharpness and romanticism of a
man who sells tea. Surtees is content (purposefully content) with this
reality. Jorrocks is as vulgar as Keats; and, as a northerner and a
gentleman, Surtees refuses to accept the improved accents of the
new-rich in the south. He exploits the rewards our class system offers
to our literature. We are continually supplying a number of vulgar
geniuses who stand out against the new snobberies which the Puritan
streak in us is liable to create; and, in the case of Surtees, there is the
anomaly that a Tory squire provides the vulgar protest. The heir of
Jorrocks is Mr Polly. Both are native protests against the mean and
successful revolutions that deny the instincts of genial, sincere and
natural men.

Surtees owes a lot to the low side of Thackeray and does seamy
society a good deal better. His dialogue is as quick and true as the
master's. He extends a robust and native tradition: the masculine
strain of English comic writing. This comedy is broad and
extroverted. It grins at the pleasures and pains of the human animal –
if it is male – and has little time for the female. Occasionally Surtees
sees a tolerable female, but very rarely. We need not suppose that he
agreed with Jorrocks that a man ought to kick his wife out of bed
three times a month, but we suspect this was only because he
regarded the act wistfully as an ideal unfortunately unattainable.
The fact is that our comic extroverts are like Mr Sponge and bring a
horse-dealer's eye to the consideration of women – 'fifteen two and a
half is plenty of height' for them. In its male world, the comic
tradition likes the misfortunes of the body, the bruises, the black

eyes, the drinking sessions, the gorging at table; prefers the low to the refined, the masterful and unreasonable to the sensitive and considerate. There is a strong regard for the impossible element in human character, for the eccentric and the obsessed. The brutes have their engaging moments. (They give the right kind of girl half a dozen smacking kisses.) But their transcendent emotions emerge in another direction. Jorrocks will quarrel with his huntsman, Pigg, but be reconciled, to the point of embracing him, at the kill. These people are dedicated. They will suffer anything, from drowning upwards, for their sport. They will experience an ecstasy which goes beyond the animal into the poetic. And, in the meantime, they will rollick. Thoroughly non-Puritan, they understand that the life of animal pleasure is the life of animal dismay and they accept it. What these writers in the masculine comic tradition dwell on is the variety of human nature. They know that action brings this out, and with a kind of mercy, they will forgive anything so long as action, not introspection, has revealed it.

Mr Aubrey Noakes has written a good brief appreciation of Surtees. It does not add to earlier studies, but it does bring out the importance of his experience with the law and his adventures in politics. Mr Noakes also goes into the interesting reluctance of the Victorians to take to him until Leech illustrated his novels. On the one hand, Surtees was a man of the eighteenth century – hence Thackeray's understanding of him; on the other, he was an amateur who dealt almost entirely with background figures, the great Jorrocks excepted. He was deeply knowing about English sporting life, the squirearchy and the law, but he did not construct the melodramas and elaborate plots of the other Victorian novelists, nor did he issue their moralisings. He often excelled them in the recording of ordinary speech and day-to-day incident. He is fresher than the masters, but he is artless. A good deal of his humour is the humour of shrewd sayings which, later on, we find in Kipling. His original contribution is in the field of invective. Surtees has a truly Elizabethan power of denunciation. Here is Jorrocks loosing off to his servant:

'Come hup, you snivellin', drivellin' son of a lucifer-match maker,' he roars out to Ben who is coming lagging along in his master's wake. 'Come on,' roars he, waving his arm frantically, as, on reaching Ravenswing Scar, he sees the hounds swinging down, like a bundle of clock pendulums into the valley below. 'Come hup, I say, ye miserable, road-ridin', dish-lickin' cub!

And give me that quad, for you're a disgrace to a saddle, and only fit to toast muffins for a young ladies' boarding school. Come hup, you preter-pluperfect tense of 'umbugs. . . . Come on, ye miserable, useless son of a lily-livered besom-maker. Rot ye, I'll bind ye 'prentice to a salmon-pickler.'

This is all the more splendid because Jorrocks keeps to the ''ard road' as much as possible, and can't bear taking a fence. He is eloquent, perhaps because he is as cowardly as Falstaff and yet as sincere in his passion. He knows what he wants to be. His is the eloquence of romance. And this is where we come to the Dickensian aspect of Surtees, too. Dickens has several degrees of comic observation. There is the rudimentary Dickens of caricature, of the single trait or phase turned into the whole man. And there is the Dickens where this is elaborated into soliloquy, in which the character is represented by his fantasy life. Like the rudimentary Dickens, Surtees feels for the man who has one idea. *Handley Cross*, *Mr Facey Romford's Hounds* and *Mr Sponge's Tours* are packed with minor eccentrics of the field, the fancy and the law; but in Jorrocks, Surtees enters upon the more complex study of people who live out the comic orgy. 'By 'eavens, it's sublime,' says Jorrocks, watching the hounds stream over a hundred acres of pasture below him. ''Ow they go, screechin' and towlin' along just like a pocketful o' marbles . . .' 'Ow I wish I was a heagle.' A 'heagle' he is, in that moment; sublimity is his condition. He has shrewdly built up his pack, he has given his uproarious lectures, he has had his vulgar adventures in country-houses; he has got the better of his betters and has outdone the new rich in vulgarity – making among other things that immortal remark about mince: 'I like to chew my own meat' – he has disgraced Mrs Jorrocks, but he has pursued an obsession utterly, so that it has no more to teach him, beyond the fact that it has damaged his credit among the accountants in the City. Fortunately, Surtees has given him power of speech. Jorrocks is never at a loss for repartee or for metaphor. He is remarkable in his duels with Pigg, and the only pity is that Pigg's dialect is nearly incomprehensible. But Pigg and his master are well-matched. They battle like theologians about the true business of life: the pursuit of foxes.

Surtees is a specialist. But he is, to an important extent, outside his speciality. He had strong views about sport. He hated the drunken-ness of sporting society and the old squirearchy. He hoped the new age would bring in something better. He was hostile to the literary conventions. His parodies of *Nimrod* show him as an opponent of literary snobbery. He disliked the obsequious regime of servants and the rogueries of the stable, the auctions and the law. It is odd that one so saturated in his world should have seen it all with so fresh an eye. Perhaps he had that morbidity of eye which is given to some men at the end of a period, when they can see things with the detachment which considerable art demands. He was too much the gentleman and amateur to construct a great novel; but he was independent enough and sufficiently instructed by obsession to create in Jorrocks a huge character who could go off and live an episodic life of his own. The Victorians were shy of Surtees's honesty. They were moving away from the notion that there was a level on which all Englishmen could be united. They were building the split-culture of our time. Surtees was trying to save England on the acres of Handley Cross.

(1961)

CHARLES DICKENS

Oliver Twist

Oliver Twist is the second novel of Charles Dickens. It was begun before *Pickwick* was finished when he was twenty-six and in the full conceit and harassing of sudden fame; and *Barnaby Rudge* was started before he got Nancy murdered and before Bill Sikes slipped by accident off the wall on Jacob's Island into his own noose. It is a novel speckled with good London observation, but the critics agree that the book which gave the word Bumbledom to the language is a gloomy and inferior work, stretched out on an incredible plot, blatant with false characters and false speech and wrecked by that stageyness which Dickens was never long to resist. The story is a film scenario full of tears and 'ham', an efficacious splurge of Cockney self-pity. On the other hand, the reader must protest that all this is no drawback to his excitement. The popular thriller is generally based on the abstraction of sinister human wishes from the common reality of life; and, willingly suspending disbelief, we can eagerly accept Fagin, even Bill Sikes and Mr Brownlow, even Nancy and Rose Maylie, as permitted fantasies. Is it because of the hypnotic fame of Dickens or because he is completely responsive to the popular taste for uninspected myth, that all his characters stay in the mind? Only the neurotic Monks and the creaking, sceptical Grimwig, have one false foot in the world of our experience.

A new edition of *Oliver Twist* has the advantage of a really brilliant, melancholy and subtle appreciation by Mr Graham Greene, himself a thorough initiate in the art of writing thrillers. It is one of those uncommon prefaces that expertly test the technical merits of a book and enlarge its suggestion. Before turning to his main points, there are two obvious yet easily forgotten virtues in *Oliver Twist* which put what might have been a total failure on its feet. For there is no doubt that *Oliver Twist* 'comes off'. In the first place it is a literary novel, nourished by Dickens's early reading. The echoes from Monk Lewis, the touches from *Jonathan Wild* in the framing of the portraits of Mr Bumble or the Artful Dodger, the preface which curiously boasts that at last we are to be given real criminals – except in the matter of bad language – and not romantic ones, are all touching and agreeable glances from a spruce young author towards his tradition. (And, as Mr Greene shows, we certainly get real thieves' kitchens and the sour poverty of criminal life, the background but not the foreground.) In the second place, the book is given a kind of authority by the frank copying of Fielding's mock heroic and disquisitional moralising. By this Fielding displayed the assurance of his sensible morality, and it is true that Dickens debases the manner by turning it into something journalistic, sprightly and even facetious; nevertheless, the manner enabled him to assume a central place in the tale, from which he could exploit, without confusion, the variety of its moods.

It was Edmund Wilson who first saw the biographical importance of the melodramatic and criminal episodes in Dickens's work. They are for the most part the least successful as literature. They are commonly over-acted and, indeed, too much stress on these and the didactic side of Dickens, is likely to take us away from his greatness. It is all very well for modern critics to neglect the comic Dickens for there, as a writer, he was completely realised. On the other hand, the impurity of Dickens as a creator is an important fact; in his confusions and concealings, strange psychological shapes are disclosed. His relation was with the public which he bowed to and upon whose not always reputable feelings he played. Upon them, as upon an analyst, he enacted a transference. Mr Graham Greene's main point is, in a sense, an extension of Edmund Wilson's into the field of religion. He suggests the religious cast of Dickens's imagination:

How can we really believe that these inadequate ghosts of goodness [Mr Brownlow and Rose Maylie] can triumph over Fagin, Monks and Sikes? And the answer is, of course, that they never could have triumphed without the elaborate machinery of the plot disclosed in the last pages. The world of Dickens is a world without God; and as a substitute for the power and the glory of the omnipotent and omniscient are a few sentimental references to heaven, angels, the sweet faces of the dead, and Oliver saying, 'Heaven is a long way off, and they are too happy there to come down to the bedside of a poor boy!' In this Manichaean world we can believe in evil-doing but goodness melts into philanthropy and kindness. . . .

And Mr Greene ends with this paragraph:

. . . Is it too fantastic to imagine that in this novel, as in many of his later books, creeps in, unrecognised by the author, the eternal and alluring taint of the Manichee, with its simple and terrible explanation of our plight, how the world was made by Satan and not by God, lulling us with the music of despair?

That *is* too fantastic, of course, as a description even of Dickens's demonic imagination, of his unconscious as distinct from his conscious, orthodox religion. The terror of *Oliver Twist* is the acted terror inherited from literature and married to personal hysteria. The Manichee is good theatre. But the suggestion is an interesting one and if we follow its lead, we must be struck by the flashes of contact between *Oliver Twist* and the Manichaean myth. The child of light is lost in the world of darkness – the terrors of childhood are the primitive terrors of the dark – from which the far-away Elect will save him. When he is saved, the end of the world of darkness is brought about – Nancy is murdered, Sikes and Fagin are hanged. We might grope farther along the strange tunnels of the Manichaean allegory and discover there a suggestion upon which the Freudian analyst of the tale of ghosts or terror will immediately pounce. These tales are now held to be artistic transpositions of the fear of castration and when one turns (as an ignorant reviewer so often must) to the authority of the *Encyclopaedia Britannica*, one indeed finds that the thriller writers have pious if tainted progenitors in the fourth century. In their belief 'primal man descends into the abyss and prevents the further increase of the generations of darkness by cutting off their roots.' What is notable (one reflects) is that the enormous preoccupation of Victorian literature for murderous melodrama – and we remember the horrifying success of Dickens in his public readings of murderous scenes – goes with an extreme sexual prudery in literature. Murder – as the saying is – is 'cleaner' than sex. We seem to see a violent age seeking a compensation for its losses.

Whether or not the imaginative world of *Oliver Twist* is without God in the Christian sense we must leave to the theologians; the interest of Mr Greene's suggestion is the inevitable implication that the emissaries of light, the Elect, are the middle classes. It is Mr Brownlow and Miss Maylie who come down, to the tune of the ineffable music of the Three Per Cents. Only by sitting at the throne of Grace could they face the abyss of darkness in which the industrial poor, the everlastingly guilty were damned and lived waiting for their doom. Only by making Rose Maylie an angel could the

existence of Nancy be assimilated; only by making kindness old-
fashioned and respectable, could Sikes be faced as a modern, sullen
and temperamental brute. It does not follow, as Mr Graham Greene
suggests, that the evil represented is stronger than the good, in the
imaginative effect; the balance between these cardboard unrealities
is perfect and a thieves' kitchen always sounds more dramatic and
'strong' than a drawing-room. And so, too, on a more reputable
plane: against the half-dreamed figures of Monks and Fagin at the
window that seemed like the imprint of a primitive memory, must be
placed those other half-waking intimations Oliver had of some
happiness in a far-away past never known. What we are convinced
of, even though by the long arm of coincidence, is the long arm of
humanity and justice.

Oliver Twist is a literary novel. Magnificent juvenilia is Mr
Graham Greene's just phrase. The plots of Dickens were to improve
and one does not know whether to put down their tedious elaboration to Mr Chesterton's belief that they were an attempt to set out
'something less terrible than the truth'. That looks like a Chestertonian
attempt to put down something more eccentric than a fact. Perhaps
Dickens in his exhibitionism wanted to put down something *more*
terrible than the truth. Either explanation sharply applies to the
disastrous passion for plot general to the Victorian novel. It is a fact
that Dickens had the greatest difficulty in inventing probabilities and
that may be related to the fantastic turn of his mind.

All the main strains of his genius are crudely foreshadowed in
Oliver Twist. There is the wonderful clean snap of scene and
episode; nearly everything is 'realised'. Mr Greene has perceived one
of those reflective passages, memory evoking or regarding its own
act, which Proust admired, and there are occasional phrases – the
absurd servant's face 'pale and *polite* with fear' – or touches of detail
that show the hand of the master. We recall things like the wisp of
human hair on Sikes's club, that sizzled for a second when he threw it
in the fire; the notices in the country village warning vagrants to keep
out. Sikes's speech is ludicrous – "Wolves tear your throats,"
muttered Sikes' – but his death is wonderful; one remembers the boy
at the window taken by surprise when the hanged body drops and
shuts off his view and how he pushes it aside. The crude London
scenes have the rattle of the streets in them; it is a novel of street
journeys.

Mr Bumble's proposal of marriage and all the sour and tippling termagants which foretell Dickens's long gallery of patchy and disgruntled women, have the incalculable quality of nature. Dickens (and Forster supported him) believed Oliver to be real; and indeed he sometimes is. He is hardly the evacuee of our time; a hundred years had to pass before the happy English middle classes were to discover what a child from the industrial slums could be like. Oliver is simply 'one of Lord Shaftesbury's little victims'. But the misery and the fear of Oliver are very real, his leaning to virtue (now so unfashionable) profoundly convincing. Why should we complain if Vice is over-exposed and Virtue over-exalted; the convention has the authority of Hogarth, and belongs to the eighteenth century, the morality of pre-industrial England. Hence – we may be tempted to think – not the absence of God or the taint of the Manichee, but the author's lingering assumption that the belief in justice, the knowledge of retribution and of the passion of mercy are self-evident in human nature, and that a good dose of terror and a long tangled plot of ill-chance and malignance will bring them out. Dickens was not the first or the last novelist to find virtue more difficult to portray than the wish for it.

(1950)

GEORGE ELIOT

Warwickshire

> She looked unusually charming today from the very fact that
> she was not vividly conscious of anything but of having a mind
> near her that asked her to be something better than she actually
> was.

It is easy to guess which of the mid-Victorian novelists wrote these
lines. The use of the word 'mind' for young man, the yearning for
self-improvement in the heroine, and, lastly, the painful, reiterating
English, all betray George Eliot. This description of Esther Lyon in
Felix Holt might have been chipped out in stone for George Eliot's
epitaph and, as we take down a novel of hers from the shelf, we feel
we are about to lever off the heavy lid of some solid family tomb. Yet
the epitaph is not hers alone. The unremitting ethic of self-improvement
has been the sepulchre of all mid-Victorian fiction except *Wuthering
Heights*. Today that ethic no longer claims the Esther Lyons of the
English novel. The whole influence of psychology has turned our
interest to what George Eliot would have called the downward path,
to the failures of the will, the fulfilment of the heart, the vacillations
of the sensibility, the perception of self-interest. We do not wish to be
better than we are, but more fully what we are; and the wish is
crossed by the vivid conflicts set up in our lives by the revolution that
is going on in our society. The bottom has fallen out of our world and
our Esthers are looking for a basis not for a ceiling to their lives.

But this does not mean that Esther Lyon is falsely drawn or that
she is not a human being. Using our own jargon, all we have a right to
say is, that the objects of the super-ego have changed; and, in saying
this, we should recall a minor point of importance. It is this. Not only
English tradition from Fielding onwards, but no less a person than
the author of the *Liaisons Dangereuses* delight in the delectable
evasions of the prig and the reserve of the prude; and it would indeed
be absurd to cut the aspirations to virtue out of characters and to

leave only the virtue that is attained or is already there. The critic needs only to be clear about the kind of aspiration that is presented to him; and here we perceive that what separates us from Esther Lyon and her creator is a matter of history. She is impelled by the competitive reforming ethic of an expanding society. One might generalise without great danger and say that in all the mid-Victorian novels the characters are either going up in the world, in which case they are good; or they are going down in the world, in which case they are bad. Whereas Goldsmith and Fielding revelled in the misadventures of the virtuous and in the vagaries of Fortune – that tutelary goddess of a society dominated by merchant-speculators – a novelist like George Eliot writes at a time when Fortune has been torn down, when the earned increment of industry (and not the accidental coup of the gambler) has taken Fortune's place; and when character is tested not by hazard but, like the funds, by a measurable tendency to rise and fall.

Once her ethic is seen as the driving force of George Eliot we cease to be intimidated by it, and she emerges, for all her lectures, as the most formidable of the Victorian novelists. We dismiss the late-Victorian reaction from her work; our fathers were bored by her because they were importuned by her mind; she was an idol with feet of clay and, what was worse, appeared to write with them. But it is precisely because she was a mind and because she was a good deal of the schoolmistress that she interests us now. Where the other Victorian novelists seem shapeless, confused and without direction, because of their melodramatic plots and subplots and the careless and rich diversity of their characters, George Eliot marks out an ordered world, and enunciates a constructed judgment. If we read a novel in order to clarify our minds about human character, in order to pass judgment on the effect of character on the world outside itself, and to estimate the ideas people have lived by, then George Eliot is one of the first to give such an intellectual direction to the English novel. She is the first of the simplifiers, one of the first to cut moral paths through the picturesque maze of human motive. It is the intimidating rôle of the schoolmistress. And yet when we read a few pages of any of her books now, we notice less the oppression of her lectures and more the spaciousness of her method, the undeterred illumination which her habit of mind brings to human nature. We pass from the romantic shadows into an explicit, a prosaic but a relieving light.

Two of George Eliot's novels, it seems to me, will have a permanent place in English literature. As time goes by *Adam Bede* looks like our supreme novel of pastoral life; and I cannot see any novel of the nineteenth century that surpasses *Middlemarch* in range or construction. With *Adam Bede*, it is true, the modern reader experiences certain unconquerable irritations. We are faced by a sexual theme, and the Victorians were constitutionally unable to write about sexual love. In saying this we must agree that no English writer since the eighteenth century has been happy in this theme, for since that time we have lost our regard for the natural man and the equanimity required for writing about him. The most we have a right to say about the Victorians is that, like the ingenious people who bricked up the windows of their houses and painted false ones on the wall, in order to escape the window tax, the Victorian novelists always chose to brick up the bedroom first.

Now in *Adam Bede* we are shocked by two things: the treatment of Hetty Sorrel and by the marriage of Dinah and Adam at the end. It is clear that George Eliot's attitude to Hetty is a false one. The drawing of Hetty is neither observation from life nor a true recasting of experience by the imagination; it is a personal fantasy of George Eliot's. George Eliot was punishing herself and Hetty has to suffer for the 'sins' George Eliot had committed, and for which, to her perhaps unconscious dismay, she herself was never punished. We rebel against the black and white view of life and when we compare *Adam Bede* with Scott's *Heart of Midlothian*, to which the former confessedly owes something of its plot, we are depressed by the decline of humanity that has set in since the eighteenth century. Humanity has become humanitarianism, uplift and, in the end, downright cruelty. The second quarrel we have with this book arises, as I have said, from the marriage of Adam and Dinah. There is no reason why a man who has suffered at the hands of a bad woman should not be rewarded and win the consolations of a good woman. If Adam Bede likes sermons, we say, better than infidelity let him have them: we all choose our own form of suffering. But George Eliot told lies about this marriage; or rather, she omitted a vital element from it. She left out the element of sexual jealousy or if she did not leave it out, she did not recognise it, because she cannot admit natural passions in a virtuous character. In that scene where Hetty pushes Dinah away from her in her bedroom, where Hetty is dressing up and dreaming her Bovary-like dreams, the reader sees something that George Eliot appears not to see. We are supposed to see that Hetty is self-willed and this may be true, but see as well that Hetty's instincts have warned her of her ultimate rival. The failure to record jealousy and the attempt to transmute it so that it becomes the ambiguous if lofty repugnance to sin, springs from the deeper failure to face the nature of passion.

This failure not only mars George Eliot's moral judgment but also represses her power as a story-teller. When Adam comes to Arthur Donnithorne's room at the Hermitage, Arthur stuffs Hetty's neckerchief into the wastepaper basket out of Adam's sight. The piece of silk is a powerful symbol. The reader's eye does not leave it. He waits for it to be found. But no, it simply lies there; its function is, as it were, to preach the risks of sin to the reader. Whereas in fact it ought to be made to disclose the inflammatory fact that the physical seduction took place in this very room. George Eliot refuses to make such a blatant disclosure not for æsthetic reasons, but for reasons of Victorian convention; and the result is that we have no real reason for believing Hetty *has* been seduced. Her baby appears inexplicably. The account of Hetty's flight is remarkable – it is far, far better than the corresponding episode in *The Heart of Midlothian* – but the whole business of the seduction and crime, from Adam's fight with Arthur Donnithorne in the woods to Hetty's journey to the scaffold, seems scarcely more than hearsay to the reader. And the reprieve of Hetty at the gallows adds a final unreality to the plot. It must also be said – a final cruelty.

Yet, such is George Eliot's quality as a novelist, none of these criticisms has any great importance. Like the tragedies of Hardy, *Adam Bede* is animated by the majestic sense of destiny which is fitting to novels of work and the soil. Majestic is perhaps the wrong word. George Eliot's sense of destiny was prosaic, not majestic; prosaic in the sense of unpoetical. One must judge a novel on its own terms; and from the beginning, in the lovely account of Dinah's preaching on the village green, George Eliot sets out the pieties which will enclose the drama that is to follow. Her handling of the Methodists and their faith is one of the memorable religious performances of English literature, for she neither adjures us nor satirises them, but leaves a faithful and limpid picture of commonplace religion as a part of life. When she wrote of the peasants, the craftsmen, the yeomen, the clergy and squires of Warwickshire, George Eliot was writing out of childhood, from that part of her life which never betrayed her or any of the Victorians. The untutored sermons of Dinah have the same pastoral quality as the poutings of Hetty at the butter churn, the harangues of Mrs Poyser at her cooking, or the remonstrances of Adam Bede at his carpenter's bench. In the mid-Victorian England of the railway and the drift to the towns, George Eliot was harking back to the last of the yeomen, among whom she was born and who brought out the warmth, the humour, the strength of her nature. We seem to be looking at one of Morland's pictures, at any of those domestic or rustic paintings of the Dutch school, where every leaf on the elm trees or the limes is painted, every gnarl of the bark inscribed, every rut followed with fidelity. We follow the people out of the hedgerows and the lanes into the kitchen. We see the endless meals, the eternal cup of tea; and the dog rests his head on our boot or flies barking to the yard, while young children toddle in and out of the drama at the least convenient moments. Some critics have gibed at the dialect, and dialect *is* an obstacle; but when the great moments come, when Mrs Poyser has her 'say out' to the Squire who is going to evict her; or, better still, when Mrs Bede laments the drowning of her drunken husband, these people speak out of life:

'Let a-be, let a-be. There's no comfort for 'e no more,' she went on, the tears coming when she began to speak, 'now they poor feyther's gone, as I'n washed for and mended, an' got's victual for him for thirty 'ear, an' him allays so pleased wi' iverything I done for him, an' used to be so handy an' do the jobs for me when I war ill an' cambered wi' th' babby, an' made me the posset an' brought it upstairs as proud as could be, an' carried the lad as war as heavy as two children for five mile an' ne'er grumbled, all the way to Warson Wake, 'cause I wanted to go an' see my sister, as war dead an' gone the very next Christmas as e'er come. An' him to be drownded in the brook as we passed o'er the day we war married an' come home together, an' he'd made them lots o' shelves for me to put my plates an' things on, an' showed 'em me as proud as could be, 'case he know'd I should be pleased. An' he war to die an' me not to know, but to be a-sleepin' i' my bed, as if I caredna nought about it. Eh! an' me to live to see that! An' us as war young folks once, an' thought we should do rarely when we war married. Let a-be, lad, let a-be! I wonna ha' no tay; I carena if I ne'er ate nor drink no more. When one end o' th' bridge tumbles down, where's th' use o' th' other stannin'? I may's well die, an' foller my old man. There's no knowin' but he'll want me.'

Among these people Dinah's religion and their quarrels with her about it are perfectly at home; and George Eliot's rendering is faultless. English piety places a stress on conduct and the guidance of conscience; and George Eliot, with her peasant sense of the laws and repetitions of nature, easily converted this working theology into a universal statement about the life of man. Where others see the consequences of sin visited upon the soul, she, the Protestant, saw them appear in the events of a man's or woman's life and the lives of others. Sin is primarily a weakness of character leading to the act. To Arthur Donnithorne she would say, 'Your sin is that your will is weak. You are unstable. You depend on what others say. You are swayed by the latest opinion. You are greedy for approbation. Not lust, but a weak character is your malady. You even think that once you have confessed, your evil will turn out good. But it cannot, unless your character changes.' And to Hetty she says, 'Your real sin was vanity.' It is a bleak and unanswerable doctrine, if one is certain that some kinds of character are desirable and others undesirable; psychologically useful to the novelist because it cuts one kind of path deeply into human nature, and George Eliot knows each moral character like a map. If her moral judgment is narrow, it enlarges character by showing us not merely the idiosyncrasy of people but propounds their type. Hetty is all pretty kittenish girls; Arthur is all careless young men. And here George Eliot makes a large advance on the novelists who preceded her. People do not appear haphazard in her books. They are not eccentrics. They are all planned and placed. She is orderly in her ethics; she is orderly in her social observation. She knows the country hierarchy and how a squire is this kind of man, a yeoman another, a teacher, a publican, a doctor, a clergyman another. They are more than themselves; they are their group as well. In this they recall the characters of Balzac. You fit Dinah among the Methodists, you fit Methodism into the scheme of things, you fit Adam among the peasants. Behind the Poysers are all the yeomen. George Eliot's sense of law is a sense of kind. It's a sense of life which has been learned from the English village where every man and woman has his definition and place.

I doubt if any Victorian novelist has as much to teach the modern novelists as George Eliot; for although the English novel was established and became a constructed judgment on situations and people after she had written, it did not emulate her peasant sense of law. Hardy alone is her nearest parallel, but he differed from her in conceiving a fate outside the will of man and indifferent to him. And her picture of country life is really closer to the country we know than Hardy's is, because he leaves us little notion of what the components of country society are. The English peasant lived and still lives in a milder, flatter world than Hardy's; a world where conscience and self-interest keep down the passions, like a pair of gamekeepers. It is true that George Eliot is cut off from the Rabelaisian malice and merriment of the country; she hears the men talk as they talk in their homes, not as they talk in the public-houses and the barns. But behind the salty paganism of country life stands the daily haggle of what people 'ought' and 'didn't ought' to do; the ancient nagging of church and chapel. All this is a minor matter beside her main lesson. What the great schoolmistress teaches is the interest of massive writing, of placing people, of showing how even the minds of characters must be placed among other minds.

When we turn from *Adam Bede* to *Middlemarch* we find a novel in which her virtues as a novelist are established and assured; and where there is no sexual question to bedevil her judgment. No Victorian novel approaches *Middlemarch* in its width of reference, its intellectual power, or the imperturbable spaciousness of its narrative. It is sometimes argued by critics of contemporary literature that a return to Christianity is indispensable if we are to produce novels of the Victorian scale and authority, or indeed novels of any quality at all; but there are the novels of unbelievers like George Eliot and Hardy to discountenance them. The fact is that a wide and single purpose in the mind is the chief requirement outside of talent; a strong belief, a strong unbelief, even a strong egoism will produce works of the first order. If she had any religious leanings, George Eliot moved towards Judaism because of its stress on law; and if we think this preference purely intellectual and regard worry, that profoundly English habit of mind, as her philosophy, the point is that it was strong, serious, comprehensive worry. A forerunner of the psychologists, she promises no heaven and threatens no hell; the best and the worst we shall get is Warwickshire. Her world is the world of will, the smithy of character, a place of knowledge and judgments. So, in the sense of worldly wisdom, is Miss Austen's. But what a difference there is. To repeat our earlier definition, if Miss Austen is the novelist of the ego and its platitudes, George Eliot is the novelist of the idolatries of the super-ego. We find in a book like *Middlemarch*, not character modified by circumstance only, but character first impelled and then modified by the beliefs, the ambitions, the spiritual objects which it assimilates. Lydgate's schemes for medical reform and his place in medical science are as much part of his character as his way with the ladies. And George Eliot read up her medical history in order to get his position exactly right. Dorothea's yearning for a higher life of greater usefulness to mankind will stay with her all her days and will make her a remarkable but exasperating woman; a fool for all her cleverness. George Eliot gives equal weight to these important qualifications. Many Victorian novelists have lectured us on the careers and aspirations of their people; none, before George Eliot, showed us the unity of intellect, aspiration and nature in action. Her judgment on Lydgate as a doctor is a judgment on his fate as a man:

He carried to his studies in London, Edinburgh and Paris the conviction that the medical profession as it might be was the finest in the world; presenting the most perfect interchange between science and art; offering the most direct alliance between intellectual conquest and the social good. Lydgate's nature demanded this combination: he was an emotional creature, with a flesh and blood sense of fellowship, which withstood all the abstractions of special study. He cared not only for 'Cases', but for John and Elizabeth, especially Elizabeth.

The Elizabeth, who was not indeed to wreck Lydgate's life, but (with far more probability) to corrupt his ideas and turn him into the smart practitioner, was Rosamund, his wife. Yet, in its own way, Rosamund's super-ego had the most distinguished ideals. A provincial manufacturer's daughter, she too longed idealistically to rise; the desire was not vulgar until she supposed that freedom from crude middle-class notions of taste and bearing could only be obtained by marriage to the cousin of a baronet; and was not immoral until she made her husband's conscience pay for her ambitions. The fountain, George Eliot is always telling us, cannot rise higher than its source.

Such analyses of character have become commonplace to us. When one compares the respectable Rosamund Lydgate with, say, Becky Sharp, one sees that Rosamund is not unique. Where *Middlemarch* is unique in its time is in George Eliot's power of generalisation. The last thing one accuses her of is unthinking acceptance of convention. She seeks, in her morality, the positive foundation of natural law, a kind of Fate whose measures are as fundamental as the changes of the seasons in nature. Her intellect is sculptural. The clumsiness of style does not denote muddle, but an attempt to carve decisively. We feel the clarifying force of a powerful mind. Perhaps it is not naturally powerful. The power may have been acquired. There are two George Eliots: the mature, experienced, quiet-humoured Midlander who wrote the childhood pages of *The*

Mill on the Floss; and the naïve, earnest and masterly intellectual with her half-dozen languages and her scholarship. But unlike the irony of our time, hers is at the expense not of belief, but of people. Behind them, awful but inescapable to the eye of conscience, loom the statues of what they ought to have been. Hers is a mind that has grown by making judgments – as Mr Gladstone's head was said to have grown by making speeches.

Middlemarch resumes the observation and experience of a lifetime. Until this book George Eliot often strains after things beyond her capacity, as Dorothea Casaubon strained after a spiritual power beyond her nature. But now in *Middlemarch* the novelist is reconciled to her experience. In Dr Casaubon George Eliot sees that tragedy may paralyse the very intellect which was to be Dorothea's emancipation. Much of herself (George Eliot said, when she was accused of portraying Mark Pattison) went into Casaubon, and I can think of no other English novel before or since which has so truthfully, so sympathetically and so intimately described the befogged and grandiose humiliations of the scholar, as he turns at bay before the vengeance of life. Casaubon's jealousy is unforgettable, because, poisonous though it is, it is not the screech of an elderly cuckold, but the voice of strangled nature calling for justice. And notice, here, something very characteristic; George Eliot's pity flows from her moral sense, from the very seat of justice, and not from a sentimental heart.

Middlemarch is the first of many novels about groups of people in provincial towns. They are differentiated from each other not by class or fortune only, but by their moral history, and this moral differentiation is not casual, it is planned and has its own inner hierarchy. Look at the groups. Dorothea, Casaubon and Ladislaw seek to enter the highest spiritual fields – not perhaps the highest, for us, because, as we have seen, the world of George Eliot's imagination was prosaic and not poetic – still, they desire, in their several ways, to influence the standards of mankind. There is Lydgate, who is devoted to science and expects to be rewarded by a career. He and his wife are practical people, who seek power. The pharisaical Bulstrode, the banker, expects to rise both spiritually and financially at once, until he sits on the right hand of God, the Father; a businessman with a bad conscience, he is the father of the Buchmanites and of all success-religions. The Garths, being country people and outside all this urban world, believe simply in the virtue of work as a natural law and they are brought up against Fred Vincy, Rosamund's brother. He, as a horsey young man educated beyond his means, has a cheerful belief in irresponsible Style and in himself as a thing of pure male beauty with a riding crop. We may not accept George Eliot's standards, but we can see that they are not conventional, and that they do not make her one-sided. She is most intimately sympathetic to human beings and is never sloppy about them. When Vincy quarrels with Bulstrode about Fred's debts, when Casaubon's jealousy of Ladislaw secretes its first venom, when Lydgate tries vainly to talk about money to his wife or Fred goes to his mad old grandfather for a loan, vital human issues are raised. The great scenes of *Middlemarch* are exquisite, living transpositions of real moral dilemmas. Questions of principle are questions of battle; they point the weapons of the human comedy, and battle is not dull. In consequence, George Eliot's beliefs are rarely boring, because they are a dynamism. They correspond to psychological and social realities, though more especially (on the large scale) to the functions of the will; they are boring only when, in the Victorian habit, she harangues the reader and pads out the book with brainy essays.

I see I have been writing about *Middlemarch* as though it was a piece of engineering. What about the life, the humour, the pleasure? There are failures: Dorothea and Ladislaw do not escape the fate of so many Victorian heroes and heroines who are frozen by their creator's high-mindedness. Has George Eliot forgotten how much these two difficult, sensitive and proud people will annoy each other by the stupidity which so frequently afflicts the intellectual? Such scruples, such play-acting! But Lydgate and Rosamund quarrelling about money; Rosamund quietly thwarting her husband's decisions, passing without conscience to love affairs with his friends and ending as a case-hardened widow who efficiently finds a second father for her family – these things are perfect. Mary Garth defying the old miser is admirable. But the most moving thing in the book – and I always think this is the real test of a novelist – is given to the least likeable people. Bulstrode's moral ruin, and his inability to confess to his dull wife, is portrayed in a picture of dumb human despondency which recalls a painting by Sickert. One hears the clock tick in the silence that attends the wearing down of two lives that can cling together but dare not speak.

The humour of George Eliot gains rather than loses by its mingling with her intellect. Here we feel the sound influence of her girlish reading of the eighteenth-century novelists who were above all men of education. This humour is seen at its best in scenes like the one where the relations of the miser come to his house, waiting to hear news of his will; and again in the sardonic description of the spreading of the scandal about Bulstrode and Lydgate. George Eliot followed causes down to their most scurrilous effects. She is good in scandal and public rumour. Her slow tempo is an advantage, and it becomes exciting to know that she will make her point in the minor scenes as surely as she will make it in the great ones. Mrs Dollop of The Tankard has her short paragraph of immortality: she had 'often to resist the shallow pragmatism of customers disposed to think their reports from the outer world were of equal force with what had "come up" in her mind'. Trumbull, the auctioneer, is another portrait, a longer one, smelling of the bar and the saleroom. Dickens would have caricatured this gift from heaven. George Eliot observes and savours. Characteristically she catches his intellectual pretensions and his offensive superiority. We see him scent the coming sale and walk over to Mary Garth's desk to read her copy of Scott's *Anne of Geierstein*, just to show that he knows a book when he sees one:

'The course of four centuries', he reads out unexpectedly, 'has well enough elapsed since the series of events which are related in the following chapters took place on the continent.'

That moment is one of the funniest in the English novel, one of those mad touches like the insertion of a dog stealing a bone, which Hogarth put into his pictures.

There is no real madness in George Eliot. Both heavy feet are on the ground. Outside of *Wuthering Heights* there is no madness in Victorian fiction. The Victorians were a histrionic people who measured themselves by the Elizabethans; and George Eliot, like Browning and Tennyson, was compared to Shakespeare by her contemporaries. The comparison failed, if only because madness is lacking. Hysteria, the effect of the exorbitant straining of their wills, the Victorians did, alas, too often achieve. George Eliot somehow escapes it. She is too level-headed. One pictures her, in life, moralising instead of making a scene. There is no hysteria in *Middlemarch*; perhaps there are no depths because there is so much determination. But there is a humane breadth and resolution in this novel which offers neither hope nor despair to mankind but simply the necessity of fashioning a moral life. George Eliot's last words on her deathbed might, one irreverently feels, be placed on the title-page of her collected works: 'Tell them', she is reported to have said, 'the pain is on the left side.' Informative to the last and knowing better than the doctor, the self-made positivist dies.

(1950)

LEWIS CARROLL

Letters

Even among the prolific letter-writing Victorian authors, Lewis Carroll is a phenomenon. He said that a third of his life seemed to go in receiving letters and the other two-thirds in replying to them – 'wheelbarrows full, almost'. He got about two thousand replies done every year but, even so, was often seventy or eighty names in arrears. The teacher of Euclid and mathematics, the ordained clergyman and Curator of the Senior Common Room at Christ Church, Oxford, was not only compulsively scribacious; he was also a systematic keeper of his postal records. From the age of twenty-nine until his death, he kept a précis of every scrap he wrote, and also a register. The recorded number of letters runs to over ninety-eight thousand, and this does not include letters concerned with college business. So fascinated was he by his addiction that he once did a kind of time-and-motion study of his flow. He wrote, he said, twenty words a minute, and took seven and a half minutes to do a page of a hundred and fifty words; an original draft of twelve pages took two and a half hours and a fair copy one and a half hours more. The learned bachelor was married to his inkpot and a harem of ingenious pens of his own invention, which included an 'electric pen' that he used for writing under the covers when at last he got into bed in the small hours of the morning. He even wrote letters that could be read only in a looking glass. He was far from solemn about his eccentricity:

> I hardly know which is me and which is the inkstand. . . The confusion in one's mind doesn't so much matter – but when it comes to putting bread-and-butter, and orange marmalade, into the *inkstand* and then dipping pens into *oneself* and filling *oneself* up with ink, you know, it's horrid.

A breakfast in Wonderland! One thing to note is that if he is obsessional he is not one of the educated indecipherables who write entirely out of self-infatuation: he wrote in a clear hand in purple ink. He was determined, on principle, to give pleasure to others.

From the tens of thousands in Carroll's 'wheelbarrow', Professor Morton N. Cohen – aided by Roger Lancelyn Green, who edited Carroll's diaries twenty-five years ago – has selected thirteen hundred letters, which have been published by Oxford in a handsome and scholarly two-volume edition. The annotation is profuse, and Carroll's photographs and drawings are diverting. The selection includes a very large number of his nonsense letters to children and many letters on his love of the theatre, the arts, and literature, on his pioneering skills as a photographer, on his interest in science and medicine; it also reflects his fastidious religious orthodoxy as he considers the manners and doubts of Victorian family practice. We are led once more to speculate on the private springs of the genius that created *Alice in Wonderland*. Carroll was a man who carried his childhood within him as a privacy all his life. It is simple to see him as the timid, pernickety don – all brain but emotionally arrested, for reasons we can only guess at. He hated publicity. He preferred to fill a monastic loneliness with fuss, puzzles, parodies, and fancies – a 'case', as so many humorists have been.

But before we try this tunnel there is the second letter in this edition to consider. It is from Carroll's father, Charles Dodgson, written to the boy when he was seven. The boy had asked for a present. The father writes:

As soon as I get to Leeds I shall scream out in the street *Ironmongers, Ironmongers*. Six hundred men will rush out of their shops in a moment – fly, fly, in all directions, ring the bells, call the constables, set the town on fire. I will have a file and a screw driver and a ring and if they are not brought directly in 40 seconds, I will leave nothing but one small cat alive in the whole Town of Leeds, and I shall only leave that because I'm afraid I shall not have time to kill it. Then what a bawling and a tearing of hair there will be! Pigs and babies, camels and butterflies, rolling in the gutter together – old women rushing up chimneys and cows after them, ducks hiding themselves in coffee cups and fat geese trying to squeeze themselves into pencil cases.

A High Churchman, from a long line of churchmen, a scholar, and a man of dominant, driving character, the father was Archdeacon of Richmond, and had his own wanton relation to the inkpot. The son's resort to fantasy is inherited. Other factors favoured its growth. He was the eldest son in a precocious family of eleven children – four boys and seven girls – living in an isolated country rectory. To see a cart pass down the road was a startling event. At home, there was the Victorian stress on brainwork. There was the lifelong stammer that afflicted Carroll and his sisters and that brought too many words to the tongue at once. There was the very conscious need for the self-control necessary to conquer whatever blocked utterance; perhaps the minds of the clever children skidded into absurdity as they paused before they hit the right word. (It is known that the character of the Dodo came from Carroll's real name, which was apt to come out of his mouth as 'Do-do-dodgson'.) If the stammer is a minor matter, it is surely important that Lewis Carroll was the eldest son in a family of many sisters, and the leader in the storytelling, the parodies, the charades, puppet shows, puns, conundrums, and other pranks of the brain that made for wit in a jolly family life in which privilege was assured and serious studies were exacted. The Archdeacon had been a double first in his time and had translated Tertullian: a first was confidently expected of Carroll, a born examinee, and of course he got it. If he was a mother's boy and a swot, indifferent to sport, he was neither namby-pamby nor a prig: he quietly held his own in the roughhouse of Tom Brown's Rugby. He worshipped Tennyson. He had a taste for poetry, though his own talent for serious poetry was wan, and he turned, as the too clever will, to parody; he ground away at mathematics and logic and amused himself, like many a Victorian polymath, with scientific gadgets. Here he was influenced by an adored Uncle Skeffington, of whom he wrote:

He has, as usual, got a great number of new oddities, including a lathe, telescope stand, crest stamp (see the top of this notesheet), a beautiful little pocket instrument for measuring distances on a map, refrigerator, etc. etc. We had an observation of the moon and Jupiter last night and afterwards of live animalcula in his large microscope: this is a most interesting sight, as the creatures are most conveniently transparent; and you see all kinds of organs jumping about like a complicated piece of machinery, and even the circulation of the blood. Everything goes on at railway speed, so I suppose they must be some of those insects that only live a day or two and try to make the most of it.

The young man has an intellect that will make the most of the detail in everything, whether he writes an exact report of a dogfight in Oxford or – inevitably – turns to mastering that new fashionable gadget the camera. Much has been made, quite naturally, of the possible unconscious sources of his genius for nonsense; but what strikes one is that he displays an extreme, perhaps obliterating consciousness. He lives for figures, words, and propositions – as a game, even a career. His fantasy has none of the melancholy of the autobiographical Edward Lear, his great predecessor, who was half in love with failure. Carroll's is a surplus of efficient, inventive intellectual energy, the positive energy of a busy child. One has to be content with attributing his fondness for little girls (he hated little boys) to the natural continuation of his love for his sisters, and his lack of emotional interest in adult love to the shock of his mother's death, when he was eighteen. He could never, after that, connect sex with love. After girls reached the age of eleven, they lost interest in him and he in them. He had only a sort of register of them in his albums of photographs. Many wrote to him when the 'Alice' books appeared – but often confessed in later life that they could not remember much about him except that he was fun.

Nothing in his diaries or his letters suggests that his interest in the scores of little girls he told stories to, played with at the seaside, and loved to take very formally to the theatre, when mothers allowed this, was other than innocent. The clergyman was strict in his religion and in the acceptance of the sexual taboos and social conventions of his time, though he did complain of Mrs Grundy. He never breaks into the rhapsodic language of a fellow-lover of girl children, the now famous and equally innocent Reverend Francis Kilvert, whom he knew. Carroll plays but he never worships. His well-known references to the torment of his 'pillow thoughts' may, of course, indicate deep sexual miseries, but one notes that the man whose overworked brain may have killed natural feeling suffered all his life from insomnia. Kilvert speaks of the 'wild passionate hearts' of his little friends; Carroll of their evanescent love – and, indeed, feeling, for him, takes the form of a nostalgia for childhood itself. Really, he is delighting in the behaviour of a species; he catches what Kilvert misses – the child's puzzled sense of growing. A superior person himself, he does not condescend but listens, knowing that children feel themselves to be superior, too, and grow by playing: they love rules, they are little bosses in behaviour. Carroll had the attraction of a conspirator in the libertinage of his grotesque theatrical invention. As he listened, he studied faces and physical peculiarities very much as children do, and then turned his observations of eyes, noses, heads, and legs into mad fancies. His manners were as proper as any child could desire. A pedant himself, he satisfied the pedant in the child. He carefully avoided the moral. Let nannies and mummies indulge in that; he would not.

Carroll's letters are packed with hidden quotations and disguised nursery verses. Having told little Agnes Hughes a satisfactorily violent story of how he knocked three cats down with a rolling pin, he adds in the next letter an appeasing dramatic sequel:

Of course I didn't leave them lying flat on the ground like dried flowers: no, I picked them up, and I was as kind as I could be to them. I lent them the portfolio for a bed – they wouldn't have been comfortable in a real bed, you know: they were too thin, but they were *quite* happy between the sheets of blotting paper . . . Well then . . . I lent them the three dinner bells to ring if they wanted anything in the night.

You know I have *three* dinner bells – the first (which is the largest) is rung when dinner is *nearly* ready; the second (which is rather larger) is rung when it is quite ready; and the third (which is as large as the other two put together) is rung all the time I am at dinner . . . In the morning I gave them some rat-tail jelly and buttered mice for breakfast and they were as discontented as they could be. They wanted some boiled pelican, but of course I knew it wouldn't be good for them. So all I said was 'Go to Number Two Finborough Road and ask for Agnes Hughes, and if it is really good for you, she'll give you some.' Then I shook hands with them all . . . and drove them up the chimney. They seemed very sorry to go and they took the bells and the portfolio with them. I didn't find this out until after they had gone, and then I was sorry too and wished for them back again. What do I mean by 'them'? Never mind.

There it is – a drama that ends pawkily in a grammatical poser. The detail of the drama is masterly in the little world in which it is enacted. It is a riotous distraction from the boredom of manners at upper-class family meals and eating what is set before you – an attack on Nanny.

Lewis Carroll was much opposed to allowing servants to bring up children. He was also critical of the absurd overdressing of children that became a form of conspicuous waste in the latter half of the century, especially at the seaside. And here we come to his troubles as a photographer of little girls: he wanted them to be as near to innocent nature as possible. The ideal, he tries to convince mothers, was to take pictures of the girls naked or as near naked as possible. There was, indeed, a Victorian cult of the idealised, sexless naked child. Painters and illustrators of fairy tales were allowed the subject. Why not the photographer? Parents were divided about this. Carroll's negotiations were elaborately tentative and polite yet also persistent. He was reassuring. No girl over the age of eleven. If necessary, he would take two girls at a time – if possible without their mothers, so that the children would be natural. It was, of course, a principle, for him (he said), never to take a frontal picture. The movement against Mrs Grundy had begun; often he got his way, but often there was a break with old friends, and eventually, in later life, he gave up photography in despair of the age he lived in. He was indignant at the questioning of his motives – *that* he never forgave. My own impression is that Carroll's pictures of the solemn, over-dressed child are better than his semi-nudes, which he hoped would embellish the walls of the parents' drawing-rooms. The overdressed girls are simply bursting with will and repressed emotion. One has the suspicion that nowadays, when the silence about sex has been broken and no one believes in the innocence of either children or adults, the opposition would be stronger. The cult of the idealised child has gone. Carroll had his own reservations. He would never have boys at these scenes in his studio; they would be too enterpris-ingly curious. Any form of sexual curiosity or marital misbehaviour shocked him. He refused to meet Ellen Terry – whom he had loved deeply when she was a child – when she left her husband for another man; many years passed before he would agree to meet her. It has been said that he'd wished to marry her.

In his biography of Carroll, published in 1954, Derek Hudson wrote that the surface life of this self-controlled man 'disguised a precarious balance. He was at once selfish and unselfish.' Perhaps the dominant will of the Archdeacon had been unnerving. The son was noted 'for statements no sooner made than they were nervously reversed'. The stammerer was a waverer. And so in the main his few letters on public and business matters are full of assertions nervously made and then half withdrawn. In religion, he could not be sure whether he was as High as his father; in his disputes with agnostics, he was the winning logician who escaped apologetically into the argument for faith, in a gentlemanly way. He was a touchy gram-marian in dispute. This comes out early, in a rather telling youthful quarrel with Tennyson. Carroll had been given a copy of an unpublished poem of Tennyson's, and he felt it would be wrong not to reveal this to the poet. Tennyson was angry and called Carroll's request to circulate the poem ungentlemanly. The proud young Carroll demanded an apology and got one – but it was grumpy and half-hearted, and he let the great man know it:

Nevertheless I accept what you say, as being in substance, what it certainly is not in form, a retractation (though without a shadow of apology or expression of regret) of all dishonourable charges against me, and an admission that you had made them on insufficient grounds.

At Christ Church, he was noted for such donnish precisions about elections, architecture, and the college wine. There came a time when the crustiness became strained. He was the loneliest of busy men.

(1970)

Trollope Was Right

The comfort we get from Trollope's novels is the sedative of gossip. It is not cynical gossip, for Trollope himself is the honest check on the self-deceptions of his characters, on their malicious lies or interested half-truths about each other. It is he, a workaday surrogate of God, sincere, sturdy, shrewd and unhopeful, who has the key. Trollope does not go with us into the dangerous region that lies just outside our affairs and from which we draw our will to live; rather, he settles lazily into that part of our lives which is a substitute, the part which avoids loneliness by living vicariously in other people. If it were a true generalisation – as some say – that the English, being unimaginative, are able to live without hope but not without the pleasure of thinking they are better than their neighbours, Trollope's are the most English of our novels. But the generalisation is not true. Trollope himself – as Mr Cockshut says in a very intelligent study – is saved by eccentricity. There is something fervent, even extreme, in his admiration of endurance. He was a man whose temper could flare up. His preoccupation with what is normal is the intense one of a man who has had to gain acquaintance with normality from an abnormal situation outside it. His special eccentricities are his mania for work and his passion for spending energy. From his point of view, novel-writing was obsessional. It convinced him that he, the outsider in a society of powerful groups of people, was justified in being alive. Even his most contented novels leave an aftertaste of flatness and sadness. He has succeeded in his assertions, to the point of conveying a personal satiety.

The plots of Trollope and Henry James have much in common. But if we compare a novel like *The Eustace Diamonds*, one of the most ingenious of Trollope's conundrums, with, say, Henry James's *The Spoils of Poynton*, we see the difference between a pragmatic gossip and an artist of richer sensibility. Sense, not sensibility, governs Trollope; it is fine good sense and, though he lumbers along, most notable for the subtlety of its timing. He is an excellent administrator and politician of private life. But whereas James saw how the magnificent spoils of the Poynton family could corrupt by their very beauty, Trollope did not envisage anything morally ambiguous in the imbroglio of the Eustace diamonds. The *Spoils* were treasure; the *Diamonds* are property. The former are made for the moral law; the latter for the courts. It is true, as Mr Cockshut says, that the brilliantly delayed climax where Dove, the lawyer, points out the stones are worthless, has its overtones. But to Trollope's imagination the diamonds are ultimately meaningless; one might defend the wicked Lady Eustace and say that she alone gave them a symbolical meaning. They at least stand for her will. But Trollope in fact dislikes her childish will as much as her propensity for lying; her poetic side is shown to be false. One wonders if he could have portrayed it if it had been genuine. She is a perjurer, a bitch and a coquette and, quite rightly, ends up as a bore; but in a novel filled with irritable and spiritless people, she is the one figure of spirit. Trollope knows simply that she is wrong.

With all his mastery, Trollope is interested only in what people are like, not in what they are for. The limitation comes out most clearly in his political novels when we see how politics work and never for what purpose, beyond those of personal career. Some critics have put down this fundamental concern of Trollope to his good-natured and sensible acceptance of mid-Victorian society, and would say that he accepted his world just as Jane Austen accepted hers. Others – and I think Mr Cockshut would be among them – point to his constitutional melancholy. It has the effect of devitalising his characters. I do not mean that old harridans like Lady Linlithgow, the delightful self-willed Lady Glencora, or Lord George in *The Eustace Diamonds* lack personal vitality; the deficiency is in artistic vitality. If we compare the portrait of Lady Eustace with Thackeray's Becky Sharp it is interesting to see how much passivity there is in Lady Eustace and how much greater is the adventuress than the stubborn fool. Lady Eustace drifts. Her wickednesses are many, but they are small. She is little more than a tedious *intrigante* who relies on chance. She, of course, succeeds with us because of her obstinacy, her wit, her courage, her seductiveness and her beauty and because her wickedness is that of a child. Indeed Lord George, the 'corsair', pats her on the head and treats her as such. Becky is a more positive and interesting figure of evil because she is grown up.

In *The Eustace Diamonds*, there are only two moments when Trollope breaks through his melancholy to write out of strong feeling. The first is an unpleasant outbreak: the antisemitism of his portrait of Mr Emilius, 'the greasy Jew'. Trollope, honest observer that he is, notes that Lady Eustace is far from being physically repelled by the preacher who is said to be repulsive. The female masochist – as Mr Cockshut says – has recognised a master, the coquette her master-hypocrite. The second outbreak occurs in describing the brutal, forced engagement of Lucinda Roanoke to Sir Griffin, and the violence with which the Amazon repels him when he tries to take her on his knee. Here the revulsion is physical. These are two disconcerting glimpses into the Trollopian alcove and both are blatant. Trollope with his blood up is better seen on the hunting field; he will be kinder there to the women who are to be humiliated.

Mr Cockshut has read the whole of Trollope and I have not. His book provides an able analysis of the novels and a fresh approach to Trollope himself. The critic might have said, with advantage, more about Trollope's curious life; Mr Cockshut is more detailed than other critics have been about Trollope's response to mid-Victorianism; he is fascinated by the moral issues which Trollope propounded, but he is apt to digress. As a critic he depends on paraphrase which is always suggestive and enjoyable though it also runs into the danger of crediting a novelist with ideas he may only dimly have discerned. Is it true, for example, that masochism is Lady Eustace's central characteristic? Surely it is a lack of interest in truth. Mr Cockshut's main point is that there are three phases in Trollope's prodigious output; the day-dream stage; the genial middle period when he accepts the world; and the final one, beginning with *He Knew He Was Right*, when he is bitterly disillusioned about the society which he has affirmed his right to. Mr Cockshut cannot think of any special reason for the change. Perhaps Trollope's leaving the Post Office and failing to get into Parliament had something to do with it. Leisure depressed, indeed terrified him and, perhaps, what Mr Cockshut calls his 'belated understanding of the changes that were coming over Victorian England' became unpleasantly observable with leisure. We need not think that hard work exhausted him, but men who are hard on themselves become harder on other people as time goes by. 'He knew he was right' could have been his device, the rightness not lying especially in his opinion, but in his choice of what might be called 'practical hallucination' as a way of living. He was perhaps reverting in late middle age to the misanthropy of his early, unhappy youth. The cycle is common enough. Dickens, too, became harsh and, to present-day taste, the harsh or obsessional phase of novelists happens to have become attractive.

He Knew He Was Right and *The Eustace Diamonds* are not genial books. There is something savage in them. The values of society are rotten, the people are fools, brutes or lunatics. Lady Eustace may be bad; but what are we to say of the virtuous Mrs Hittaway, the social climber, who does not scruple in the name of virtue to employ Lady Eustace's servants to spy upon her and who is so morally exalted by her own slanders that she does not even want to consider the evidence for them? These people are a nasty, grubbing lot, no better than they should be. Their story is redeemed and 'placed' by Trollope's smiling remark that the scandal managed to keep the old Duke of Omnium alive for three months and gave everybody in London something to talk about at dinner. Trollope may be pessimistic, but he was too alert a comedian to be misled into rancour. His good nature was truthful if it grew less and less hopeful. Himself morbidly subject to loneliness and boredom and capable of portraying characters who were destroyed by these evils, he never fell into exaggeration – nor indeed rose to it.

The Eustace Diamonds is a triumph of ingenious construction and of story-telling. Trollope is a master of that dramatic art which the English novel seems to have inherited from its early roots in the theatre; the art of putting the right in the wrong and the wrong in the right. He also understands Society and the difference between the weary meaninglessness of the conventional and the vicious aimlessness of the unconventional. The fast set and Grundys such as Mrs Hittaway, are opposite sides of the same coin. Yet if, as Mr Cockshut's analysis patiently shows, the gossip is morally organised, it is not schematic. The characters are various in themselves. A dull man like Lord Fawn becomes fascinating. We see the figure of Frank Greystock in all the colours of a merely moderate honesty. Each character is brought to its own dramatic head. Will Greystock jilt the governess and marry Lady Eustace? Trollope is not content to stop at answering that question, but goes one better and shows Greystock falling asleep in the train, bored stiff by a flirt who had captivated him. Trollope's observation can make even a Commissioner of Police interesting. Nor does the comedy remain on one level. The love affair of Lucinda and Sir Griffin approaches the grotesque and the horrible and the sharp financial deals and recriminations of Lady Eustace and Mrs Carbuncle are as savage as anything in *Jonathan Wild*. Trollope is a remorseless exploiter of fine points. If he had been a mere plotmaker he would have been satisfied to expose the perjuries of Lady Eustace in the court scene, but he squeezes more than that out of it. He sees to it that a sadistic counsel, powerless to be other than cruel, makes the liar tell the truth a dozen times over, unnecessarily. And when the bogus preacher proposes, Lady Eustace doubts if he is bogus enough.

The critic must admire these skills. He must admire Trollope's knowledge of the groups in the social hierarchy. He must notice how fertilising was Trollope's own dilemma: that he was a man of liberal mind crossed by strong conservative feeling. There remain the serious limitations that his manner is slovenly, repetitive and pedestrian, that his scene has no vividness, that – as Mr Cockshut says – the upper steps of his moral stairway are missing, that he lacks fantasy. There will be sin but no sanctity. It is, after all, Lady Eustace's crime that she was not the average woman and it is supposed to be Mrs Hittaway's justification that *she* is. And so, when we emerge from Trollope's world, we, at first, define him as one of the masters who enables us to recognise average life for what it is. On second thoughts, we change the phrase: we recognise that he has drawn life as people say it is when they are not speaking about themselves.

One of the chronicler's 'failures' – *The Prime Minister* – was the penultimate volume of what Trollope considered his best work: the series which begins with *Can You Forgive Her?* and runs on to the Phineas novels. As Mr Amery says in his introduction to the attractive Oxford Crown edition, it raises the question of politics in the novel. The failure of *The Prime Minister* is, of course, relative; no novel containing Lady Glencora could be called dull. But this one has no personable young hero like the frank and susceptible Phineas Finn and Emily Wharton is a bit of a stick as the meek but obstinate young bride in love. On the other hand, Lopez, the speculator and fortune-hunter, is a genuine figure of the age; drama is created by his shifty fingers, he is bold and credible. The only bother with Lopez is that he is made the vehicle of Trollope's peculiar dislike of 'outsiders' and foreigners – he loathed Disraeli really because he was a Jew – and a hostile lecturing tone comes into Trollope's voice when he writes of him, which is absent from the portrait of that other rapscallion, Burgo Fitzgerald. Yet Trollope tries very hard to be fair to Lopez, who is presented with objective care and is never all of a piece. He has courage, for example, and one notices that he does not lie until he is kicked when he is down. Only his suicide, at the end, is out of character, for obviously a man like Lopez will always start again from the bottom. He perfectly illustrates what a novelist like Galsworthy would have made a lot of moral fuss about: that in a rich oligarchic society, the Lopezes will always be sacrificed when their heads are turned or when it is a question of class-solidarity and self-defence. Trollope is very accurate as a psychologist of the uncomprehending rogue; a little cynical as he shows how mad it is to think of succeeding in England if you use your imagination and disobey the rules. It is a tremendous moment when Lopez attempts to blackmail the Duke of Omnium and the best kind of surprise: the brilliant Lopez has lost his head. We had forgotten how stupid cleverness can be. Finally, in the major conflict between the lofty-minded Prime Minister and his wife, Lady Glencora, whose whole idea is to exploit her husband's political eminence socially, there is wit, and drama too.

Where is the specific failure, then? I do not mean the general criticism of Trollope that he is commonplace, that reading him is like walking down endless corridors of carpet, restful to walk on, but in the end enervating. What is the failure within Trollope's own honest terms? The reader is bound to agree with the experienced opinion of the politician who introduces the book: as Mr Amery says, it was possible for Trollope to write about the Church without engaging in religious controversy, because this is only fitful in religion and, anyway, is only one aspect of it. But controversy is the living breath of politics, and Trollope leaves it out altogether. He purposely makes the Duke of Omnium Prime Minister of a Coalition, in which controversy is momentarily quiet. The fact is that Trollope the civil servant despised politicians and the Duke of Omnium is really a Treasury official, plus an immense sense of rank and a vast income. And so, though we hear in detail of the machinery of Parliament, the intrigues for safe seats, the machinations of the drawing-rooms and have an excellent picture of political comedy and humbug, we have no notion of politics as anything more than a career disputed between the 'ins' and the 'outs'.

It infuriated Trollope to see that Disraeli's political novels were more highly thought of than his own. He wrote of them: 'Through it all there is a feeling of stage properties, a smell of hair-oil, an aspect of buhl, a remembrance of tailors, and that pricking of the conscience which must be the general accompaniment of paste diamonds.' Even so, Disraeli's *Sybil* and *Coningsby* are far more convincing as political novels. They burn with the passions of the day and if there is falsity in the lighting, that is an essential political quality. Disraeli presents politics as prophetic dogma; he understands that politics grow out of beliefs, interests and conditions, though they degenerate into expedients. The working class are not excluded as Trollope excludes them; and though Trollope lived in a quieter political period, it can hardly be said that the workers were without voice. Disraeli's vision of politics in his novels was exotic and perhaps no purely English novelist is capable of this, any more than he has been capable of the dialectical fantasies of Shaw; to write well about politics one has got to believe in them in the abstract and to regard them as a possible imaginative world. Trollope hated the idea of such a thing, and in consequence, though he gets the surface brilliantly, he misses the reason for its existence.

Character is the whole interest of Trollope and if his portrait of the Prime Minister, the Duke of Omnium, is meant to be a picture of the perfect gentleman and statesman, it is neither idealised nor forced. The Duke's skin is too thin, he has scruples, he is moody, morose and capable of ducal temper. Though he is in conflict with his wife, who gives a fantastic house party – forty guests a night for six weeks, and none to stay more than forty-eight hours; think, says the housekeeper at Gatherum Castle, as if she had Arnold Bennett at her elbow, of the towels and the sheets! – the Duke clearly understands that if she is a woman with no scruples, she is kept straight by her feelings and convictions. And Trollope is expert in crossing the intentions of his people with the accidents of life. The climber Lopez might have got his safe seat, if only the bumptious Major Pountney – 'a middle-aged young man' – had not annoyed the Duke on another matter. But we get, I think, a better idea of the political entanglement in the earlier book, *Phineas Finn*. Phineas is not an outsider, and therefore Trollope is in a better temper. He is the ingenious, penniless, handsome young fellow, going into politics against the author's affectionate advice and we are led with him step by step into his career. There are even glances at the Irish Question. We see Phineas funking his first opportunity to speak and making a mess of it when he does get up, full of indignation, on another occasion.

There are shrewd portraits of the Whips – but there is nothing to equal Disraeli's wonderful libellous sketch of Croker – and Trollope knows how to grade his politicians according to the condition of their careers. There is a hostile portrait of John Bright. He is Turnbull, who is contrasted with Monk, an imaginary Radical 'ever doubting of himself, and never doubting himself so much as when he had been most violent and also most effective, in debate'. But Turnbull-Bright has no doubts:

I think that when once he had learned the art of arranging his words as he stood on his legs, and had so mastered his voice as to have obtained the ear of the House, the work of his life was not difficult. Having nothing to construct he could always deal with generalities. Being free from responsibility, he was not called upon either to study details or to master even great facts. It was his business to inveigh against existing evils, and perhaps there is no easier business. . . . It was his work to cut down forest trees, and he had nothing to do with the subsequent cultivation of the land. Mr Monk had once told Phineas Finn how great were the charms of that inaccuracy which was permitted to the opposition.

That is all very well, but the very irony at the expense of politicians shows the failure to rise to the imaginative opportunity. As Mr Amery says, Disraeli would have plunged for the excitements of foreign policy. He would have risked.

Indeed, although *Phineas Finn* is an amusing guide to Parliamentary life as it then was, it interests us really for things like the famous portraits of the violent red-eyed Lord Chiltern – this plunging, dangerous man would be the hero of a contemporary novel, not a minor character – the superb Mr Kennedy, so gloomy, so evangelical, who adroitly lengthens family prayers when he is jealous of his wife's lover:

[He] was a man who had very little temptation to do anything wrong. He was possessed of over a million and a half of money, which he was mistaken enough to suppose he had made himself. . . . He never spoke much to anyone, although he was constantly in society. He rarely did anything, though he had the means of doing everything. He had seldom been on his legs in the House of Commons, though he had been there ten years. He was seen about everywhere, sometimes with one acquaintance, sometimes with another – but it may be doubted whether he had any friend . . . though he would not lend money, he gave a great deal – and he would give it for almost every object. 'Mr Rbt. Kennedy, M.P., £105' appeared on almost every charitable list that was advertised. No one ever spoke to him as to this expenditure, nor did he ever speak to anyone. Circulars came to him and the cheques were returned. The duty was an easy one to him and he performed it willingly. Had any moment of inquiry been necessary it is possible the labour would have been too much for him.

That is a close study of something not often observed: the neutrality, the nonentity of rich men. And then there are the women of the book who all talk so well and who are very well distinguished from each other. The stress on sex in the modern novel has meant that women have lost their distinctiveness as persons. Trollope excels in making the distinctions clear.

Trollope is a detailed, rather cynical observer of a satisfied world. Honest, assertive, sensible, shrewd, good-humoured, he is content. As Henry James said, he gives us the pleasure of recognition. But content is, so to speak, a summit that he has attained, not a torpor into which he has fallen. He grew worldliness like a second skin over the raw wounds of his youth, and the reason why he describes what is normally observable about people so well, is that he longed merely for the normal. He had been too insecure to want anything more than that security, and it was by a triumph of personal character that he attained it. Trollope might excusably have become a neurotic – and without talent. It is maddening to see the themes of Henry James taken back to the platitude of their starting point and left there; strange to have to recognise that what are called 'things as they are' can be soothing. It is dangerous to marry for money, but it is also dangerous to marry for love; it is dangerous to commit adultery for society will drop you, yet society is greedy and hypocritical. It is bad to borrow; it is mean not to lend. One is listening to human nature muddling along on its old rules of thumb. The only pattern we can discern is that made by the struggle of the individual within his group: politics, the law, the Church. It is not a passionate struggle. It is mainly a question of faintly enlightened self-interest. We feel about his people what we feel about our relatives: the curiosity that distracts us from a fundamental apathy. The sense of danger and extremity which alerts us in the war-like compositions of Jane Austen, is dulled. His novels are social history, without the movements of history; life as we see it without having to think about it. It has no significance beyond itself; it is as pleasant, dull and restful as an afternoon in an armchair. The footpads in the London parks, the frightened family of the crooked bankrupt, the suicide on the suburban line, are there, not to frighten us unduly, but to give further assurance to normal people that normality is stronger than ever. Can we wonder, in these times, at the Trollope revival?

(1963)

Fordie

'I once told Fordie that if he were placed naked and alone in a room without furniture, I would come back in an hour and find total confusion.' Ezra Pound's joke about Ford Madox Ford hits the mark. Confusion was the mainspring of his art as a novelist. He confused to make clear. As an editor, as a source of literary reminiscence, he attracts because he is always sketching his way from inaccuracy to inaccuracy in order to arrive at some personal, translucent truth. His unreliability may have annoyed, but it is inspired.

As a novelist – and he wrote some thirty novels, nearly all forgotten – he is one of those whose main obstacle is his own talent. A Conrad cannot invent; a Lawrence cannot narrate: such deficiencies are fortunate. They force a novelist to compensate, with all his resources, so that we shall hardly be aware of what is lacking and shall, in any case, think it unimportant. Ford is obstructed less by his defects than by the effusiveness of total ability. He has been called brilliant, garrulous and trivial, but what really happened was that, with the exception of *The Good Soldier*, parts of the Tietjens trilogy and most of *The Fifth Queen*, he never sank into the determined stupor out of which greater novelists work. It is comforting to think that the unduly brilliant may eventually have their stroke of luck: *The Good Soldier* is a small masterpiece.

Interest in Ford's work is now reviving in England and in the United States, where technicians are studied with a useful if exhausting piety. Mr Richard Cassell has got in early with a handy, basic investigation, *Ford Madox Ford*. He is alert to the peculiar effects of the Pre-Raphaelites on Ford, the French influence on the English novels of the period, and so on, but does not discuss the curious romanticising of the idea of 'the gentleman' which has made Ford seem tiresome and false to the modern reader. The dilemma of 'the

gentleman' preoccupied Shaw, James, Conrad, Galsworthy, and has
even been revived in the latest novels of Evelyn Waugh. It was once a
burning topic – one that Forster, with his marvellous aversion from
burning topics, ignored. But there are overtones in Ford's writing on
the subject which recall his own criticism of what the Pre-
Raphaelites felt about love – they swooned. Swooning about love
was a way of not knowing the facts. Ford swooned about the country
gentry, and nothing dates so much as fashion in love.

Still, *The Good Soldier* survives the swooning over the character
of Colonel Ashburnham and does so because, for once, Ford had his
excessive gifts under control. For once he remembered that if he was
to be an Impressionist writer, he had better not confuse writing with
painting. The confusion of memory need not be coloured; indeed, in
writing, if the parts are too prismatically brilliant, the whole will
become grey instead of luminous. As this novel shows, Ford was
equipped by intelligence and by grief to be a moralist once he could
be freed from the paint-box and, above all, from High Art. Conrad
must have been a very bad influence on a man who had already too
much vagueness in him; Henry James can have only been harmful to
one with already so much consciousness. To them Art did nothing
but good; the idea is excellent in itself; but it is dangerous to a man of
talent who only very seldom in a laborious literary life hits upon a
subject that draws out all his experience.

The Good Soldier and *The Fifth Queen* succeed. The former has
the compact and singeing quality of a French novel; it is a ruthless
and yet compassionate study in the wretchedness of conventional
assumptions and society's war upon the heart. The latter is a
historical romance and tells the story of Henry VIII and Katharine
Howard; it suffers a little from Ford's chronic allusiveness, but a
great issue is at stake and the ambiguities in it awaken all his interest
in intrigue. His mind was one that hated conclusions, not because it
was a sceptical mind but because it wanted to be put to one more test.
From this spring his ingenuity as a story-teller – a gift so rare that it is
often scorned – and his constant concern with technique. Critics
have usually praised this technical capacity, but have said that this
was all he had; yet it is – and one ought not to have to say so – a
capacity of enormous importance. (Imagine that Jane Austen had left
Sense and Sensibility in its epistolatory draft!) One can see that to a
mind as given to confusion and to posture as Ford's was, technical
capacity was his one reality. He asks nothing better than to be seen

making difficulties work for him. The famous device of the 'time-shift', which was a mania with him, enabled him to begin his scene in the middle and yet arrive with a whole tale of suspense that was thick with suggestion and memories caught on the way ashore.

In *The Good Soldier* the time-shift enabled him to effect those dramatic revaluations of people which give his novels their point. We had supposed, for example, that Leonora was vulgarly jealous when she slapped Mrs Maidan's face; but in a page or two we dart back in time to discover that there was another and stronger motive, one that exposes a hidden part of Leonora's nature: her shocked frigidity, her greed for money. When that is threatened, her passion for appearances collapses. In choosing for the narrator a dull and unemotional man who fumbles his way through a tale of passion which leads to death and madness, Ford has found someone who will perfectly put together the case of the heart versus conventional society, for he is a mild American Quaker perpetually astonished by Catholic puritanism. Meanwhile his own do-gooding wife is, unknown to him, a destroyer and nymphomaniac. Ford is often accused, by the hospital nurses of criticism, of triviality, but in this book the trivia are sharp and enhance the awful dull force of the tragedy.

Re-write *The Good Soldier* in straightforward narrative and Ford's vision of life as a minutely operating process of corrosion vanishes, and with that, of course, his particular Catholic outlook. Corrosion, as it is presented in this novel, means that we have more parts to our lives than one and that they work fatally upon each other. One has a quiet, extraordinary sense in the book of the minds of people perpetually thinking away their heartbeats.

Ford's preoccupation with technique – point of view, time-shift, *progression d'effet*, rendering and so on – was both a godsend and a curse, for he was constitutionally distracted, impatient and shy of coming to terms. By concentrating on the *means* of creating an impression he seems to have hoped, in some of his novels, to find that the means would suggest an End darker, more inscrutable and mysterious, than anything in the author's mind at the outset. Life was an intrigue that was never resolved, a meaningless experiment. This approach might lead, as it does in the works of Conrad, to fogginess; in Ford it could lead only to an excessive high-lighting of detail and to staginess. The secret, Romantic Ford leans too much on the ominous and sardonic outsider, the shadow figure breathing heavily down the neck of the reader, Art pretending to be Destiny. But when Ford is at one with his subject, as he is in *The Fifth Queen*, he stages well. His delight in playing fast and loose with time, in beginning a scene in the middle of a broken sentence, dropping it and picking it up again until the crisis is built up, his whole patterning and puzzling, are vividly justified.

He succeeds, more often than not, in his ingenious system of getting at the inside of things by looking intensely at the surface alone. This, of course, he inherited from the painters. He may see more than we can in the way people's hands lie in their laps, or how their legs look when they are kneeling, or how much of Henry VIII appeared as he went upstairs; and in the larger pictorial actions – Tom Culpepper rushing up drunk from Greenwich to Smithfield eager to see some martyrs at the stake because he'd never seen a burning before – the sense of daily life dancing by in a man's mind is wonderfully conveyed. Ford was a master of episode. If he is stagey, he does not ham. We notice, for example, that Tom Culpepper doesn't in fact see the actual burning because he gets into an absurd brawl. As a story-teller Ford recognised life when he saw complication and chance. His brutal scenes are benevolently comic; his women are originals; wherever there's human naivety and deviousness he is as happy as Kipling was, but with compassion. And throughout there is no detail that fails to bear on the religious quarrel which is his central subject. He responded very much in all his work to the margin men and women leave in their minds, to their long-headedness; and one can see that he found a parallel between the corruption of the Reformation and that of the Edwardian world which had killed the heart, he would have said, by reducing virtue and honour to the condition of masks.

No doubt *The Fifth Queen* is too close to the eye in a cinematic way to have the spacious historical sense of a great historical novel like *Old Mortality*; it hasn't the coolness of Mérimée's superb short novel, the *Chronicle of Charles IX*; but it makes most of our historical fiction up to 1914 look like the work of interior decorators. Literature for Ford was a passion; its rituals were sacred. But there is no doubt about his moral seriousness or the cumulative effect of the main story. How, by what stages, will Katharine bring the King to the point of making his submission to Rome? How will the King procrastinate? What lies will trap the Queen? Will the King, for once, be able to escape from his changeable and fatally political nature? What belongs to Caesar, what to God – and what to Good Learning? There is nothing allusive in the handling of this massive central conflict and it is brought to its climax without melodrama. One thing Impressionism could do was to catch the day as it passed through the minds of the actors in it. It could record confusion by a scrupulous and ingenious use of the means of art. Allowing for Ford's pleasant vanity in the imposture, this bravura piece – as Graham Greene calls it in his introduction to the Bodley Head collection of Ford's stories – is rather fine.

Half-English, half-German and, by fancy, French, Ford Madox Ford was nature's expatriate. His only country, he said, was literature. To be precise, it was 'the Novel'. He simply lived for it. Consider him as an incurable and dedicated work of fiction, one of the most diverting yet serious and instructive of 'living lies', and he becomes comprehensible. As a brilliant human being he was self-dispersing, moving from one hallucination to another, dumping his luggage in the hotel room of two or three cultures; he reassembled himself, for a while, in words and stories and in them he believed with an industrious and short-lived intensity. He succeeded in only three remarkable stories – *The Good Soldier*, the *Fifth Queen* trilogy and *Parade's End*. They vindicate his happy yet tortured incapacity to go straight from a starting-point, for he had none. They put his lack of self-confidence, his shortness of spiritual breath, his indolence, to use. They brought out and exploited with full resource the price he had to pay for his extraordinary cleverness: the emotion of anguish. One is tempted to say 'passion' also – but one has to hesitate here. The writers who convey passion also convey the terrible calm of its purgation and aftermath and Ford is too full of his own skill and ironical humour to allow that. But he does leave us with an indignant sense of unforgettable pain. One always finds that at the bottom of the baggage Ford left about the world.

Some pain is self-sought – the pain, for example, of our choice of impossible incarnations. It is hard, here, to separate the factitious from the inevitable. When he became incarnate as Tietjens in *Parade's End*, Ford could not obliterate Ford. One does not want him to do so, for Tietjens is Ford's anguished hallucination. No novelist can completely become another character; in Tietjens Ford constructed an English gentleman as only something like German romanticism or idealism could see him. Ford was no gentleman; he was a fine artist. He seems minutely to have observed the type, and at the same time to have loaded him with history and an inhuman willingness to suffer everything for the sake of suffering. So often one has seen expatriates find their home in a past that has not existed: Ford's plain feudal Yorkshire squire, with his love of the pre-industrial way of life, his scorn of the vulgar modern world, his dislike of ambition, his irritable abstention, his martyred sense of decency, looks today like a romancing not about a man but a code.

When Ford created Tietjens the dilemma of the gentleman was very much the fashion, as I have said. These talented agrarians existed. The coarse businessmen, speculators and careerists were breaking in on them, the press had turned yellow, the conventions were shocking when they worked and even more shocking when they did not. If Tietjens and his scruples about sex and society seem odd now, they did not fifty years ago. Rock-like before the unanswered slanders of his bankers, his military friends, his father, his cold, promiscuous wife who tricked him over the paternity of his child, Tietjens was exactly the figure to expose by his silence and his suffering the rottenness of Edwardian society. Further, he was not a Roman Catholic but his wife was, and the curse on the Tietjens family is thought to go back to the Reformation and the thieving of Roman Catholic lands. This adds to Tietjens's martyrdom, a touch of destiny which is pretty gamey stuff. That old row has been hung too long to be digestible. One is rather exasperated by Tietjens's stubborn determination to collect all the slings and arrows going; after all, where does the family get its millions from? From the sacred soil of a great estate? Hardly. Towards the end of the novel there is a hint that the family controls a lot of industry in Middlesbrough. Tietjens is just as much a child of the industrial revolution as anybody else. He may not like the men of the new order who were coming in just before 1914: not being gentlemen they were certain to cheat. But isn't he simply an idealiser of convention? One has a sneaking sympathy for his wife, who at one moment complains that her husband is trying to be Jesus Christ as well as the misunderstood son of a great landowner. Her cruelties are an attempt to turn a martyr into a man.

In creating Tietjens, Ford chose a character utterly unlike himself and did the detail admirably. He caught the obtuse pride of the social masochist. He caught the spleen of the gentleman because this accorded well with the ironic spleen that Ford himself felt as an artist, even when it was a pose. The gregarious, voluble, intelligent nature of Ford could not be prevented from mingling with the Yorkshire squire; what one does not accept in Tietjens is the romantic German aura. Any German can do a better job of being an English gentleman and Tietjens is just a Germanised squire. He is even a classical scholar.

Two more able American critics, John Meixner and Paul Wiley, have written studies that will stimulate the Ford addict, and both agree that *Some Do Not* is the best of the Tietjens novels. It is a complete 'Affair'; the famous time shifts are well-patterned. And both understand that Ford, being an indolent man with little self-confidence and an observer before everything else, was best at beginnings. Any paragraph is better than a page. All the good things, large or small, are beginnings. The boredom we experience in Ford comes, indeed, from the strain of reading innumerable beginnings on every page. So these critics find that Tietjens does not grow. His wife turns melodramatically wicked as the book goes on. I don't entirely agree with the first part of the verdict: Tietjens may be better done in the earliest volume but he becomes more representative and important as a human being in the account of the war in France, and especially because his puzzling private life is in abeyance.

Ford's response to the war brought out his highest quality: his historical sense and his exactitude. He surveyed with sardonic relish the chaos of the staff officer's labours: the numbering and allotting, the terrible paper-work in a war no one understood. The Canadians are going up the line, but where are they? They have been held up somewhere by a train smash. What is to happen to the men they are supposed to relieve? Ah, now the Canadians have been found! And now we've got them, the orders have been countermanded. The intrigue and the rot at the Base produce a natural defensive reaction: the chaos is intended by the politicians, the *embusqués* at home. And who are they? The new men, of course, the climbers and careerists. (This certainly was the legend of the period.)

The general picture of a whole society floundering is done with a wonderful precision and not in the form of easy diatribe. Tietjens is just the right kind of numbed Homeric figure to record the sudden killing of a man in the staff dugout, a man to whom he had refused leave; or the explosion of a mine and the rescuing of the buried. As a character Tietjens escapes from the cliché of almost all the war novels of that time in which the hero conveys that the whole war has been declared against him personally. Tietjens knows that a civilisation, or at any rate a class, is sinking. Responsible and capable, Ford-Tietjens has an unselfed and almost classical sub-Olympian view of the experience. Although he was self-consciously an impressionist, Ford has some inner sense of a moral order. Or, if not that, a moral indignation at the lack of it. Or, if not that, a taste for the moral consolations of defeat. He brings not only an eye but a judgment to what he sees.

There is something odd but also – from a novelist's point of view – tolerant about this judgment. A craftsman, through and through, in everything, Ford is interested in the way things are done. Even corruption has its curious status. What are gunners like, what are their interests, their follies, what is the *virtu* of the trade? He is deeply interested in the idle detail of human nature and his own lazy aloofness enabled him to catch the detail perfectly. A variety of scenes comes to mind: the death of O Nine Morgan or the astonishing scene where a gunner chases a solitary German with shells.

His antics had afforded these gunners infinite amusement. It afforded them almost more when all the German artillery on that front, imagining that God knew what was the matter, had awakened and plastered heaven and earth and everything between them for a quarter of an hour with every imaginable kind of missile. And had then abruptly shut up.

And it had all happened merely because Tietjens had lightly told a gunner that any Italian peasant with a steam-plough could pulverise a field at a cost of thirty shillings, which was cheaper than the cost of high explosives. As a craftsman the gunner had been put on his mettle.

That incident is anecdotal, but Ford could create the people who lived the anecdotes. His art – particularly the theory of the time shift – was in part based on an analysis of talk, the way it plunges and works back and forth. The method was perfected in *The Good Soldier*; in the later, Tietjens novel, it does not succeed so well. It often becomes a device for refusing to face a major scene. One has only a confusing notion of what went on in the hotel bedroom when the drunken General broke in on Tietjens and his wife at a crucial point in their sado-masochistic relationship, when it is important that we should know all. Ford's view seems to have been that no one ever quite knows what goes on at the crucial moments of life. His craftsmanship becomes obscurely crafty at such moments, as though, with tiresome cleverness, he had decided that it was the business of art to impose chaos on order. At his worst, he turns never saying Yes and never saying No into an aesthetic neurosis.

Where do we place Ford in relation to the contemporaries he admired – James and Conrad? For Mr Meixner Ford was 'locked in the prison of his own theories' and lacked 'the personal audacity, the conquering boldness' required by a masterpiece. He was a penetrating historian, a man of fundamental insights, but he did little with them; his ingenuity made him intellectually thin. *The Good Soldier* succeeds because it is done in the first person, which allows him to rid himself of the stiff aloofness and impersonality he thought he was copying from the French – by a paradox this is his unmistakably French novel. He has not the range of a James or a Conrad, nor the mass of good work; but Conrad's characters are 'static and inert', despite the subtlety and penetration of his analysis; and Ford (for Mr Meixner) surpasses Conrad in *The Good Soldier* and *Some Do Not* because Ford's people have great inner life, are more various, more real, more fluid and more pleasing and more moving. I would have thought Conrad's sceptical moral sense, as a *déplacé*, was richer than Ford's. Compared with James, Ford goes deeper (for Mr Meixner) into the range of spiritual terror and anguish. If, after a lot of wrangling, one came to agree with this last point, one would have to qualify it by saying that the very nature of Ford's methods made these depths brief and rare; and that they came as a result of calculated shock. We feel the shock felt by Tietjens when O Nine Morgan is killed before his eyes; we are startled by the picture of Tietjens trying to recover his memory when his brain has been affected by bombardment – but these episodes remain superb fragments.

Mr Wiley is good at showing the consistency of Ford's career as a novelist and as theorist of the novel and pays a lot of attention to the forgotten works. Although the discussion of Ford's methods, in his last novel, *Vive le roy*, is interesting, it does not succeed in making this maddening work more readable. Like a first-class teacher Ford gives his ideas the force of his personal life. But, except in his two best books, he had so many ideas that he was exhausted by the time he got to the page. He had not the breath. He creates the spell of someone always on the move; the pen itself was expatriate. His theories, in the end, become devices for postponing the novelist's task: which is to settle and confront. Impressionism – and with it a desire to impress –

becomes an unconscious journalism. One sees him, and his characters also, wearing themselves out by continually changing trains.

(1962)

ARNOLD BENNETT

The Five Towns

It is a long time now since the earth seemed solid under the feet to our novelists, since caprice, prophecy, brains and vividness meant less than the solid substance of time and place. And Arnold Bennett, in books like *The Old Wives' Tale* and the Clayhanger trilogy, seems to be the last of the novel's four-square gospellers. I return to him often and always, once I get into him, with satisfaction. A book like *Clayhanger* has the sobriety as well as the tedium of a detailed engraving; and there is, oddly, enough of the connoisseur in Bennett to induce our modern taste. He is not a dilettante in the ego's peculiarities and he is without interest in elegance; he is the connoisseur of normality, of the ordinary, the awkward, an heir – one might say – of the makers of the Staffordshire figures who thought Moody and Sankey as good a subject as equestrian princes of the blood. We speak of the disciplines of belief, of art, of the spirit; Bennett speaks of the discipline of life itself, reveres its frustrations, does not rebel against them; kneels like some pious behaviourist to the drab sight of reflexes in process of being conditioned. He catches the intolerable passing of time in our lives, a passing which blurs our distinctiveness and quietly establishes our anonymity; until our final impression of him is as a kind of estate agent's valuer walking with perfunctory step through the rooms of our lives, ticking his inventory and treating us as if we were long deceased. He cannot begin – and I think this is his inheritance from the French naturalists – until we are dead, until we and our furniture have become indistinguishable evidence. I find this very restful. Frustration – *pace* Mr Wells – is one of the normal conditions of life, and calming is the novelist who does not kick against the pricks.

Fidelity and sincerity are the words one puts first to Arnold Bennett's work. Some years ago there appeared an anthology called *The English in Love*, containing love passages from the English novelists, and I was much struck by the superiority of Bennett's contribution to the work of specialists like Meredith and D. H. Lawrence. Bennett was not describing passion; but against his quiet exactitude and sincerity, the lyricists looked forced and trite. The very matter-of-factness of Bennett made him one of the best portrayers of women we have had. The vices of romanticism or of misogynist satire passed him by in his best work completely. What other words come to mind when we think of him? They are his own words: 'detracting' is one, 'chicane' – a great favourite – is another; but there is a sentence in the early pages of *Clayhanger* which contains a volume of criticism on him. He is writing of young Edwin Clayhanger coming home from his last day at school in the Five Towns: 'It seemed rather a shame,' Bennett says of Edwin, 'it seemed even tragic, that this naïve, simple creature, immaculate of worldly experience, must soon be transformed into a man wary, incredulous and detracting.' The essence of Bennett's mind is packed into that awkward sentence with its crick in the neck at the feeble beginning and the give-away of its three final words. Bennett had borrowed the manner and methods of the French naturalists without being seriously formed by the scientific, political and philosophical ideas which made them naturalists and gave them their driving force. Timidity rather than conviction is behind the brevity of his address. The result is that the apostle of will, efficiency and success appears to us hesitant and uncertain; he is between two stools; he cannot make up his mind whether life is 'rather a shame' or 'tragic'. And when we compare *Clayhanger* with the contemporary French *Les Thibaults* – which, like *Clayhanger*, contains a prolonged study in fatal illness and is also concerned with the relation of father and son – we feel at once, though we recognise the conscious artist, Bennett's lack of imaginative stamina and resilience. What Bennett observes will be truthfully, almost litigiously, observed. Hazard will set the points wrongly in the lives of humdrum people and push them off the rails. Time will get its teeth into them more deeply year by year. We shall feel, as Edwin felt, that we must 'brace ourselves to the exquisite burden of life'. We shall feel we are interpenetrated 'by the disastrous yet beautiful infelicity of things'. What we shall miss is the sense that life is conceived of as anything in particular, whether it be the force that makes the Five Towns or forms the bleak impetuosity of Hilda Lessways. We shall not feel that life is much more than a random collection of *things*.

Admitting the absence of a frame, allowing for some lagging of narrative which the modern novelist would speed up, everything else in *Clayhanger* is good. Bennett, as I have said, was the connoisseur of the normal, the ordinary and the banal. Where other novelists add, he – as he said – detracts. For example, how easy for the novelist to identify himself with the sixteen-year-old Edwin and to exaggerate that sense of being alone with the universe which the boy had when he sat in his room alone at night. Bennett collects that emotion, astutely yet compassionately – but he collects it, labels it – it becomes part of the collection of human samples which make up Edwin Clayhanger's life. Bennett's pursuit of the normal is even better illustrated by his treatment of the character of the hard, impulsive, passionate figure of Hilda Lessways. Here he uses a characteristic device: he makes two full-length portraits of her from two different points of view, a method which gives a remarkable suspense to the story. The first portrait of Hilda is romantic and mysterious outline. In the second, with enormous dramatic effect, he fills in the plain reality of her life. That second appearance of hers, as she cleans the house and quarrels with her mother about money, is a remarkable portrayal of the relationship of two women. As spectators of Hilda's character we might easily exaggerate, romanticise and misread her disaster; but Bennett's gift as a novelist is to abolish the rôle of spectator. He almost painfully domesticates the reader, puts him in the slow muddle, murmur and diurnal perturbation of a character's life, so that the reader knows no more than Hilda knows, where she is going or why she is going there. Where most novelists live by a sort of instinct for imaginative scandal, Bennett – by some defect of imagination which he is able to turn to advantage – clings like a cautious puritan to sober likelihood. He doesn't bet: 'It's a mug's game.' The result, in the portrait of Hilda, is a staggering probability. There is a passage when she discovers her husband is a bigamist and a crook, that the child she is expecting is illegitimate, and that she will be left penniless in their boarding-house at the mercy of bailiffs. She is faced by ruin. How do people face ruin? Variously, unexpectedly; they traipse, protected by conviction, through their melodramas. Bennett seems to reply:

Hilda in a curious way grew proud of him. With an extraordinary inconsequence she dwelt upon the fact that was grand – even as a caterer, he had caused to be printed at the foot of the menu forms which he had instituted the words: 'A second helping of all or any of the dishes will willingly be served if so desired.' And in the general havoc of the shock she began to be proud also of herself because it was the mysterious power of her individuality that had originated her disaster.

The determination to avoid the dramatic has led to something far more dramatic: revelation, a new light on character, the unexpected vistas in ordinary life.

Bennett's characters have three dimensions; the slow but adroit changing of the light that is thrown upon them makes them stereoscopic and gives them movement. And this movement is not the swift agitation of the passions but the dilatory adjustment to circumstance.

One of the reasons why bad novels are bad is not that the characters do not live, but they do not live with one another. They read one another's minds through the author. In *Clayhanger*, we feel at once that the characters are living together because, quite without prompting and entirely in the course of nature, they misunderstand one another. Edwin never understands his father because he does not know his father's past. The father cannot understand the son because the father's whole attitude to life is that his rise from barbarous poverty is a primitive miracle. He is primitive, the son is rational. Each one bumps awkwardly along in the wonder of his own nature. When the father is stricken by fatal illness the son becomes the tyrant. Their emotions about each other are strong; but the two men do not feel these emotions for each other at the same time. The fierceness of the father's battle for life in the long, grey death scene startles the son – and yet he feels how strange it is that a dying man should be strong enough to return again and again to the struggle, whereas he, the son and slave, should be at the point of collapse. A writer with little poetic feeling, Bennett thinks of our awkwardness with each other, of the unbridgeable gaps of time, experience and faculty which separate us, and not of our ultimate isolation. That is why he is a pathetic and not a tragic writer; one who feels uncertainly that 'it is rather a shame', that we have to bear time's burden of 'beautiful infelicity'.

Bennett's collector's passion for ordinariness is a kind of poor relation of Meredith's passion for the fantastic. It is amusing to make an irreverent comparison between Meredith's chapter *On an Aged and Great Wine* with Bennett's fervent hymn to building materials and plumbing in *Clayhanger*. This tedious literalness of Bennett's culminated in that nightmare of deified gadgets, *Imperial Palace*. But the virtues of Bennett lie in his patient and humane consideration of the normal factors of our lives: money, marriage, illness as we have to deal with them. Life, he seems to say, is an occupation which is forced upon us, not a journey we have chosen, nor a plunge we have taken. Such a view may at times depress us, but it may toughen us. Bennett really wrote out of the congenital tiredness of the lower middle class, as Wells wrote out of its gambling spirit and gift for fantasy; and in the end, I think, Bennett's picture, with its blank acceptance of the Sunday School pageants, the Jubilees, the Band of Hope, the fear of the workers, the half-baked attempts at culture, is the more lasting one. It is history. History presented – when we glance back at Bennett's French masters – with the dilettante's and collector's indifference to any theory of what history may be about.

(1965)

Mr Forster's Birthday

'May I never resemble M. de Lesseps', E. M. Forster wrote when he considered the famous statue by the Suez Canal on one of his journeys to India. 'May no achievement upon an imposing scale be mine.' He has indeed been a haunting absence in the English novel, but on the occasion of his eightieth birthday, we can allow ourselves to dress up our prose in the boater and blazer of 1905 and think of his silence, since *Passage to India*, as 'a rotten business', without a moral – like Harold's dropping of the oars and dying, in *The Point of It* – and of Forster's survival in our literature as a 'cert'. How does one survive if one does not impose? Forster has survived so far by interposing. Where his elders, Shaw, Wells, Kipling, imposed by sheer efficiency and manpower, Forster has interposed and influenced by a misleading slackness, by the refusal to speak in a public voice. This has given the personal a startling strength. He has had, one guesses, more influence on the educated middle classes than any other English writer in the last thirty or forty years; for it is he who has taught them to disengage themselves from their inherited official, not to say imperial, personality. The Empire Kipling celebrated, Forster destroyed, and by a handful of out-of-date novels – for it was his fate to have a great deal of his material pulled from under his feet by the 1914 war. In saying his say against imperialism, he exhausted in advance what he could have said, as a novelist, against totalitarianism. He was kind enough to write articles.

One can rely on English life to produce these personal voices: a Samuel Butler, a Mary Kingsley, a Forster; in our own generation, a George Orwell. Their voices are direct, natural, distinct and disengaged, malignly flat. The machine stops when they start talking. We are so used to various sorts of 'side' in English life, that we are startled and pleased by the note of authority from nature. Outside of our poetry we find that voice hard to hit upon. Forster's gift has been just that: the private voice, carrying without effort, in the public place. The refusal to be great; the attack on the will and the bad heart; the two cheers instead of the usual three for democracy, the third being reserved for 'love the Beloved Republic, which feeds upon Freedom and lives'; the belief in personal relationships – 'the heart signs no documents' – and an aristocracy of 'the sensitives, the considerate and the plucky'; the debating-point plea for a 'period of apathy, inertia and uninventiveness' – these are not withdrawals. Some are principled assertions of the supreme value of individual life; some are there to redress a balance. None is a brilliant paradox put down by a consuming brain. The apologist for softness is intellectually hard; the liberal who has been forced out of economic *laisser faire* and who believes that, nevertheless, *laisser faire* is the only doctrine that 'pays' – a favourite ironic word – in the world of the spirit, is not proposing to let us do what we like. No one is let off in Forster's novels; like Jane Austen, he is a moral realist. Leonard Bast, the prototype of the Angry Young Man, will get a rap on the knuckles for being a crushed soul. Having a chip – a maiden aunt seems to say – is no excuse for hysteria and making messes. Mr Wilcox catches it for being a soul-crusher. No tears, I seem to remember, are shed in Forster's novels. The sins of the heart, the failure to 'connect', don't pay: they end in emptiness and panic. Those are better words than the jargon we have learned to use since the nervous breakdown, if only because they imply the moral imperative which is necessarily lacking in scientific studies of the mind.

There is the voice of the decided moralist in Forster; fortunately for the English novel, it has been transposed into the accents of the brusque and off-hand sanity which is in the central tradition of our comedy. Like Shaw's – though in the private interest, being more concerned with intimate feeling than with justice – Forster's is a comedy of ideas, and the danger there was that it would be expressed in a comedy of types or that he would have chosen people possessed of too great a skill in debate. He escaped this danger by his brilliant use of people who had been thoroughly unfitted to deal with their situations; like so many of Henry James's characters they are null or dull. Looking again at the early short stories which try out the themes to be taken up by *Where Angels Fear to Tread* or *Howards End* one is, at first, shaken by their pedestrian characters. How faded the people are now; they were born faded. Everyone outside Cambridge, one suspects, had to bear that accusation. Pompous, shabby, fussy

suburbans they are, a collection of dim widows, daughters genteel or
bossy, sons emasculated or emotionally congested. There are the
mild, mechanical soldiers and all are liable to the blood-pressure, the
wilfulness or the frostbite of a class-consciousness that has passed
out of our knowledge. Formidable to deal with, these injured
families are in danger of suffering (as Gissing's characters do) from
an initial social pathos which is unforgivable in works of art. (Class
theories play the part of the famous pathetic fallacy.) But, at second
glance, the pathos goes. For these unlikely dullards are suddenly
shaken by issues that had never occurred to them as existing; they are
tripped up by melodrama, and their dullness makes their situation
more arresting. They are made to skip and look lively. Mr Forster's
beliefs are gentle, but he has no sentimental indulgence for weakness,
and we remember that behind the fineness of his spiritual scrutiny lie
the scrupulous traditions of the Clapham Sect; working in him is a
spirited agnosticism and he does not see why the moral stakes for
these muddled gamblers should not be put very high or why the
upper middle classes should not have to risk all. In a way, he treats
the English as if they were foreigners – a good idea considering how
anti-foreign we have always been. His people swing between two
states of mind – the disinterested and the benighted; and they fall
into four foreign groups: the Teutonic, heading towards suicide in a
sea of general ideas; his Latins – vulgar, avaricious but redeemable
because they have not been castrated by good taste, are in the sink-
or-swim of the instinctive life, and are liable to racial memories of
Mediterranean paganism; the Oriental – passive, touchy and affron-
ted; and the inhabitants of Tonbridge. Where have we seen the
Forster situations before? In the novel-poems of the poet Clough, but
whereas Clough is torn in half and is half-guilty, half-aggressive
about his passivity and his escape into abstract thought, Forster
presents the picture of a united personality who knows his mind. He
knows what he is committed to.

This is not like the committal of Shaw or Butler – with whom he
has, however, some affinity – nor any of the other committals of
those who attacked the official late Victorian or Edwardian personality. His comedy is not freakish; it is not accommodating; there
is no comfort in his scepticism. He is not scabrous and not at all the
satirist, even if he caricatures; he is without the orgiastic sense of the
full comic writers who revel in meaninglessness. He is not very
sociable. His comedy is positive and spiritual; it has one most

alarming trait: assurance. It is lonely. It has courage. He has always got his deadliest effect from a pretence of soppiness, from a casual, slangy disregard of the spirit of composure, or from a piece of parenthetical bathos. That opening argument about the cow in *The Longest Journey* is an example. If he is casually disrespectful, he is also casually abrupt about matters of life and death: the echo in the cave, Gino's outbreak of physical cruelty at the crux of sorrow in his child's death, young Wilcox getting three years for hitting someone with an old sword, Leonard dying perfunctorily because a bookcase falls on him, the baby falling out of the carriage, and those brief, dismissed sudden deaths in boats, playing fields and at the level-crossing. The intellectual must face causality; but he had better remember casualty and the inexplicable. None of these famous incidents will 'do' in a realistic novel; the shock is too great and one might attack them as pointers to a suspicion that Mr Forster has exaggerated the device of not belonging to the world, and even that he grew up so quickly because he refused to join it. But these incidents, of course, succeed in romance where the writer has the licence to load his dice as he wishes. He has, also, a hankering after the pagan acceptance of mercilessness and the absence of tears.

Since his time, anyone in the nature of a personage has vanished from the English and American novel. The official has gone. The conversational, the vernacular voice has come in, but only in the interests of naturalism. It is common now to read novels in which physical life is rendered so clearly that we have the impression of seeing it before our eyes like the pebbles of a clear running stream. That impression can be had from Mr Forster's novels also – but with an important difference. It is the moral life that has the pebble-like clarity in *his* writing; he has made it tangible and visible. He has, so to say, speeded up the process of contemplation by making clear what, in his view, needed to be contemplated. The plain conversational style is truly conversational in the sense that we feel several people are talking and trying to find out; in spite of James's influence, there is no sense of monologue. Forster's talk, like all good talk, has the quality of surprise.

It is easy enough to demonstrate that Forster represents the end of something. He has almost said so himself, though not quite: civilisations are a string of intermissions in the anger of time. He speaks at the end of liberal culture and, since there is no other, there is no implicit accusation. He agrees that this firm attachment owes something to privilege and we all know the dogma that, in its penultimate phase, a culture sees spiritual order in art alone; in its ultimate post-Forsterian phase it crumbles into a sort of Byzantine pedantry.

Forster's contribution to our present collective society is the reminder that it will be an arid and destroying desert if we remove the oasis of private life. But he is a dangerous master. All very well for him to refuse to be great: he had to fight the portentous. Educated and inured by the powerful, he was free to develop apathy and softness as an unexpectedly useful muscle. He had something pretty unscrupulous to disbelieve in. Does he feel, now, the burden peculiar to famous old age, that an age has caught up with him? Does he feel that, in England at any rate, a younger generation is carrying the cult of privacy and personal relationships to the lengths of whimsicality and eccentricity? It often strikes one that far too large a portion of educated energy is going into running England as a kind of private joke, an ingenious personal crossword. We are more gentle with one another, but we spend an inordinate amount of time being gentle; we are bathed to the point of sleep in tolerance and understanding. Forsterian teaching has been taken on without our recognising that it had the virility of a reaction. It is very pleasant to relax, as he taught us, and to believe (for example) in his notion that the bucket drops down into the unconscious and brings up the substance of the work of art. It is true. But isn't it Mr Forster's old enemy, the will, that has turned the handle and let the bucket down? It is a mistake to take this infertile and original writer literally. Thus his 'apathy' really means 'integrity'. One other writer of his generation, Boris Pasternak, has it, and has demonstrated its phenomenal spiritual strength. Like him, Forster hands back the ticket, bored by the verbosity of the strong-willed, knowing that there is a creative force in the secrets of life. He is fresh because he is unable to conceive of a life without free choice; perhaps we would think him more than courageous, and actually great, if his novels had conveyed the other half of the argument: that we have to choose for others and that choice is made by others for us. But this is to ask for an inrush of ungoverned emotion beyond the scope of comedy.

(1962)

EVELYN WAUGH

Club and Country

Many good writers live on their nerves and can turn to anything. Clever, they have only one self. This is not the case with Evelyn Waugh; he has many selves, deeply embedded, on which to draw. He might have settled down with Lady Metroland and tippled away at a mixture of the *Bab Ballads*, the cautionary tale and Firbank; but his real line was the prose, not the poetry, of outrage. The wild, feathered feminine scream of that last master was not for him. His temperament was sober. He moved to the hard-headed traditions of English satirical comedy; one glance at the English upper classes, imposing their private fantasies on whatever is going on, treating everything from war downwards as if it were all happening in one of their country houses, has been enough to provide comedians with material for a lifetime. Mr Waugh went on next to be inconvenienced by his Sir Galahad and St George complexes; but after *Brideshead Revisited* and a brief return to the outrageous in *The Loved One*, the gentleman moralist appeared, a clubbish writer assiduously polishing his malign sentences, daily persisting with the stings of mortifying circumlocution. His early books spring from the liberating notion that human beings are mad; the war trilogy, a work of maturity, draws on the meatier notion that the horrible thing about human beings is that they are sane.

For better or worse, there is a masculine vein in English comedy, a vein which is sociable and not intellectual, sensible rather than sensitive. It shows us willingly paying the price of misanthropy for the pleasure of making a go of life in clubs – day and night – parsonages, public schools, villas, furnished apartments and other privacies of the national masochism. It required a nerve on Mr Waugh's part to treat the war as something which could or could not be known socially in these terms. It also required the accomplishment of a lifetime to bring off those three volumes. It is true that they have the formal melancholy of a memoir, and that Sir Galahad strikes a few unattractive poses; but the comic invention is strong: and there is an advance towards a compassionate study of human nature. Crouchback's bad wife would once have been seen as a vile body; she is now discerned as a displaced person.

The melancholy note persists in the first volume of Mr Waugh's autobiography, *A Little Learning*. In his dire way he has done what he can to pass himself off as a fossil. Like his father – as he appears in this volume – the son is a considerable impersonator. His prose is set to the felicities of misleading. This book is of great importance to students of his novels – though he does not yet discuss them – for it shows how long-established his preoccupations as a man and writer have been. An outstanding quality of his work has been its care for cadence in English prose and his regard for craftsmanship as a moral duty; he comes of a line of clergy and doctors, some of whom were minor writers; his background is literary and unassumingly sedate. The youthful taste for working at medieval script is another sign of the craftsman to come and a sign too of that feeling for Romance which has been the less successfully manifested aspect of his work. (His father was also romantic; he would refer to the 'stout timbers' of the villa he built for himself as if it were some galleon anchored in the North End Road and never forgave the local authorities for incorporating his then rustic part of Hampstead into the ugly and socially ambiguous brashness of new Golders Green.)

As for religion, Mr Waugh was always interested in theology and never at all bored by church. There is nothing to suggest that his later conversion to Catholicism was Romantic; everything to suggest that theological ingenuity was an important appeal. A relative in the Bengal Lancers brought in the St George touch and the nostalgia for swords and regalias. The designs of the nursery wallpaper were medieval: it was a taste of the period. The boy's upbringing was quiet, instructed, entirely happy. No Oedipal struggles appear. There was nothing to provoke the later sense of outrage, nothing – apparently – to titillate the psychiatrist except the mildness of it all. Even at the end of the volume, when he plans to drown himself after coming down from Oxford, full of debts and depressed about lost fun, Mr Waugh takes the view that this was a normal adolescent gesture, abandoned at once when he swam into some jellyfish.

What provoked the taste for outrage? Mr Waugh is a thoughtful rather than an intimate autobiographer, in this volume. He keeps the lid on. His aim appears to be the desire to conform, no doubt ironically, to a carefully prepared conventional pattern and to repose, almost masochistically, upon a belief in the Unremarkable. Clearly this, in so dashing an imagination, suggests a conflict. His marvellous feel for the disreputable comes from a man with a family addiction to the neutral yet aspiring. But one thing *did* go wrong. There was no woodshed. But home was so happy that to leave it for school made him 'nastier' (on the general principle that all school-boys are 'nasty'?) And then there was the despoiling of England.

As one who belongs to his generation, though coming from a very different background, I understand something of what Mr Waugh means when he writes of the shock caused by the ruin of rural England. It would seem all the worse to a literary suburban:

This is part of the grim cyclorama of spoliation which surrounded all English experience in this century and my understanding of the immediate past (which presumably is the motive for reading a book such as this) must be incomplete unless this huge deprivation of the quiet pleasure of the eye is accepted as a dominant condition, sometimes making for impotent resent-ment, sometimes for mere sentimental apathy, sometimes poisoning love of country and of neighbours. To have been born into a world of beauty, to die amid ugliness, is the common fate of all us exiles.

The evil, then, was the sense of exile. Most, indeed I would say all writers, have this sense anyway. It was exacerbated for him, as for many schoolboys, by the frustration of 'being out of the war'. It was his brother Alec Waugh, not Evelyn, who would be the hero. One was reduced to dreamy, hungry, insubordinate futility. In some respects Mr Waugh's exile is snobbish. Mr Waugh, senior, was an industrious and kindly reviewer of the old school who hated the new thing in the best jocose tradition of elderly criticism; Mr Waugh, junior, turns rancorous: 'There are the State-trained professional critics with their harsh jargon and narrow tastes.' Mr Waugh senior has his jargon too. Of D. H. Lawrence's art he wrote: 'his fancy is half asleep upon a foetid hot-bed of moods.' But, as his son truly says, as a critic the elder Waugh was no snob. His limitation was the 'common enough inability to recognise the qualities he loved unless they were presented in familiar forms'. Mr Waugh's own 'State-trained' reveals a similar inability.

Prep school, public school, university: these now tedious influences standardise English autobiography, giving the educated Englishman the sad if fascinating appearance of a stuffed bird of sly and beady eye in some odd seaside museum. The fixation on school has become a class trait. It manifests itself as a mixture of incurious piety and parlour game. (Some of Mr Waugh's contemporaries are now writing or have written their autobiographies and are watching each other like chess-players. What was Rugby doing when Sherborne saw Waugh go to Lancing and did Eton care?)

Cautious, lonely, observant at first at Oxford, Mr Waugh eventually kicked out, did the right thing by drinking a lot and coming down deep in debt, and was ready for a far more interesting life than appears in this opening volume. One must hope that his feeling for impersonality will not become so subtle as to make the irony too sober. The best things in the present volume are those that recover the detail of a period. One recognises this room:

The dining-room was dark and full of oil-paintings. The drawing-room was much cluttered with small tables, draperies, screens and ornaments on carved brackets. It contained two cabinets full of 'curiosities' – fans, snuff-boxes, carved nuts, old coins and medals; some of them unremarkable, such as, carefully wadded, encased and labelled, the charred tip of a walking stick with which some relation had climbed Mount Vesuvius and a lock [unauthenticated] of Wordsworth's hair.

There was even a phial containing a specimen of 'White Blood' from a patient dying of anaemia. Tourists' trophies had not yet become standardised.

Mr Waugh is a master also of the compressed portrait. There are three maiden aunts – an extinct genus now, as Mr Waugh points out:

My Aunt Connie sat on the bench when women became eligible as magistrates and was much distressed by the iniquities there revealed to her. All three had the prudishness proper to maiden aunts, though Aunt Elsie in old age developed a tolerance of very slightly indelicate fiction.

The portrait is good, the prose embroidered here with the facetious parlance – is that the word? – of clubs. This is the trouble with club Mandarin – it becomes flunkeyish. Better write like Wooster than like Jeeves. The crisp manner used in describing W. W. Jacobs is preferable:

In person he was wan, skinny, sharp-faced, with watery eyes. Like many humorists he gave scant evidence of humour in private intercourse. In losing the accents of Wapping he lost most of his voice and spoke through the side of his thin lips in furtive, almost criminal tones, disconcerting in a man of transcendent, indeed of tedious respectability. He was a secular puritan, one of those who 'have not got the Faith and will not have the fun'. . . .

Except for the last sentence, the portrait is exact. The little man was skipping up and down, as merry as popcorn, when I once caught sight of him at a suburban 'hop'. It must be remembered that all humorists suffer from overwork.

The gentle portrait of the author's father is the longest in the book. It is interesting chiefly as an example of a quality that is generally overlooked by admirers of the son's comic originality. The wit, the hilarious transitions, the pace and savagery of his comedies, deceives us into seeing Mr Waugh as a writer who jumps with inspired carelessness from one fantasy to the next. The dialogue alone, his early forte, should undeceive us. Its quality is accuracy; in fact a grave exactitude has been the ground of his comic genius as it is of his serious writing in travel and biography. He can be accurate to the point of testiness. Indeed he is only bad when he is not accurate, that's to say when St George, panache etc. come in and make him slur.

Mr Waugh's eye for the fact enables him to catch the changing impressions so important to the faithful memorialist. Until he was sixteen he had supposed that his father was simple and prosaic; then a friend came down and said: 'Charming, entirely charming and acting all the time'. He was. Between bouts of coughing he would cheerfully call upon Death for release; declare in the middle of signing a cheque he was being driven to a pauper's grave. He talked aloud to imaginary people continuously. He assumed, without knowing it, Dickensian roles. Before the 'ingratitude' of his sons he became Lear. His sighs could be heard across a theatre. He had talent as an amateur actor and, on the evidence of his son's prose – on the confessions of Pinfold and the anecdotes that trickle down from the West Country about his histrionic mischief – one would guess that Evelyn Waugh's sobriety is a genuine impersonation. It is unsafe to trust the elegiac tone of this volume; he may also be trying out his own funeral in advance, to see what a literary demise could look like. Autobiography is a way of dressing up the past.

So far we have been reading about the unknown Evelyn Waugh. In the last chapter the frosts of youth vanish; the young sparkler appears. We see contemporaries who were later to become famous or notorious, among them Gerald Gardiner, Harold Acton, Robert Byron and Brian Howard. Of the last two we have striking, not to say pungent, preliminary sketches. Brian Howard, particularly, was one of those dangerous, destructive and seminal nuisances, a plaguing character of wasted talent who begins to barge about in the corridors of Mr Waugh's early fancy. Grimes turns up in Wales, an effusively homosexual schoolmaster. We have reached the verge of *Decline and Fall*, when Mr Waugh began to rise and shine.

With *Unconditional Surrender* Evelyn Waugh brought his wartime trilogy and Guy Crouchback's love affair with military servitude to a civil end. The infatuation had begun in *Men at Arms*. It was romantic, strenuous and hilarious, set in the glorious days of the Molotov-Ribbentrop treaty when Crouchback, a Catholic gentleman, no longer very young, was being taught to polish his sword and train for a St George-and-Dragon battle with the fundamental enemy: 'the Modern Age', i.e. everything between the days the family property went in the reign of Elizabeth I and the Nazi-Communist pact. He joined the Halberdiers, hung about Bellamy's Club. The comedies of military discipline and chicanery absorbed him; the tedium was relieved by minor campaigns, the war about Apthorpe's portable thunder box, his liability to bouts of 'Bechuana tummy'. Apthorpe was one of Waugh's richest comic creations.

The next phase – *Officers and Gentlemen* – was ambiguous. The Communists were on our side now and that rather muddled St George's objective. Also, a number of officers who were not gentlemen turned up – the shady and resourceful ex-hairdresser, Trimmer, for example. Bellamy's still stood but Turtle's, further down St James's, caught fire in the Blitz and the whisky poured down the street. Air Marshal Beech, not quite our class, was found over-staying an air raid under a billiard table. There were exercises on a Scottish island where the far-seeing Laird, choked by peat smoke in his Castle, was intriguing for supplies of gelignite for a private purpose. He had a daughter who was pro-Hitler and got Crouch-back into prolonged trouble. Trimmer, in these rough days, was looking for a woman and picked up Guy Crouchback's ex-wife, a nymphomaniac, and, later on – being a ranker-officer – behaved with absurd cowardice on a Commando raid. For this he naturally became a national hero – the Press having been told to find one in order to impress our doubting Allies, the Americans. Later, in Crete, Crouchback experienced disaster. His *liaison dangereuse* with the military dragged on between farce, boredom, status quarrels, and ended in a few days of nightmare. He escaped from Crete in an open boat.

At the beginning of *Unconditional Surrender*, Crouchback's

apathy is complete; but his capacity for pain has been noted by the gods. He persuades himself that it is his duty to remarry his ex-wife because she is going to have a child by the gaudy Trimmer who, punch-drunk with international publicity, has vanished. After a period of parachute training under another ranker, Ludovic, who – again, no gentleman – has murdered his C.O. in the flight from Crete, Crouchback is nagged by an ex-schoolmaster in Yugoslavia. On top of that there is the double-dealing of partisan warfare. He is obliged to watch helplessly the persecution of a party of homeless Jews and to see his discreet attempt to better the lot of two of them turn into the lunatic evidence that will send them to the People's Court and the firing squad. Crouchback's apathy breaks when he realises that a sense of the futility of life is not enough, for life has culminated in the monstrous. It is perhaps the final, mortifying irony of the book that Crouchback survives and prospers. He even has the pleasure of seeing Box-Bender, his extremely unlikeable Protestant brother-in-law, having trouble with his son. The boy talks of becoming a monk.

Evelyn Waugh has a genius for very specialised social effrontery and its delight in outrage. It required a nerve to treat the war as a sordid social jamboree of smart and semi-smart sets, who are mainly engaged in self-inflation and in climbing up the ladder, to present it as a collection of bankrupt sideshows. But Mr Waugh has more nerve than any of his English contemporaries, and large portions of the last war were exactly as he describes them.

The war is not, of course, presented as anything more than heightened (or deflated) personal experience; the trilogy is a memoir rather than a novel. Other books about the war have gone straight for the conventional – the battle. He, too, can negligently turn out a battle, but his interest is, fundamentally, the moralist's. His eye is trained on the flat detail of human folly, vanity and hypocrisy; and although he can be rightly called a wounded Romantic, he is a most patient and accurate observer. His glances at London life during the period are laconic and just. The last war saw the birth of the organisation man and Mr Waugh was in, all eyes and ears, at the dreadful *accouchement*.

There are, we know, two Evelyn Waughs: the satirical blessing who wrote *The Loved One* and the appeasing, even tender comic moralist, the accomplished, testy, courteous, epigrammatic man of letters who wrote *A Handful of Dust*. (Crouchback characteristi-

cally takes Anstey's *Vice Versa* to read on his campaigns.) The
trilogy is in his humane and perfectly finished manner. His scorn is
modulated, his sentences are distillations. Most comic writers like to
think they could play it straight if only their public would let them.
Waugh is able to be grave without difficulty for he has always been
comic for serious reasons. He has his own, almost romantic sense of
propriety. His snobbery, when he is in this mood, is an amusing and
acceptable mixture of High Romance, Puritan decorum and tartness,
and has a professional sense of the rules of the English class game. To
object to his snobbery is as futile as objecting to cricket, for every
summer the damn game comes round again whether you like it or
not.

Only one kind of snobbery is affronting in Mr Waugh: the violent.
It is ugly, theatrical and falsely generalised. Even if we accept that
ranker-officers are envious, calculating, unsure showmen and on the
make, must we add cowardice, lack of nerve and – as in the case of
the minutely observed Ludovic – crime? Is the envy of the lower
classes any more likely to lead to dishonesty and cowardice than the
conceit of the uppers? It is here that Mr Waugh's High Romance
becomes vulgar sentimentality. In this book he throws Ludovic away
as a recognisable human being and an original type rarely attempted:
the solemn, climbing, half-sinister, half-hurt queer with shattering
gifts as a bad writer. I do not deny that Mr Waugh uses him with
malign masochistic skill when he shows him writing a novel that
falsifies a good deal of Crouchback's experience, for Ludovic has
watched Crouchback like a cat.

Amid the antics of brigadiers, generals, politicians, socialites,
partisans, wives and mistresses, the dry and stoical Crouchback is a
frosty figure. His apathy makes him a perfect focus. He is given a
nullity that, on the one hand, may represent the gentlemanly ideal:
the whole of life will be vulgar to him. On the other hand, he is subtly
endowed with the reticence and decency that suggest a life profoundly satisfied by the pains that have been inflicted on it, and by the
one or two affections that remain.

Virginia, the faithless wife and good-time girl, is beautifully
understood. The comedy of her conversation, full of four letter
words, with the almost virginal Uncle Peregrine is exquisite. He had
never heard a lady use such language; it astounds rather than
displeases; it also misleads, for he has the flattering illusion that she is
making a pass at him and is piqued when he finds she is not. What she

is after is re-marriage to her ex-husband who has come into money, for she is at the end of her tether. It is the measure of Mr Waugh's sympathy that he lets out no savage laugh at the cynical proposition and yet is not sentimental about it. The war has, at any rate, taught Crouchback to recognise a 'displaced person' when he sees one. He does not love her. She does not love Trimmer's child when it is born: she calls it 'that baby'. Crouchback does not weep when she is killed in an air raid, which lets him off some of the awkward consequences of playing so straight a bat in the sex Test. And when, at the end of one novel, his awful brother-in-law complains that things have turned very conveniently for Guy, we muse happily on the richness of Mr Waugh's point. His comedy has always been hard, perverse and shocking; but that in no way prevents it from reproducing the human heart with delicacy, or at any rate, that portion of the heart that, however shallow, can still feel wrong and pain.

Only two episodes in this final volume strike me as being tame: the strange, dull set-piece when Ludovic files past the Sword of Stalingrad in Westminster Abbey. As symbolism, irony, fragment of war chronicle, whatever it is, this scene is in the way. Later on, Ludovic goes to a party given by the editor of a literary monthly whose grubby camel-hair coat and sharp Sultanic orders to the girls will bring back sentimental memories to knowing readers; but again, this is a tame jest. The vanities of the military and social servitudes are Mr Waugh's subject; it is good, of course, of Mr Waugh to call and all that on his Bohemian friends, but somehow the visit falls flat. No literary figure can compete with an Apthorpe, a Trimmer, an Uncle Peregrine or any of the huge list of exquisitely touched-in characters who fought the war with chits, passes and top secret reports, in Mr Waugh's terse *Who's Who* of the National Peril.

St George Crouchback ends by reassessing his views on the dragon. Mme Kanyi, a Hungarian Jewess, says to him:

'Is there any place that is free from evil? It is too simple to say that the Nazis wanted war. These Communists wanted it too. It was the only way in which they could come to power. Many of my people wanted it, to be revenged on the Germans, to hasten to the creation of the national state. It seems to me there was a will to war, a death wish, everywhere. Even good men, thought their private honour would be satisfied by war. They could assert their manhood by killing and being killed. They would accept hardships in recompense for having been selfish and lazy. Danger justified privilege. I knew Italians – not very many perhaps – who felt this. Were there none in England?'

'God forgive me,' said Guy, 'I was one of them.' It was after being told, by an enthusiastic little bureaucrat, of her arrest, that Crouchback was tempted to strike an officer.

(1949)

Temperament of Genius

To the present-day reader who can know 'Bloomsbury' only by hearsay, and for a critic like myself who read Virginia Woolf's works as they came out but who had no acquaintance with the older survivors of the set until their middle age in the Second World War, they must seem like the natives of some lost tropic of this century's early history. One is apt to forget that they were not the only distinguished writers, artists, thinkers, Puritans, or hedonists of the time. After 1939 that phase of our civilisation, sometimes known as the sunset of the high bourgeois culture of Europe, had clouded over. As the dramatis personae reappear in *The Diary of Virginia Woolf*, patiently annotated by Anne Olivier Bell, in the *Letters*, edited by Nigel Nicolson and Joanne Trautmann, and in Quentin Bell's *Life*, their voices, with their cool antique accent, come back.

We now have the sixth and last volume of the wonderfully talking *Letters*; we have already had the third volume of the *Diary* covering the years 1925–1930: the final volume is yet to come. (It is therefore impossible to match the *Letters* with the *Diary*, in which Virginia talks to herself, but events rarely correspond with her private musings. In the *Letters* she carelessly and hastily gave away the projected self of the hour; in the *Diary* she contemplated herself and her work more searchingly, often more gloomily. Her truthfulness was, as is usual in diaries, a truth to the moment, as her observation of people changed from one day to the next. The unguarded candor on which 'Bloomsbury' prided itself had the malice of artificial comedy, and she was known to have the sharpest tongue of all. But the cult of friendship was reckoned to be strong enough to stand the militancy. The artist was forgiven, the Kensington lady not always.

Virginia Woolf was a compulsive letter writer. The 'humane art', as she once wrote in an essay on letter writing, was a way of warding off loneliness by keeping conversation going with the absent, at a time when conversation had revived as an art in itself. She did not much care for the solitude she needed but lived for news, gossip, and the expectancy of talk. She was a connoisseur of manners and gestures, and had the habit of asking a question and breaking off to ask another. If she wrote to captivate her friends and to keep the affection she so strongly needed, the other purpose of letter writing was to stir the mood for serious writing (Balzac also recommended this). Nigel Nicolson adds a passage that cannot be bettered:

She described people as if they had no substance until their differences from other people had been analysed, and events as if none had really taken place until it had been recorded, in a manner unmistakably her own, imagining the smile, the frown, of the recipient, rarely repeating a phrase, so grateful for the wealth of the language that she scatters it wilfully, as lavish with words as a pianist is with notes, knowing that it is inexhaustible.

It must be said that if her pace had always been fast, it often became a shade frantic in her fifties. This is because she worked harder than ever when she became famous, as gifted writers do – what else is there to do but write? – but also because for everyone younger or older than herself the Thirties were a period of oppressive anxiety. The *fear* of yet another great war was at any rate removed when war became real, though – as she noted in an ominous phrase – it was henceforth impossible 'to lift the fringe of the future.' Her history of madness, the tragedies of her early life had made her familiar with terror. One may even feel that her imaginative prose has wildness in it and that her laughter, as she breaks life down into moments, is a skirmish with alarm. In the third volume of her *Letters*, in which her great energies are more robust than in the present one, her will was on terms with the venture she was committed to. To Vita Sackville-West she wrote in 1928:

I believe that the main thing in beginning a novel is to feel, not that you can write it, but that it exists on the far side of a gulf, which words can't cross; that it's to be pulled through only in a breathless anguish. . . . Only when one has forgotten what one meant, does the book seem tolerable.

There is confidence and experience in those words.

In 1936 she had finished *The Waves* and *Orlando*, a volume of *The Common Reader* was behind her, and she was struggling with the enormous novel *The Years* and her tormenting biography of Roger Fry. It tormented because biography has to bow to research and fact. (Those who sneered at her, as Q. D. Leavis did, as 'an idle social parasite' might bear in mind the immense reading her criticism in

The Common Reader demanded and that, for example, even a short essay on Mrs Thrale was rewritten eight times. If she could not resist Society, which her husband thought dangerous for her, her plunges were not pure vanity and may have relieved an overactive brain). And London was not all vapid dissipation: her own circle were deep in political committees – she could hear them droning away in the next room at Tavistock Square – as Hitler went into the Rhineland and the Spanish Civil War began and was brought close to home by the tragedy of Julian Bell's death there. There was the relief of the guilt, the fear, the hysteria of Munich as she went back to Rodmell to her familiar headaches. Civilisation, said Leonard and everyone else, was at an end. 'Bloomsbury' was coming to an end. The younger generation questioned the solitary obsession that kept her going.

In the third volume of the *Diary* (1925–1930) we do hear of a 'brush with death' when she falls down unconscious during a walk with Lydia Keynes. She writes:

Had I woken in the divine presence it wd. have been with fists clenched & fury on my lips. 'I don't want to come here at all!' So I should have exclaimed. I wonder if this is the general state of people who die violently. If so figure the condition of Heaven after a battle.

Earlier still she had felt 'that old whirr of wings in the head which comes when I'm ill so often.'

If violence was latent in her genius and nature, the letters show her as the mistress of comedy. It is the one certain excellence, and perhaps supreme, in the English essayists and novelists, for our affections are entwined with our militancy. In the present volume, as the familiar Bloomsbury chatter goes on, the startling figure of Ethel Smyth thumps in and out. This seventy-year-old feminist and musician who is at war with the whole male sex and whom Virginia freely addresses as 'my uncastrated cat' falls in love with her. Ethel Smyth is a sort of deaf Britannia who bawls out her hatred of Bloomsbury like some blustering figure out of Rowlandson.

'What a rackety race you Smyths are,' Virginia writes to her. 'Bankruptcy, Sapphism, hunting, suicide, all in one gulp. How then did you keep so d—d military upright and brass-buttoned? Explain.'

At first afraid that Ethel will put a portrait of her in one of her autobiographical works and maddened by the almost daily bombardment of letters, Virginia fights back in defence of her friends. Ethel is quite unlike the adored Vita Sackville-West who can be called upon to 'pluck a swan and dip its feather in green ink' and touch mind and heart in her letters. Virginia writes to Vita:

Oh Ethel! I could not face her, though she was passing our door. Her letters sound as if she was in a furious droning mood, like a gale, all one note. . . . [All about the hostility of the male-governed world] Deafness I daresay. . . . She can't get rid of her mind in talk.

But she excuses herself to Ethel when *The Waves* is getting out of focus:

But this explains perhaps certain absences of mind, and cannon bolts down the telephone – Lord! how I like the thud of my abuse upon your hide. I think I shall make a practice of it. 'Ethel, d'you know you're a damned Harlot – a hoary harpy – or an eldritch shriek of egotism – a hail storm of inconsecutive and inconsequent conceit. That's all.' And I shall ring off.

But, cooling down after a row about Maurice Baring:

How you grow on me. Isn't that odd? Absence; thinking of someone – then the real feeling has room to expand, like the sights that one only sees afterwards. Is that peculiar to me, or common to all? Anyhow, lying in bed, or listlessly turning books I could hardly read, over and over again I've thought of you, and dwelt on your affection. . . . And then how I adore your broad human bottom – how it kindles me to think of you, worried and bothered, yet lunching at a party of 12 and I'm convinced keeping the table in an uproar; and plunging like a blue Italian Dolphin into all the nets of the Sitwells, always battling and battering – and with it all keeping a mushroom sensibly intact.

All the letters are fictions in embryo – this particular running portrait Dickensian caricature. She is treating Ethel with far more affection in her wicked wit than Dickens showed Americans in his *American Notes* or *Martin Chuzzlewit*, for Ethel was half an outsider, and escaped the fate of what the Woolfs called the under-world beyond their circle.

We notice deep unchanging devotion toward her husband, her sister, her nephew Julian, and her adored niece Angelica. She fought back hard when Benedict Nicolson – Vita's son – attacked Roger Fry for his supposed failure to 'educate the masses' – that general charge of social isolation and lack of committed social conscience which the young were bringing against their elders.

The war-time letters are valuable as historical day-to-day evidence. The war frames the letter to Benedict Nicolson so that it is like a long short story, for as she takes up Fry's defence, bombers come over: 'I went and looked at them. Then I returned to your letter.' Her defence begins to blister with sarcasm about Ben's privileges, which Fry had not had. 'The raiders began emitting long trails of smoke. I wondered if a bomb was going to fall on top of me; I wondered if I was facing disagreeable actualities; I wondered what I could have done to stop bombs and disagreeable actualities. . . . Then I dipped into your letter again.' The argument continues as she is telling him she admires his honesty but warns him against looking for scapegoats. It was particularly searing for her to have to remind Ben that Fry had to deal with insanity and death in his own home. 'I know you're having a worse time [in London] than I am. . . . Another siren has just sounded.' The letter is fierce as argument and story. It worried her afterward that perhaps she had misunderstood his argument.

Being in the 'front line' for air raids and possible invasion at Rodmell gave her, as it did elsewhere to others, a gambler's exhilaration to her fears: there was the awful sense of 'the suspended sentence', the possibility that 'the sense of the future by which we live' had gone. The most shattering intimate aspect of the war for her was the destruction of the little streets and great sites of ancient London which, more than any other place, and far more than the serene marshes and downs of Sussex, had fed her sparkling sense of people and place. The London of her late Victorian girlhood, of the talkers of the eighteenth century and the gestures of the gorgeous Elizabethans, had been the mother of her genius.

What was the future? One has the impression that what haunted her at this time was another fear, the one that hunts the gifted as they age: that their talent may be vanishing whether their world is or is not collapsing. Illness, exorbitant, compulsive work might perhaps be exhausting not her talent, but the great strength of her will, except the will – and that would be rational – to kill herself. But the noises and dreaded voices in her head had begun.

When we turn back to Volume Three of the *Diary* we see her at the height of her matured powers, wryly conscious of the deceits of fame. She was basking in the lark of *Orlando*, the fantastic love letter to Vita Sackville-West, and was agonising as she went on to *The Waves*, a very different matter. The 'tug and suck' are at her; why, she asks, could she not be as spontaneous as she had been in *Orlando*? But,

. . . the idea has come to me that what I want now to do is to saturate every atom. I mean to eliminate all waste, deadness, superfluity: to give the moment whole; whatever it includes. Say that the moment is a combination of thought; sensation; the voice of the sea. Waste, deadness, come from the inclusion of things that don't belong to the moment; this appalling narrative business of the realist: getting on from lunch to dinner: it is false, unreal, merely conventional. Why admit anything to literature that is not poetry – by which I mean saturated?

She is disquieted by 'the remorseless severity' of her mind. It never stops reading and writing. Is she too much a professional, 'too little any longer a dreamy amateur?'

She goes to see Thomas Hardy, who impresses by his vitality. Writing poetry, he flatly said, was a question of physical strength. A kind, sensible, sincere man, who held his head down like a pouter pigeon, he made one good Hardyesque remark: 'None of my books are fitted to be wedding presents.' She goes to see H. G. Wells, who had the red cheeks and jowls of a butcher, liked rambling and romancing about people, but who reeked of lust. The virtues he admires, he says, are courage and vitality. ('I said how ghastly.') He replies nothing is ghastly where there is courage. He gets drowsy after lunch. She goes to see Arnold Bennett – no love here. He's too pleased with his clothes.

'And you drop your aitches on purpose,' I said 'thinking that you possess more "life" than we do.' 'I sometimes tease,' said B. 'But I don't think I possess more life than you do.'

She is blind to Bennett and certainly didn't grasp that *Riceyman Steps* is a masterpiece that has lasted. The old men she likes best are those like George Moore and Yeats who kept their minds flying.

There is a painful meeting with Eliot and his first wife. Mrs Eliot, who is 'sane to the point of insanity,' all suspicion and looking for hidden meanings, says Virginia has made a signal for them to go. When they've left Virginia says, 'This bag of ferrets is what Tom wears round his neck.' And there are the weeks of long personal gloom.

One goes down the well & nothing protects one from the assault of truth. Down there I can't write or read; I exist however. I am. Then I ask myself what I am? & get a closer though less flattering answer than I should on the surface – where, to tell the truth, I get more praise than is right. But the praise will go; one will be left alone with this queer being in old age. I am glad to find it on the whole so interesting, though so acutely unpleasant.

The next day she cheers up a little, reflecting on the mystical side of solitude.

How it is not oneself but something in the universe that one's left with. . . .

And out comes that sudden, wild, mysterious image –

One sees a fin passing far out.

Perhaps that shark-like fin is a hint of how the impulse to write *The Waves* first came to her. Quentin Bell calls the *Diary* a masterpiece: it is, indeed, among the great diaries, and is a huge, sharply peopled autobiography of the temperament of genius.

(1984)

MAX BEERBOHM

A Dandy

Among the masked dandies of Edwardian comedy, Max Beerbohm is the most happily armoured by a deep and almost innocent love of himself as a work of art. As the youngest child of a large and gifted family of real and step-brothers and sisters, he seems to have adroitly decided to be an adult Enigma from the cradle onwards and to be not merely an old man of the world as early as possible, but even to pass as ancient man, possibly on the principle that the last shall be first. If he could not be as tall as his eldest brother, the world-famous actor Beerbohm Tree, he could cultivate the special sparkle and artifices of the diminutive so that one now has the impression that he must have worn a top hat and a swallowtail coat in his pram. One understands the point of Oscar Wilde's question: he asked a lady whether Max ever took off his face and revealed his mask. Max had no face; or if he did have one it was as *disponible*, as blank as an actor's is. If he had a secret it lay in his quite terrific will and the power to live as if he and the people he saw were farcical objects.

In his essay on 'Dandies' Max Beerbohm asks whether a dandy's clothes can be seen responding to the emotion of the wearer. Needless to say, an instance of this sartorial melancholia is known to him:

I saw with wonder Lord X's linen actually flush for a moment and then turn deadly pale. I looked again and saw that his boots had lost their lustre. Drawing nearer, I saw that grey hairs had begun to show themselves in his raven coat. It was very painful and yet, to me, very gratifying. In the cloakroom, when I went for my own hat and cane, there was the hat with broad brim and (lo!) over its iron-blue surface little furrows had been ploughed by Despair.

'Deadly pale', 'lost their lustre', 'gratifying': only such epithets from a dead usage could release the protest of fantasy that is alive. The art of Max in that passage is shown in a single word: the grey hairs appear 'in' the coat, not 'on' it, as many a comic, careless of the full terror of his effect, would have said.

Beerbohm's detachment must have owed something to the fact that his father came of a distinguished Baltic German family. He had had two English wives: one died, so he married her sister secretly in Switzerland – it was illegal in Great Britain to marry a deceased wife's sister at that time. The father was an amiably slack and cultivated man: the mother engagingly eccentric with a talent for erratic minor alterations in English metaphors. She would say 'I feel as old as *any* hills' – to be old, seemingly, was as important to her as it was to her youngest son. The foreign strain was just the thing to give an edge to Max's talent and that of the family. Expatriation allows one to drop a lot of unwanted moral luggage, lets talent travel lightly and opens it to the histrionic. For his own talents Max Beerbohm could not have chosen a better time. Putting aside, for the moment, such matters as Dandyism, the Aesthetes, the Decadents, the acquaintance of Oscar Wilde, Beardsley, the fading Pre-Raphaelites and the last remorses of the Romantic Agony, no place could have been luckier than London for the wits. The city had many clever newspapers and reviews, the theatre had Shaw and Ibsen to deal with, Pinero and others to insult. It was the time for the fancy of the essayist, for fantasy, the comedy of manners, hoaxes, impersonations, caricature and for carrying on an artist's war with England's fleshly Philistinism, led by a Prince of Wales who looked like a licentious grocer, and for attacking the blustering side of British imperialism, by exaggerating the size of Kipling's chin and the bushiness of his eyebrows. Max's eyebrows were impeccable question marks. The amount of theatre criticism and essay writing he did as a young man, and the delightful trouble it stirred up among the respectable, is remarkable.

The famous 'Defence of Cosmetics' written when Max was still at Oxford, and his closeness to the Wilde and Beardsley set, led some to suspect that Max was on the then dangerous edge of homosexuality. In fact, Max was horrified by the scandalous intimacies of the flesh; his sexual temperature was low – perhaps, as Lord David Cecil suggests in *Max: A Biography*, because he was the last child of elderly parents whose vitality had declined. His temperament was narcissistic – as his innumerable caricatures of himself show – and he seems not even to have attained the narcissism of adolescence, but to have sat with the scrupulous prudence of the demure child in front of any mirror he could find, experimenting in poses and grimaces.

He lived by the eye and – as one can see by his drawings – discreetly beyond touch of hand. Two caretaking wives looked after him in middle and late life and – to all appearances – treated him tenderly if overwhelmingly, as a dangerous toy. And then – how typical this is of an intelligent and sensitive man who is without roots – he turned to literature and the arts for his nationality. Among other things, in the wide-eyed persona he invented, there is sadness. Was it the sadness of not being a genius on the great scale, like his admired Henry James? Possibly. Was it the sadness of knowing that his work must be perfect – as that of minor writers has to be – because fate made him a simulacrum? Or was he simply born sad?

And now to Beerbohm's centenary year in times that are so unsuited to him. Piously Rupert Hart-Davis has done a large catalogue of all Beerbohm's caricatures that have been framed or suitably reproduced, a volume useful to collectors. (It is amusing that Beerbohm's devastating caricatures of Edward VII and George V, done in his 'black' period, are among the treasures in Windsor Castle.) A selection of essays, *A Peep into the Past*, has also been made by Hart-Davis, and serves to show the development of the essayist. In later essays the charm has become benign and thin, but three of them are excellent: the remarkable spoof portrait of Wilde done when Beerbohm was still an undergraduate and suppressed after the trial, in which occur the well-known lines: 'As I was ushered into the little study, I fancied that I heard the quickly receding *frou-frou* of tweed trousers, but my host I found reclining, hale and hearty, though a little dishevelled upon the sofa.'

The other, written on *De Profundis*, denies the comforting view of many English critics of the time that Wilde had undergone a spiritual change after his imprisonment. Beerbohm saw him as still an actor but with a new role.

Yet lo! he was unchanged. He was still precisely himself. He was still playing with ideas, playing with emotions. 'There is only one thing left for me now,' he writes, 'absolute humility.' And about humility he writes many beautiful and true things. And, doubtless, while he wrote them, he had the sensation of humility. Humble he was not.

And there is the hilarious pretence in another essay that a powerful bad poet of the period – Clement Shorter – had spent his life writing love poems not to a lady but to one of the awful British seaside resorts.

The best American essay on him, in my opinion, was by Edmund Wilson, dry and to the point. There was no mellifluous English nonsense about the 'inimitable' and 'incomparable'. I feared what would happen to Max if he was put through the American academic mangle. There seems to be a convention that this machine must begin by stunning its victim with the obvious, and when I found Mr Felstiner saying, in his study *The Lies of Art*, about the notorious essay on cosmetics that 'Cosmetics were a perfect choice to join the teachings of the moment, aestheticism and decadence,' I understood what Max meant when he said that exhaustive accounts of the period 'would need far less brilliant pens than mine'. But, as I went on, I found Mr Felstiner a thorough, thoughtful, and independent analyst of Max as a caricaturist and parodist. He has good things to say about Beerbohm's phases as an artist in line and water colour, about his absolute reliance on the eye. He is admirable on the parodies in which Max reached the complete fulfilment of his gifts, and his comments on *Zuleika Dobson* are the most searching I have ever read.

Beerbohm caricatured Americans, the working class and the bourgeoisie automatically as part of the impending degradation of civilisation and the arts.... John Bull is the crucial figure throughout, shaming himself in Europe, vilely drunk or helpless in the face of British losses, and deeply Philistine. On the evidence of these cartoons, Shaw called Beerbohm 'the most savage Radical caricaturist since Gillray'.

His Prince of Wales is a coarse, tweedy brute, imagining a nunnery is a brothel. His pictures of royalty were savage:

What angered Beerbohm during the Boer War was not Britain's damaged empire – he was indifferent to that: 'the only feeling that our Colonies inspire in me is a determination not to visit them.' It was the self-delusion and debasement of conduct at home, the slavish reliance on grandiose national myths.

But he was no Gillray, nor was he a Grosz. He 'enjoyed with an eye for what men are individually – for their conceits, contradictions, deadlocks, excesses. Beerbohm drew more for fun than in the hope of changing attitude or behaviour. In fact he depended as man and artist on the survival of the context he satirised.'

Edwardian literature has many, many sad stories, stories whose frivolity half discloses the price a culture is paying for its manners and illusions. *Zuleika Dobson* is one of the funniest and most lyrical and sad of these tales. As in all Beerbohm's fantasies, literary cross-references are graceful and malign. Fantasy states what realism will obscure or bungle.

Yet in comparison with previous jocular or sentimental treatments, he could claim to have given 'a truer picture of undergraduate life'. His book points to real elements of conformity and sexual repression. . . . By chance the river itself has the name of Isis, Egypt's greatest goddess, all things to all men. So what emerges is an allegory of Youth forsaking Alma Mater, the Benign Mother, for the consummating love of woman.

Zuleika seems to have been modelled in part on the famous bareback rider whom Swinburne knew, and she has a close connection with 'the Romantic Agony'. She is a 'Volpone of a self-conceit: her mirror is the world', i.e. she is the male dandy's opposite number. Mr Felstiner writes of her rapture when she is spurned by the Duke:

All the world's youth is prostrate with love but she can only love a man who will spurn her. . . . 'I had longed for it, but I had never guessed how wonderfully wonderful it was. It came to me. I shuddered and wavered like a fountain in the wind' – sounds like the joys of flagellation. The Duke even finds himself wanting to 'flay' her with Juvenalian verses. 'He would make Woman (as he called Zuleika) writhe.'

The element of parody insures the tale: Beerbohm's excellence and his safety as an artist are guaranteed because, unfailingly, he is writing literature within literature. Parody, as Mr Felstiner again puts it, is a filter. It drains both literature and life.

Beerbohm rarely drew from photographs. He drew from memory. The recipe for caricature was 'The whole man must be melted down in a crucible and then, from the solution, fashioned anew. Nothing will be lost but no particle will be as it was before.' So Balfour's sloping body becomes impossibly tall and sad in order to convey his 'uneasy Olympian attitudes'. Carson, who prosecuted Wilde, is a long curve like a tense whip, whereas Balfour is a question mark. Beerbohm thickened Kipling's neck and enlarged his jaw to stress the brutality he saw in him. Pinero's eyebrows had to be 'like the skins of some small mammal, just not large enough to be used as mats'. One difficulty, he noted in *How They Undo Me*, is that over the years a subject may change – the arrogant become humble, the generous mean, the sloppy scrupulous. Yeats had once seemed like a 'mood in a vacuum' but the youthful aspect changed: 'I found it less easy to draw caricatures of him. He seemed to have become subtly less like himself.' As Mr Felstiner adds, a shade unnecessarily, 'The truth is that he [Yeats] had become more like himself. . . . An evolving

discipline made his themes and his style more tough-minded, idio-
matic, accountable.'

Mr Felstiner has noticed that in Max's caricatures the eyes of the
politicians are generally closed – public life has turned them into
blank statues in their own life-time – but the eyes of the writers and
artists are open. The eyes of James are wide open – sometimes in
dread. Beerbohm wrote a sonnet to him: 'Your fine eyes, blurred like
arc lamps in a mist'. Beerbohm's admiration for James and his
closeness to his belief in the primacy of art are responsible for the
excellence of his well-known parody in *The Christmas Garland*. It
required an art equal – if for a moment only – to James's own to get
so keenly under the skin; and, like all good things, it was not
achieved without great trouble. Indeed, Max added to the famous
Christmas story, one more turn of the screw.

He constantly revisited his subjects. His parodies are indeed
criticisms and the silent skill with which nonsense is mellifluously
introduced, without seeming to be there, is astonishing. James's
manner has often been mimicked, but never with Beerbohm's gift for
extending his subject by means of the logic of comedy. I do not share
Mr Felstiner's admiration for the Kipling parody: Max was blind to
Kipling's imagination though he was daring in suggesting there was
something feminine in Kipling's tough masculine worship of
obedience. Max here disclosed a violence on his own part. Kipling
was as good an actor as he; had been brought up by a pre-Raphaelite
father and had as much regard for form and style as Beerbohm had.
But, of course, like greater artists, the parodist celebrates his own
blindnesses as well as his power to see.

He could even show open schoolboy coarseness in a way that is
surprising in one of his circumlocutory habit. There are a few lines on
Shaw, an old love-hate, in J. G. Riewald's edition of rhymes and
parodies, *Max in Verse*:

I strove with all, for all were worth my strife,
Nature I loathed, and next to Nature, Art;
I chilled both feet on the thin ice of Life,
It broke and I emit a final fart.

This book has some of Beerbohm's best things: the parody of
Hardy's Dynasts, the pseudo-Shakespeare of Savonarola Brown –
only Max could have seen what could be done by splitting iambic
pentameters into banal dialogue. The Shropshire Lad is told abruptly
to go and drown himself, and for those puzzled about the origins and

pronunciations of English place names like Cirencester, there is a gently malicious ballad. Thirty-four of these poems have not been published before, partly because Max was very tactful, at the proper time, about hurting people's feelings – he repressed the keyhole James until after James's death – and partly because he knew when his own juvenile phase had lasted too long.

(1984)

Conrad and Destiny

Conrad exists in English literature, but he is a harsh exotic who can never quite be assimilated to our modes. No English novelist has his peculiar accent in psychological and moral curiosity; it is like the knowing accent of Kipling, a foreigner's acquired slang, but expressing a far more elevated sensibility than Kipling had; only Henry James, another alien, with his pursuit of fine consciousness, approaches Conrad's fencing with extremes. Yet here all Conrad's critics have been dissatisfied. They have felt, as Forster did, that he was following extremes into a fog of argument or rhetoric; or they have been obliged to agree with the comment of Dr Leavis – the most substantial of Conrad's critics – on the inequalities of *Heart of Darkness* and that 'he is intent on making a virtue out of not knowing what he means. The vague and unrealisable, he asserts with a strained impressiveness, is the profoundly and tremendously significant.'

Even in *Nostromo*, where Conrad's powers of concretion were married to a great subject, we shall not exactly know where we stand. We are always liable in his work to lapse from the certainties of art into the restless brilliance of opinion, to find the matter in hand being explored with the cleverness of the café writer and the moral dilettante. We shall be haunted by the special and tragic brilliance of the exile who, as he exhibits himself and plays his role, is never unconscious of the fact. As Mr Douglas Hewitt says in *Conrad: A Reassessment*, his novels are not tragedies – they *resemble* tragedies. They are, generally speaking, one must add, inhibited from tragic fullness by his famous, defensive and histrionic irony. He is, at bottom, a rather sadistic and sardonic writer. His irony is ultimately perverse – or, as earlier critics used to say, morbid – because it is a personal irony and does not always lie in the nature of the events he describes. Is *Nostromo* a great classical novel or a brilliant commentary? That is to say, superb as it is, does it not strike one as being a commentary on the kind of novel or dramatic work that could, at some time, be written on its subject?

Nostromo is the most strikingly modern of Conrad's novels. It might have been written in 1954 and not, as it was, in 1904. All the issues of the economic exploitation of a backward country are here; the politics of Costa-guana over two or three generations are telescoped in depth without losing the focus on the present. We see both the ideal and fraud in colonial exploitation, in the fight for liberalism, progress, reform, the bent to revolution and the advent of a foreign power. Even the rise of two of the now dominant forces in his kind of situation is clearly noted: the desire of America to take over everything in the world and, against or with that, the rise of the masses. Conrad did not set these things down in a political or historical essay, nor in a novel of propaganda, but in the impure detail of a large sceptical and imaginative work. Every moment is physically realised not by a right-minded and insensitive political reporter with a mind hardened-off (or softened) by his programme, but by an artist dealing, as art must, in the waste, the elusive, the incalculable. It is one of the prophetic felicities of this work that it is pervaded by a profound, even morbid sense of insecurity which is the very spirit of our age, and that sense is (as it must always be) personal. Before anyone else – though we may pause to give Mr E. M. Forster his due – Conrad the exile foresaw that in half a century we should all become exiles, in a sense.

One or two reflections follow from our astonishment with *Nostromo*. The first is a general reflection on the social soil in which the modern English novel is planted. The great English subject – one is inclined to say – and at any rate the great subject which includes a picture of society, lies outside England, simply because English life itself has for long been parasitic on life abroad and does not wish to recognise the fact. 'Abroad' is where English institutions have been put to the test and not in South Wales, Tyneside, Birmingham or Surrey. As I say, apart from Conrad, only E. M. Forster seems to have known this; possibly Lawrence, too, in a book like *Kangaroo*. The second reflection is one that throws a light on some of Conrad's defects as a novelist. He suffers from being before his proper time. It is a freak of time that he is a Romantic. Even in small yet not unimportant matters like the use of dialogue, Conrad was unlucky. If he could be writing *The Secret Agent* or the bandit pages of *Victory* now, he would certainly not write the wooden Cockney or the ludicrous melodrama of his gangster's dialogue; the intellectual energies of the refugee would not have been spent on acquiring literary English, but the English of speech.

Conrad is a man in what we may call the post-1940 situation, but who is obliged to conceal the fact under a dramatic fog of rhetoric. He loved rhetoric, of course, and became – as Mr Hewitt says – more prone to it when his talent went to pieces from *Chance* onwards; vaguely emotive words like 'unspeakable', 'nameless', 'inscrutable', 'horror', 'pure evil', 'mystery', 'Woman' are the well-known pedals of the Romantic organ. Behind them lay things which, a generation or so after, he could have named, and as an incipient nihilist he would have been bound to name them. He would have been obliged to live or set down in precise physical detail, the nihilism which he feared so much in his nature. It would have been drawn out by a nihilist age. The case of Kurtz in *Heart of Darkness*, the case of Heyst in *Victory*, or Decoud in *Nostromo*, is contemporary, but now the full glare of the interrogator's lamp is on their faces. Conrad would have been drawn out of the grandiloquent shadows that exasperate us and which seem to exasperate him; he would have found less to opine upon and, more cruelly, to state. The morbidity of which early critics complained – quite rightly; before 1914 certain values seemed impregnable – would not strike one in our imaginary Conrad who had been drawn out by times that would fit his temperament like a glove. Betrayal, guilt, isolation, the double self, corruption, the undisguised sadism that has appeared in our life, the anarchy, are not matters of speculation and pious lament. They are contemporary facts.

Mr Hewitt is of the opinion that the decline of Conrad's work which began with *Chance*, comes from a failure to see any secure or positive values which could counter the force of his negative criticism. The alternative was to plump for popular Romance and an unreal, black and white world of wholly good or wholly evil people. These later books are simply the early rhetoric expanded. Mr Hewitt's book is a short one which sticks to the text of a few of the novels and is concerned with the specific moral health of Conrad's genius at different times; it is far from comprehensive and though its main points are excellent, one misses a sensibility to detail. Gould and his wife, for example, are scarcely realised characters in *Nostromo*: they are states of mind, like the Dukes who hold the

Court in a Shakespearean drama. Why in comparison does Mr Hewitt find Heyst's conversations with the girl on the island less acceptable than Mrs Gould's conversations with Decoud in *Nostromo*? The dialogue is wooden in both instances but the matter is allusive and subtle. Is not the difference between Gould and Heyst simply that one is a practical and obsessed solitary scheming for his mine, whereas Heyst is a passive solitary? Mr Hewitt warns us of the danger of paraphrasing Conrad, but Conrad paraphrases himself in characters like Gould, Heyst and Decoud. They are attitudes, not people, though they are attitudes lit up here and there by the novelist's power to give them flashes of individual life. The fact is that Conrad was a writer of restless and changeable conceptions, but he was poor in invention. His imaginative eye did not easily move; it was fixed upon brilliant detail so that the sound of a thing like the clank of railway trucks, with its suggestion of prisoner's fetters, becomes so powerful as an image, that it is more real to us than the people who have to be explained or 'talked on' in brilliant but ultimately elusive colloquies. He is a jumpy, attitudinising, artificial writer, bedevilled by his eye. The selection of the isolated subject is, in part, the expression of his maddened desire for a subject that can be made to stand still so that it can be forcibly elaborated. The pattern of *Nostromo* is wonderful. It is like some grim brocade; yet was it necessary to be so elaborate in order to get the utmost out of the subject? And did Conrad get the utmost? On the level of a great tragic conception, I think, it must at last be thought he did not. We are overburdened by detail, by a too constant intensity. We are hypnotised. We 'come to', but there has been no purgation.

The Secret Sharer, in Mr Hewitt's opinion, marks the deciding crisis in Conrad's life as a novelist. In this excellent tale he thinks Conrad exorcised his personal devil and thereafter turned away from the central conflict which had fertilised his art. Leggatt, the man who takes refuge in the young Captain's cabin, has killed a man in some squabble, and he plays the part of the Dostoevskian 'double' as Gentleman Brown had done to Lord Jim. Leggatt is the hidden transgressor in the unconscious, an embodiment of the fear 'that there are parts of himself which he has not yet brought into the light of day' and which may interfere 'with the ideal conception of one's own personality every man sets up for himself secretly'. The Captain is put to a strain leading almost to madness by his secret partnership and actually risks his ship; but having pushed the pact to the limit, he conquers and sails off, free at last, where Kurtz, Gentleman Brown of *Nostromo* and Lord Jim represent failures in this struggle with the unconscious. It is a shrewd point of Mr Hewitt's that *Chance*, with its optimism of black-and-white Romance and reliance on the sailor's simple code immediately follows these histories of failure. Conrad's pessimism, his lack of a positive scheme of spiritual values, clearly left him, as a Romantic artist, in an intolerable situation.

Exile, the fact of being uncommitted, is at the bottom of Conrad's triumphs and his failures. He is a writer of great vanity. One has the impression of a writer more suited to the theatre than to the novel. The wonderful faceting of *Nostromo* is essentially theatrical in effect; self-consciousness, artifice, the sense of his role which every Conrad character feels, including Marlow himself, strengthen our impression. Of course, he was no more a dramatist than Henry James was, but there is this straining towards the drama. It is, indeed, the self-dramatising, evasive, speculative quality in his own comments on his work which make him an unusually unreliable guide to his achievement.

Two things strike us about Conrad. The first is that despite his life of action, his true heritage was political and literary. He took to the sea, as a writer might, if he had a good stomach, out of a romantic passion for travel and geography. He was not a born seaman who eventually takes to writing as another form of extroversion. Conrad's father was a well-known if minor literary figure in Poland, a dilettante of reckless political nerve, and the son's decision to go to sea was a violent break with the formative influences of his upbringing. It was a protest, an adventure, could almost be thought an aberration, and was likely to recoil. Secondly, we must note the immense importance of politics and especially of political defeat in his life. He saw defeat lived out in tragedy, in the death of his father and mother after their exile in Russia. He was with them there; he nearly died there. He learned exile as a child. The 'gloom' of Conrad was not the broad, passive gloom of the Russians which seems to arise from the dull excess of space; he disliked being called a Slav. He was a Westerner who despised the Dostoevskian Russian. Conrad's 'gloom' – as his biographer says – began with his early schooling in sorrow. It grew, later on, into something hard and sardonic. It is the bitter irony of the active man of strong imagination who sees, with personal indignation, the relativeness of experience. The exile has the illusion of moral freedom and becomes a connoisseur of the ironies of his situation.

There is some parallel in the lives of Conrad and his father. The dangerous political gestures of the father were patriotic, noble, passionate and romantic, but they were carried on in the futile void created by an all-powerful tyranny. There was a total lack of prospect. It was oceanic. In the life of the son the conception of tyranny that wastes life has changed into the embittering notion of Destiny. There is something odd about Conrad's idea of Destiny; so often it is merely exasperating, when it should surely be dreadful; perverse when it should be impassive. The men of the generation of Conrad's father knew evil by direct experience. The police rapped on the door. The arrest was made. The lies were told. The trial took place and the protests. The sentence to Siberia, which was really a sentence to fatal illness and the loss of everything valued in life, was a fact – to Conrad's father. To the son, when he grew up, evil was a bad dream, a sinister memory, a dark rhetorical suggestion. Again and again in his work, the evil thing becomes diffused and generalised into an indefinable reek of corruption. Indeed Conrad's special contribution to the English novel is to have insinuated into it the sense of an atmosphere of evil which is notoriously lacking; but as Dr Leavis has fairly said: 'he is intent on making a virtue out of not knowing what he means. The vague and unrealisable, he asserts with a strained impressiveness, is the profoundly and tremendously significant.' On the other hand, we have to note that Conrad is better at the evil fact – the cannibal helmsman lying dead in the wheelhouse in *Heart of Darkness*; the crew disappointed that they cannot eat the body – than he is at evil in the general sense. There are times when the belief in original sin sounds either histrionic or professional; and in *Heart of Darkness* far too much play is made with words like 'inscrutable', 'unfathomable', 'impalpable', 'mysterious', 'inconceivable' in a manner that suggests an attempt to create a system or dogma of evil by sheer rhetoric. Conrad's description of the Congo is unforgettable, but his moral reflections look like stage-drawings or temporary constructions. I think the exile's temperament gave Conrad his obsession with the allusive. He could never resist a symbol; and his images tend to submerge his people at their crisis, as if they were evasions. Even so, such a concern for texture does not really explain why 'Mistah Kurtz', the whole focus of *Heart of Darkness*, is a ghost or figment. His extreme lusts – what are they? What unnamable things did he do? Was he a cannibal? He murdered, we suppose. It is curious that when Marlowe actually sees the heads on the poles outside the hut, he sees them not by the defenceless naked eye but by the magnifying intervention of binoculars. At the very crisis of the story we do not directly face the fact; we are given the distortion.

Kurtz is, of course, made into an ubiquitous, diffused, romantic symbol in this manner and is the symbol of two kinds of corruption: the primordial, and the disgusting aspect of colonial exploitation in its first greedy rush. The Whites have gone mad with greed. Kurtz has simply been logical. He has gone over the borderline into 'complete freedom'. He has accepted the union of 'desire and hate'; he has split into the prim hypocrite citizen and the savage lunatic. In love (we are led to conclude) he found 'horror'. All this is psychologically absorbing, for Conrad means it to apply as a potential to all of us; but it is mere hearsay in the novel. The novelist does not show us an instance of it in action.

Conrad was concerned with fear, guilt, remorse and the tincture of corruption in good things. He is preoccupied by betrayal. It is the rootless who betray. His greatness lies in the handling of a large range of moral types who suffer these evils each in a different way, so that we feel he understands a universal condition. The preoccupation stirred up certain Polish critics years ago. What crime or betrayal had Conrad on his conscience? Why did he write *Lord Jim*? What about *The Secret Agent*? His work is close to personal experience – did he commit some fault at sea? It seems certain that he did not. He may have felt, as a foreigner, the morbid anxiety that he might not come up to codes of the nation he had made his own. The Poles suggested that Conrad felt the guilt of the *emigré*, a guilt all the sharper because he was the son of a man who had been a national martyr. Conrad did not evade the criticism and answered it very sensibly. He was especially unlucky, because he reached forward prophetically to a time when exile has become, to our sense, a general experience.

(1964)

Among the Ruins

In person Cyril Connolly was a gift to the rueful moralists and extravagant gossips of every kind in his generation, but above all to himself. He was an egoist and actor with many parts and impersonations. I often thought of him in middle age as a phenomenal baby in a pram, his hands reaching out greedily for what he saw, especially when it was far beyond him, or, if he got it, delighted for a moment and then throwing it out and crying to get it back. Marvellous at amusing us, lost or sulky when alone: a baby talked about by the nannies, principled, spiteful, or bemused, who, of course, gathered around the resourceful only child. He disarmed by parodying others and himself. He had his moods. 'I have always disliked myself at any given moment,' he wrote. 'The total of such moments is my life.' Yet soon he would be saying that his life was 'a chain of ecstatic moments'.

One of his roles was the bohemian. Not as bohemian as all that, as David Pryce-Jones notes in his portrait, but rather dressy, a man who knew his tailors, almost a dandy, negligently upper-class. At his best, charming, formidable in knowledge, at his worst bad-mannered when he did not like his company. In these middle years he turned on himself. 'A fat, slothful, querulous, greedy, impotent carcass,' he wrote in *The Unquiet Grave*; 'a stump, a decaying belly washed up on the shore'. But, as David Pryce-Jones continues, there was pleasure in the words: the festive pleasure 'latent in the vocabulary . . . suicide by aphorism . . . He was not going to deprive himself either of the joys of excess or of the atonement which topped them off.' He could be very grave.

A fine critic, compulsive traveller, and candid autobiographer, author of *Enemies of Promise* and *The Unquiet Grave* – vocabulary was the making of him. It fitted him to crave, at least, to write 'a masterpiece'. On that he laid down the law for all writers who wanted to count. He was extremely well educated. The Latin classics had been drummed into him at Eton, he had read widely in French, Spanish, and other languages. It would be a crime, he held, not to be a Baudelaire, a Flaubert, a Rochester, a Pope, Congreve, or Dryden, even a Sterne, where his English tastes lay, or an elegiac Roman poet. He had read them all and – as his critical writing shows – he had imagination and decisive images flashed with the speed of wit in his mind. What checked him? The pursuit of pleasure, dining out, chasing women, his spendthrift habits, even his love of conversation – he lists all the notorious traps. He adds his life's grudge: writers without private means or patrons fall back upon reviewing other people's books and it stultifies their creative gift. Like himself, they become, at best, men of letters; at worst, newspaper hacks who go public.

But, as David Pryce-Jones says, there is another buried theme in *Enemies of Promise* – the loss of will-power and failure of nerve in the upper-class English of his generation, who had exhausted that will after the huge achievement of the Victorian age and the 1914 war. By the Thirties the high bourgeois culture had lost its place and its grip. It had become a minority affair of coteries on the one hand – Connolly was a natural coterie figure – or had drifted into commercialism on the other. Not to mention the rise of fascism. A putative Connolly of today would groan that the man of letters is now 'out' and that the sciences and, above all, the levelling effects of technology were driving out any hope of the masterpiece. Its public has gone.

The most startling and effective chapter in *Enemies of Promise* are those in which he analyses the state of English prose and its past cycles: 'The vocabulary of a writer is his currency but it is a paper currency and its value depends on the reserves of mind and heart which back it.' Journalists, politicians, and advertisers devalue this currency:

There was a time . . . when it was impossible to write badly. This time I think was at the end of the seventeenth and the beginning of the eighteenth century, when the metaphysical conceits of the one were going out and before the classical tyranny of the other was established. . . To write naturally was a certain way of writing well.

Until Addison ruined everything by making prose 'artful, and whimsical . . . sonorous when sonority was not needed, affected when it did not require affectation'. Connolly's early tastes were for

the natural mandarins: for Dryden, Pope, Congreve, and Rochester.
Addison turned it into a popular industry. 'The quality of his mind
was inferior to the language which he used.'

At this we turn to Peter Quennell's selection of Connolly's essays,
to one on Sterne written when the critic was a mere twenty-three. He
knew all about Sterne's insincerity and smirking and that *Tristram
Shandy* 'must be the slowest of any book on record', so that it often

reminds one . . . of the youthful occupation of seeing how slowly one can
ride a bicycle without falling off; yet such is Sterne's mastery, his ease and
grace, that . . . [we feel] he will always keep his balance and soon there will
follow a perfect flow of words that may end with a phrase that rings like a
pebble on a frozen pond.

The clinching gift for images like that is one that Connolly never lost,
when he cleared up his own early mandarin passages. If slothful, he
was not so as a reader or in what he wrote. Rather, he was a
perfectionist of a special kind: 'I stay very close to the text – no
soaring eagle, but a low-swung basset who hunts by scent and keeps
his nose to the ground.' And so much depends on style,

this factor of which we are growing more and more suspicious, that although
the tendency of criticism is to explain a writer either in terms of his sexual
experience or his economic background, I still believe his technique remains
the soundest base for a diagnosis, that it should be possible to learn as much
about an author's income and sex life from one paragraph of his writing as
from his cheque stubs and his love letters.

Enemies of Promise was a book of warnings. From the mandarins, as
he said goodbye to them, one could 'borrow art and patience, the
striving for perfection, the horror of clichés, the creative delight in
the material, in the possibilities of the long sentence and the
splendour and subtlety of the composed phrase.' We must reject such
things as 'woolly profundities . . . whimsy . . . archaism, pedantic
usages'. The list is long. There should be no 'when all is said and
done', no 'to my way of thinking', no 'I must aver', no 'adventurers
among their books', no coy references to personal habits, no armchair. Among 'the realists, the puritans, the colloquial writers' one
must reject 'the flatness of style . . . the cult of a violence and
starkness that is masochistic'. 'Construction' is what we can learn
from the realists, 'that discipline in the conception and execution of a
book, that planning which gives simply-written things the power to
endure.' And 'pruning': without that 'the imagination like a tea-rose
reverts to the wilderness.'

It is very odd indeed that, except for a reference to Tolstoy, he has nothing to say, in the books before me, on the Russian novelists, little about the Victorians. He was thinking only of his English contemporaries – Forster, Joyce, Firbank, Virginia Woolf, Lawrence – and always under the shadow of Flaubert.

Did Connolly think of his own 'masterpiece' as being a novel? He wrote one, *The Rock Pool*, and is said to have tried another. Reading it again, one sees that it keeps to the text of his addiction to the fashionable Mediterranean and the passing dissipations of foreign artists in Cagnes. It shocked English publishers in the Twenties because it portrayed one or two lesbians. It caught the jargon and the spell under which the dizzy exiles of this Rock Pool lived. It is more interesting for its send-up of the typical sententious English youth down from public school and Oxford on his first spree; its theory of the permanent adolescence of this English type, pompous, snobbish, and mannered. The story connects with the attack on the concern with 'character' and preparing for high office and rule at these schools in his time and fits very well with Connolly's response to his and Orwell's youth at Eton in *Enemies of Promise*. But if *The Rock Pool* dates it does establish lasting matters in his life: his inherited restlessness and love of travel; the obsession of aggressive or romantic islanders. (Always make your fortune overseas and release your 'id' abroad. Even left-wing 'little Englanders' have adopted Blake's wish to establish a mystical Jerusalem 'in England's green and pleasant land' as their ideological anthem.)

Connolly's forebears were English military men, always on the move, with Anglo-Irish, i.e., colonial, connections. Travel began when he was a child sent on long stays to southern Ireland where he was spoiled, and where he found Anglo-Irish castles and ancestral talk of Norman blood romantic. He even started to learn Gaelic but came to fear the lowering influences of the Celtic Twilight. He was taken twice to South Africa and often to France. These places, and particularly their landscape, with everything luscious and strange in nature, intensified his powers of minute observation. Exotic flowers, fruits, animals, birds, and insects were, so to say, his first 'texts'. When he grew up he longed to return to the privileges of the Grand Tour; he tried a 'modern' Grand Tour. He loved modern luxury. The great sights excited: he had little interest in the inhabitants. And despite his lifelong complaint that Eton's old method of teaching Latin concentrated on endless construing of the sentences of the ancients, he identified himself in Italy with the Rome of Virgil, Tibullus, and Petronius: every site brings the art and literature and the importance of history to life.

So he is a discursive traveller, and those who condemned him for being a self-indulgent French and Mediterranean buff will find from his diaries and notebooks that he was a close observer of the streets of London, and not only the fashionable or elegant: he was often doing an anti-Grand Tour in the East End, not as a topographer and social observer, but more as a collector of life stories.

He is always present in these wanderings, a man with an eye on his dinner, but bent on the great or extraordinary site – see the excellent essay 'In Quest of Rococo'. He is always candid when he is bored or disappointed, very briskly himself, speculating on the relation of art to life and life to art. He never leaves out his own nostalgias and guilts, so that we come to see that if he ever wrote the indispensable masterpiece that 'will last ten years' it would not be a poem or a novel but something compulsively autobiographical: the exposure of a temperament.

On mature travel, as Peter Quennell says in his introduction to the essays, a piece called 'The Ant-Lion' is striking. Connolly is on the edge of Provence. At Albi he is looking at the extraordinary blood-red cathedral. Inside 'the pious buzz like cockchafers.' The landscape is magnificent, the site on the cliff looking down on the Garonne is dramatic. But outside, Connolly, the naturalist, has been distracted by the gruesome sight of a fight to the death between two insects – the 'ant-lion' and a gadfly. He goes on to the Bishop's Palace. It is attached to the cathedral and astonishingly houses the pictures of Toulouse-Lautrec. The collector of the bizarre wakes up. The powerful mother of the painter had obliged the cathedral to turn the palace into a *musée* for the work of her dwarfish son: La Goulue, the Moulin Rouge in this holy place! The painter, he notes, is to Degas what Maupassant was to Flaubert, not of the first rank; he recalls an 'artificial' world because 'it excludes the sun,' and yet for all that he has 'force and intelligence'. But an ant-lion on holy ground!

The wandering moralist lets his speculations run on. Holy ground? This is the country of the Albigensian heresy, the Cathari, who were massacred, who believed in abstinence from food. The Elect or Perfecti held procreation to be evil, were heretics who dreamed that when all men were equal and free they would live in static bliss and would cease to kill for a living. Well, lately we have had the story from Ladurie's *Montaillou*, but Connolly's imaginative leaps of association dramatise the scene. Characteristically, the cathedral, which had amazed, now disappointed him.

It turned out, indeed, that Connolly's 'masterpiece' was to be a travelling affair, an autobiographical myth, one of his own fables.

'Dry again?' said the Crab to the Rock-Pool. 'So would you be,' replied the Rock-Pool, 'if you had to satisfy, twice a day, the insatiable sea.'

Forty years after it was published, we come again to *The Unquiet Grave*, Connolly's mythical confession and elegy which we notice he very characteristically called 'A Word Cycle'. In the Fifties it was attacked as being a mere anthology, done by a lazy man, borrowing from others and his hoarded notebooks. It was abused for *outre-mer* snobbery and self-indulgence by the colloquial generation who found it morbid and depressing. In a revised introduction Connolly pointed out that it was written during the war when Londoners were indeed tired, depressed, and battered. But why drag in Virgil and the Palinurus myth? It turns out that Connolly had been haunted by it when he was a young man and had even mentioned Palinurus in his very first essay. Reading the book again Connolly did not find it morbid. He excused what he rightly considered the weakest part – the speculative passages concerned with depth-psychology; still they were worth it, 'even if a loss to literature'. He denied the morbidity: he had set himself free.

All grief, once made known to the mind, can be cured by the mind, the manuscript proclaimed; the human brain, once it is fully functioning, as in the making of a poem, is outside time and place and immune from sorrow.

In Dryden's translation of Virgil, Palinurus is the pilot of the ship that carries Aeneas away from Dido. He falls asleep during a storm and is thrown overboard, taking the rudder with him. It becomes his raft. The ship founders on the shore and the gods do not save the crew, who with Palinurus are butchered by the inhabitants. Later the gods repent and allow a minor Cape to be named after him. The juxtaposition of Connolly's own griefs and tastes, his lusts, his failures, his moralisations, with the long quotations from the masters that orchestrate or comment on his experience enhances his private dilemmas. (Mere anthologies do not orchestrate.) His wit and his fantasies have their play: 'My previous incarnations: a melon, a lobster, a lemur . . .' or 'It is better to be the lichen on a rock than the President's carnation.'

His curiosity, especially in natural history, flashes out:

Why do ants alone have parasites whose intoxicating moistures they drink and for whom they will sacrifice even their young? Because as they are the most highly socialised of insects, so their lives are the most intolerable.

There is the satire in bravura passages on the Thirties:

Ah, see how on lonely airfield and hill petrol-station the images of Freud and Frazer are wreathed in flowers! From Wabash to Humber the girls are launching their fast-perishing gardens of Adonis far out on to the stream; with sacred rumbas and boogie-woogies the Id is being honoured in all the Hangars.

Or 'Our memories are card-indexes consulted and then returned in disorder by authorities whom we do not control.' Or more piercing, at the age of forty:

Everything I have written seems to date except the last lines I set down. These appear quite different, absolute exceptions to the law – and yet what dates in them does not vary but remains the same – a kind of auto-intoxication which is brought out by the act of writing.

Was *The Unquiet Grave* a work of auto-intoxication? Yes, but also an ordered cure by mythologising in four parts, curing himself of guilt. The terrible sayings of Pascal dominate the first; in the second there is grief and remorse over loss of love and youth; in the third Sainte-Beuve (whom he more than half resembles) and Chamfort bring cynicism, philosophical resignation, and drive off the suicidal ravings of Nerval; in the final section of catharsis he relives the early stages of his love affair. Goodbye, Sainte-Beuve. There is an apology for the pursuit of happiness and he affirms the values of humanism. The epilogue is a pastiche of psychoanalytical jargon and Jungian exegesis, and then he fusses happily with the scholarly disputes about the story of Palinurus. For example – how did Palinurus, the pilot, manage to fall off the ship? How could he so conveniently carry the rudder with him so as to be able to use it as a raft?

Connolly has earned his minor cape.

(1984)

EDITH WHARTON

New York, 1900

A novel by Mrs Wharton in her best period is a correcting experience, a pain when the correction seems to be directed at ourselves, a pleasure when it is being handed out to other people. She is – so many of the important women novelists have been this – a mother-figure, determined, pragmatic, critical and alarming. How inevitable not to come up to her moral, intellectual, above all her social standards. Once we get out of the room where we have been sitting alone with the formidable lady, we foresee that we shall break out or go downhill once more. We know she is no fool; she can startle us by her range of observation; but we shall suspect that what she calls discipline is really first cousin to puritanism and fear, and that what she calls the Eumenides are really projections of the aunts who run the conventions and man the barricades of the taboos. The acerbity of a novelist like Mrs Wharton is *mondain* before it is intellectual; it denotes a positive pleasure in the fact that worldly error has to be heavily paid for spiritually. Her sense of tragedy is linked to a terrifying sense of propriety. It is steely and has the hard efficiency of the property market into which she was born. When, in *The House of Mirth*, Lily Bart is told that she will have to choose between the values of the smart set in New York and the 'republic of the spirit', we are not absolutely convinced that this republic is not a new kind of puritan snobbery. The men who belong to this republic signally fail to rush the women off their feet into this excellent world, and Mrs Wharton is drily aware of their failure. In its first decades the rise of American Big Business created an upper class whose sensitive men cut themselves off from a crude society that shocked them and which was dominated by women. She noted this in her autobiography and it is plain in all her books. Her own interesting situation is that there is an emotional force held back in her, which resents the things her mind approves of and it is this dilemma that gives her mind its cutting edge – at any rate in the books she wrote before she found personal happiness. That happiness, it now seems, dulled her talent.

There is, of course, more than all this to Mrs Wharton, both as person and novelist. She elaborated the balance sheet of renunciation and became the accountant-historian of a rich society, and nothing passed her merciless eye. She wrote best when the pressure had been hardest to bear, even though that pressure may have frozen the imaginative and enhanced the critical character of her talent. Her prose has a presentable cold pomp: 'The cushioned chairs, disposed expectantly under the wide awning, showed no signs of recent occupancy.' Under great bitterness and frustration we have learned to expect outbursts of sentimentality – as a far greater writer, like Mauriac, has shown us – and when she drags the Eumenides into three or four melodramatic pages of her best novel, *The House of Mirth*, we are embarrassed. But it is exceptional for her control to go. Her study of rich New York in the early 1900s in that book will pass for smart sets anywhere and at any time, for even in our day, when most conventions have gone, when people no longer behave like 'deaf mutes in an asylum', the cheerless figure of the socialite remains. The smart set is the quintessential dust bowl. In a later comment on this novel Mrs Wharton wrote 'that a frivolous society can acquire dramatic significance only through what its frivolity destroys. Its tragic implication lies in its power of debasing people and ideals.' The idea is Jamesian and if the execution of it lacks the poetry, the heightened recitative of Henry James, we do get from Mrs Wharton the hard, unpitying moralist who will forgive but not forget, and the derisive critic of social architecture.

Indignation about the sins of another social class is, of course, easy money, and does not, of itself, get a novelist very far. One slightly suspects that Mrs Wharton did not like new people getting rich. But she did examine her subject with scientific efficiency, and in Lily Bart she created the most rewarding kind of socialite: one who was morally a cut above the rest of her circle, but who had been fatally conditioned from the first. Lily Bart is a beautiful and very intelligent girl, delightful company and really too clever for any of the men her society was likely to offer. On the lowest level, she is hopeless about money, about pushing her way in first, about intrigue, about using people, about the main chance. Her own view is that she behaves as she does, because she has no money. It is Becky Sharp's cry: virtue on

five thousand a year. But this is only half her case. She is a superb
artist in the business of being in the swim, a brilliant contriver of
success; she has a wonderful sense of timing – when to be in the
spotlight and when not. Her startling weakness is that she sows but
she does not reap. At the last moment she is wrecked by the sudden
boredom and carelessness of the very clever. On the day of victory
she oversleeps. Her self-confidence is such that she does not bother to
play her ace; and she imagines her gift for dispensing with success at
the last minute will make her impervious to her enemies. It does not.
Selden, who wants to marry her, imagines that her last-minute
failures are signs of grace, impulses from the unconscious. They
make her very likable, but they must be considered as opportunities
for further displays of courage and sangfroid rather than happy,
non-social back-slidings into 'the republic of the spirit'. Her courage
is half vanity. So low are the standards of her set that she is
encouraged thereby to mistake thrilled nerve for an access of
intelligence: 'She . . . listened to Ned Silverton reading Theocritus by
moonlight, as the yacht rounded the Sicilian promontories, with a
thrill of the nerves that confirmed her belief in her intellectual
superiority.' Theocritus is, in short, the right poet, at the right
moment, among the right people, at the height of the season. A venial
folly; after all, are we quite sure that the enlightened Selden is any
better for cutting himself off from the life of his country and reading
La Bruyère?

Lily Bart has the beauty and vanity which George Eliot thought so
wicked in women, but Lily's attractions are energy, an occasional
capacity for honesty and innocence. She is not ashamed of her
cunning in getting money out of a married man like Gus Trenor, for
she has used her brains; what really shocks her is the price demanded. Her match is Rosedale, the rich rising Jew who reads her
character perfectly, who puts his price up as hers goes down and, in
the end, out of sheer admiration for her abilities, is willing to behave
disinterestedly. But he is defeated by her gift for last-minute failure:
she refuses to silence the women who have ruined her. Pride or a
sense of virtue? Neither, I think – and here Mrs Wharton is very
penetrating: those who believe in their star believe also in despair.
Lily Bart is a gambler. One enjoys her as one enjoys the electric
shocks of roulette, as one enjoys the incorrigible and the plunger.
And one enjoys her also because Mrs Wharton turns her inside out:
'Moral complications existed for her only in the environment that

had produced them: she did not mean to slight or ignore them, but they lost their reality when they changed their background.' Or, when it is a matter of getting a financial 'tip' out of Trenor: 'She was always scrupulous about keeping up appearances to herself. Her personal fastidiousness had a moral equivalent and when she made a tour of inspection in her own mind there were certain closed doors she did not open.'

The only element missing from Lily Bart's character is her obvious sexual coldness to which, when the novel was written, Mrs Wharton could hardly have referred even if – to suppose the impossible – she had desired to do so.

New York's social scene is expertly set down in *The House of Mirth* with an anthropologist's thoroughness and the novel is remarkable for its skilful visits from one smart set to the smart set on the stair below. These tours are conducted with all Mrs Wharton's superlative snobbery. 'Mrs Bry, to Mrs Fisher's despair had not progressed beyond the point of weighing her social advantages in public.' There was smart hotel society:

Through this atmosphere of torrid splendour moved wan beings as richly upholstered as the furniture, beings without definite pursuits or permanent relations, who drifted on a languid tide of curiosity from restaurant to concert hall, from palm-garden to music-room.

Here reigned Mrs Hatch, the simple lady who, surrounded by beauty specialists, wished to soar socially; the Bovary of the gossip columns, who wanted to do what was 'nice' and to be taught how to be 'lovely'.

Mrs Wharton hated the smart set she had been brought up in and she is good in this novel no doubt because she is anatomising the monster whose stupidities and provincialities might have crushed her. But the making of her as a novelist is her power to create incident and to conduct great scenes. Strangely enough her ironical power and gift of surprise often recall those of an utterly different novelist – Thomas Hardy. She has – usually under iron control – a persistent sense of fate, a skill in entangling her characters before striking them down. The scene at Gus Trenor's when this magnate turns nasty and looks like going to the point of sexual assault is wonderfully handled and Lily is marvellous in it; every cliché in this well-known situation is avoided, every truth in it discerned and the end is perfect. And Bertha Dorset's revenge on Lily: this is as brilliant a *volte-face* and surprise as one can remember in any plot in social comedy. Mrs

Wharton did not touch these heights afterwards, though even in her weaker novels, there is the same astringency, the same readiness of invention.

Again and again we find that novelists who have attacked the conventions because they stultify the spirit, who attack the group for its cruelty to individuals, will end by pointing out the virtues of submission. Mrs Wharton may have hated old New York, but she hated the new New York even more. She disliked the prison of silent hypocrisy, but she drew in her skirts when candour came in. Especially after her long life, *en grande luxe*, in Europe. What indignation denounces creeps back in the name of sentiment. *The Age of Innocence* shows a man giving in, loyally marrying the conventional girl he does not love, throwing over the Europeanised woman who is his natural equal. It is the surrender to the established bourgeois standard. No great harms come of it; only dullness and disappointment. The sweet young girl he was engaged to was slyer than he thought. She became like her mother-in-law to whose face 'a lifelong mastery over trifles had given factitious authority'. Perhaps, after all, her husband reflects, the old New York which would not 'know' a divorced woman, was rather charming and quite right. Better renunciation than a hole-in-corner affair. Mrs Wharton always believed in the sterner condition; but her brain resented it. Not even snobbery and respect for 'factitious authority' could get her into the Catholic Church at the end of her life. The old Puritan worldling stood out firmly for patching, for facing unpleasantness, making the second best of things, refusing accommodations. Worry, culture and character were the thing. One imagines God wondering if he dared leave a card. The strange thing is that we mistrust her at once when, late in life, she becomes benign.

(1955)

MARK TWAIN

The American Puritan

After reading Hemingway and Faulkner and speculating upon the break of the American novel with its English tradition, we go back to the two decisive, indigenous Americans who opened the new vein – Mark Twain and Edgar Allan Poe. Everything really American, really non-English comes out of that pair of spiritual derelicts, those two scarecrow figures with their half-lynched minds. Both of them, but particularly Twain, represent the obverse side of Puritanism. We have never had this obverse in England, for the political power of Puritanism lasted for only a generation and has since always bowed if it has not succumbed to civilised orthodoxy. If an Englishman hated Puritanism, there was the rest of the elaborate English tradition to support him; but American Puritanism was totalitarian and if an American opposed it, he found himself alone in a wilderness with nothing but bottomless cynicism and humorous bitterness for his consolation. There has never been in English literature a cynicism to compare with the American; at any rate we have never had that, in some ways vital, but always sardonic or wretched, cynicism with its broken chopper edge and its ugly wound. We have also never had its by-product: the humorous philosophers; Franklin's Poor Richard, the Josh Billingses, the Artemus Wards, the Pudd'nhead Wilsons and Will Rogerses with their close-fisted proverbs: 'Training is everything. The peach was once a bitter almond: cauliflower is nothing but a cabbage with a college education.' Or: 'Consider well the proportion of things. It is better to be a young June bug than an old bird of Paradise.'

I say we have never had this kind of thing, but there is one exception to prove the rule and to prove it very well, for he also is an uprooted and, so to speak, colonial writer. Kipling with his 'A woman is always a woman, but a good cigar is a smoke' is our first American writer with a cynicism, a cigar-stained humour and a jungle book of beliefs which, I think, would be a characteristic of our literature if we become seriously totalitarian in the future. For English totalitarianism would create the boredom and bitterness of the spiritual wilderness, as surely as Puritanism did in America.

When Mark Twain turned upon the religion of his childhood because it was intolerable, he was unaware that it would destroy him by turning him into a money-grubber of the most disastrously Puritan kind. Fortunately the resources of the imagination are endless even when a fanatical philosophy wrecks human life, genius and happiness. Out of the mess which Twain made of his life, amid the awful pile of tripe which he wrote, there does rise one book which has the serenity of a thing of genius. *Huckleberry Finn* takes the breath away. Knowing his life, knowing the hell from which the book has ascended, one dreads as one turns from page to page the seemingly inevitable flop. How can so tortured and so angry a comedian refrain from blackguarding God, Man and Nature for the narrow boredom of his early life, and thus ruin the gurgling comedy and grinning horror of the story? But an imaginative writer appears to get one lucky break in his career; for a moment the conflicts are assimilated, the engine ceases to work against itself. The gears do not crash and *Huckleberry Finn* hums on without a jar. America gets its first and indisputable masterpiece. The boyhood of Huck Finn is the boyhood of a new culture and a new world.

The curious thing about *Huckleberry Finn* is, that although it is one of the funniest books in all literature and really astonishing in the variety of its farce and character, we are even more moved than we are amused by it. Why are we moved? Do we feel the sentiment of sympathy only? Are we sighing with some envy and self-pity? 'Alas, Huck Finn is just what I would have been in my boyhood if I had had half a chance.' Are we sorry for the vagrant, or are we moved by his rebellion? These minor feelings may play their part; but they are only sighs on the surface of the main stream of our emotion. Twain has brought to his subject far more than this personal longing; he has become the channel of the generic American emotion which floods all really American literature – nostalgia. In that brilliant, hit-or-miss book, *Studies in Classical American Literature*, which is either dead right or dead wrong, D. H. Lawrence called this feeling the longing of the rebel for a master. It may be simply the longing for a spiritual home, but it is as strong in Mark Twain as it is implicit in Hemingway. One finds this nostalgia in Anglo-Irish literature which is also colonial and, in a less lasting way, once again in the work of Kipling. The peculiar power of American nostalgia is that it is not only looking back to something lost in the past, but suggests also the tragedy of a lost future. As Huck Finn and old Jim drift down the Mississippi from one horrifying little town to the next and hear the voices of men quietly swearing at one another across the water about 'a chaw of tobacco'; as they pass the time of day with the scroungers, rogues, murderers, the lonely women, the frothing revivalists, the maundering boatmen and fantastic drunks, we see the human wastage that is left behind in the wake of a great effort of the human will, the hopes frustrated, the idealism which has been whittled down to eccentricity and mere animal cunning. These people are the price paid for building a new country. The human spectacle is there. It is not, once you have faced it – which Dickens did not do in *Martin Chuzzlewit*, obsessed as he was by the negative pathos of the immigrant – it is not a disheartening spectacle; for the value of a native humour like Twain's is that it records a profound reality in human nature: the ability of man to adjust himself to any circumstance and somehow to survive and make a life.

Movement is one of the great consolers of human woe; movement, a process of continual migration is the history of America. It is this factor which gives Twain's wonderful descriptions of the journey down the Mississippi its haunting overtone and which, naturally enough, awakens a sensibility in him which is shown nowhere else in his writings and which is indeed vulgarly repressed in them:

> . . . then we set down on the sandy bottom where the water was about knee-deep and watched the daylight come. Not a sound anywhere – perfectly still – just like the whole world was asleep, only sometimes the bull-frogs a-clattering may be. The first thing to see, looking away over the water, was a kind of dull line – that was on the woods on t'other side – you couldn't make nothing else out; then a pale place in the sky; then more paleness, spreading around; then the river softened up, away off, and wasn't black any more but grey; you could see little dark spots drifting along, ever so far away – trading scows . . . and such things; and long black streaks – rafts; sometimes you could hear a sweep screaking; or jumbled-up voices, it was so still, and sounds come so far; and by-and-by you could see a streak on the water which you know by the look of the streak that there's a snag in the swift current which breaks on it and that streak looks that way; and you see the mist curl up off the water, and the east reddens up, and the river, and you make out a log cabin in the edge of the woods, away on the bank t'other side of the river, being a woodyard likely, and piled by them cheats so you can throw a dog through it anywheres. . . .

And afterwards we would watch the lonesomeness of the river, and kind of lazy along and by-and-by, lazy off to sleep. Wake up, by-and-by, and look to see what done it, and may be see a steamboat, coughing along upstream, so far off towards the other side you couldn't tell nothing about her only whether she was stern wheel or side wheel; then for about an hour there wouldn't be nothing to hear nor nothing to see – just solid lonesomeness. Once there was a thick fog, and the rafts and things that went by was beating tin pans so the steam boats wouldn't run over them. A scow or a raft went by so close we could hear them talking and cussing and laughing – heard them plain; but we couldn't see no sign of them; it made you feel crawly, it was like spirits carrying on that way in the air. Jim said he believed it was spirits; but I says, 'No, spirits wouldn't say "dern this dern fog".'

(Note the word 'way' in this passage; it is a key nostalgic word in the American vocabulary, vaguely vernacular and burdened with the associations of the half-articulate. It is a favourite Hemingway word, of course: 'I feel *that way*' – not the how or what he feels of the educated man.)

The theme of *Huckleberry Finn* is the rebellion against civilisation and especially against its traditions: 'I reckon I got to light out for the Territory ahead of the rest, because Aunt Sally she's going to adopt me and sivilize me and I can't stand it. I been there before.'

Huck isn't interested in 'Moses and the Bulrushers' because Huck 'don't take no stock of dead people'. He garbles European history when he is discussing Kings with Jim, the negro. Whether Huck is the kind of boy who will grow up to build a new civilisation is doubtful; Tom Sawyer obviously will because he is imaginative. Huck never imagines anything except fears. Huck is 'low down plain ornery', always in trouble because of the way he was brought up with 'Pap'. He is a natural anarchist and bum. He can live without civilisation, depending on shrewd affections and loyalty to friends. He is the first of those typical American portraits of the underdog, which have culminated in the poor white literature and in Charlie Chaplin – an underdog who gets along on horse sense, so to speak. Romanticism, ideas, ideals are repugnant to Huck; he 'reckons', he 'guesses', but he doesn't think. In this he is the opposite of his hero, Tom Sawyer. Tom had been telling 'stretchers' about Arabs, elephants and Aladdin's lamp. Huck goes at once 'into a brood'.

I thought all this over for two or three days, and then I reckoned I would see if there was anything in it. I got an old tin lamp and an irony ring and went out into the woods and rubbed it till I sweat like an Injun, calculating to build a palace and sell it; but it wasn't no use, none of the genies came. So then I judged that all that stuff was only just one of Tom Sawyer's lies. I

reckoned he believed in the A-rabs and elephants, but as for me I think
different. It has all the marks of a Sunday school.

That is, of American Puritan civilisation, the only civilisation he
knew.

'Ornery', broody, superstitious, with a taste for horrors,
ingenious, courageous without knowing it, natural, sound-hearted,
philosophical in a homely way – those are the attributes of the
gorgeous, garrulous Huck and they give a cruelly extravagant
narrative its humanity. He obliges you to accept the boy as the
devastating norm. Without him the violence of the book would be
stark reporting of low life. For if *Huckleberry Finn* is a great comic
book it is also a book of terror and brutality. Think of the scenes: Pap
with d.t.'s chasing Huck round the cabin with a knife; Huck sitting
up all night with a gun preparing to shoot the old man; Huck's early
familiarity with corpses; the pig-killing scene; the sight of the frame
house (evidently some sort of brothel) floating down the Mississippi
with a murdered man in it; the fantastic events at the Southern house
where two families shoot each other down in a vendetta; the drunken
Boggs who comes into town to pick a quarrel and is eventually coolly
shot dead before the eyes of his screaming young daughter by the
man he has insulted. The 'Duke' and the 'King', those cynical rascals
whose adventures liven up the second half of the story are sharpers,
twisters and crooks of the lowest kind. Yet a child is relating all this
with a child's detachment and with a touch of morbidity. Marvellous
as the tale is, as a collection of picaresque episodes and as a
description of the mess of frontier life, it is strong meat. Sometimes
we wonder how Twain's public stomached such illusionless reporting. The farce and the important fact that in this one book Mark
Twain never forced a point nor overwrote – in the Dickens way for
example – are of course the transfiguring and beguiling qualities. His
corpse and coffin humour is a dry wine which raises the animal
spirits. Old Jim not only looked like a dead man after the 'King' had
painted him blue, but like one 'who had been dead a considerable
time'.

Judiciousness is carried to the comic limit. And then, Mark Twain
is always getting the atmosphere, whether he picks up the exact
words of loafers trying to borrow tobacco off one another or tells a
tall story of an hysterical revival meeting.

Atmosphere is the decisive word. *Huckleberry Finn* reeks of its
world. From a sensitive passage like: 'When I got there it was all still

and Sunday-like, and hot and the hands was gone to the fields; and there was them kind faint dronings of bugs and flies that makes it seem so lonesome and like everybody's dead. . . .' to descriptions of the silly, dying girl's ridiculous poetry, the sensibility draws a clear outline and is never blurred and turned into sentimentality. One is enormously moved by Huck's view of the world he sees. It is the world not of Eden, but of the 'old Adam', not the golden age of the past, but the earthly world of a reality which (we feel with regret) we have let slip through our fingers too carelessly. Huck is only a crude boy, but luckily he was drawn by a man whose own mind was arrested, with disastrous results in his other books, at the schoolboy stage; here it is perfect. And a thousand times better than the self-conscious adventures of Stevenson's *Treasure Island* and *Kidnapped*.

Is *Huckleberry Finn* one of the great works of picaresque literature? It is, granting the limits of a boy's mind in the hero and the author, a comic masterpiece; but this limitation is important. It is not a book which grows spiritually, if we compare it to *Quixote*, *Dead Souls* or even *Pickwick*; and it is lacking in that civilised quality which you are bound to lose when you throw over civilisation – the quality of pity. One is left with the cruelty of American humour, a cruelty which is softened by the shrewd moralisings of the humorous philosophers – the Josh Billingses, the Artemus Wards, the Will Rogerses. And once Mark Twain passed this exquisite moment of his maturity, he went to bits in that morass of sentimentality, cynicism, melodrama and vulgarity which have damned him for the adult reader.

(1941)

WILLIAM FAULKNER

The Hill-Billies

The vogue of Faulkner in France at the present time is easily understandable. Writing after 1918 about a society which had not recovered from the Civil War and which was to be marked by the demoralisation of the period of Prohibition and the gangsters, Faulkner anticipated some of the circumstances of the lawless life which rose in France under the Occupation and in the Resistance. Society was paddling in general crime, publicly selling the law at every street corner, and the college boy and his girl in *Sanctuary* were vicious replicas of the adolescents who had first appeared in Gide, and who, in the last war, moved beyond civilised judgment. The only comment possible came from the Negroes – the verse occurs in *Sartoris*:

> Sinner riz frum de moaner's bench,
> Sinner jump to de penance bench;
> When de preacher ax 'im whut de reason why,
> Say, 'Preacher got de women, jes' de same ez I.'
> Oh, Lawd, oh Lawd.
> Dat's whut de matter with de church to-day

And the women had got the moonshine whisky.

Faulkner's obscure and rankling genius began to work at the point when, failing to find a place from which to make a judgment, he set to writing about people from the whirlpool inside them, floating along with experience as it came out. His confusing, difficult, punch-drunk novels are in fact elaborately patterned and, as time has gone by, they have become (I think, ingeniously) didactic; but they fill the demand made by some Existentialists for a novel without a centre and which works outwards from the narrator in all directions at once. They exploit 'the absurd', the cruel meaninglessness of existence and they hope, by making every instant of any character's consciousness a life and death matter, to collect at the end a small alluvial deposit of humanism.

Faulkner is an affected but seminal writer for those who are in situations similar to his. In England, because the situation does not exist or because our overwhelmingly strong social instinct can still fairly successfully cover-up and deal with disintegration at the same time, Faulkner's vogue has passed. He was admired for his devices and as a romantic and exotic; he seemed to have opened rhetorical or poetic avenues into popular life and speech and to have caught a kind of Elizabethan dramatic spirit. In the end, Southern misery and his mannerisms palled. We had heard enough of hill-billies for a lifetime and he seemed to be an obsessed provincial stewing too long in his own juice.

Soldiers' Pay is Faulkner's earliest work in prose. Reading it again, one sees immediately, it is much fresher than the later, ruminating and didactic Faulkner. It has the lyrical hardness, the mark of experiment, the crispness of design which were to be found in *Light in August* and *The Sound and the Fury*, and is written before Faulkner became so deedily engrossed in his own complexity. He belongs to the period of difficult writing, obliquity, the self-propagating image that grows like a brilliant fungus all over his prose. And when this Southern dandyishness is given up, he is apt to convey the agony of the South in an agonising prose which appears to be chewed like tobacco and occasionally squirted out, instead of being written. The total effect is, however, hypnotic. After being trained for a generation since Joyce on difficult, associative writing, we ought not to be set back, and I can only suppose the English reader lacks the necessary links with the Southern Negro and poor white cultures. But there *is* more than that to the difficulty of Faulkner: it is not that he is allusive or perpetually putting fresh obstacles in the way of his vision, but that he gives all his allusions and obstacles the same value. I will quote a long passage from a late book, *Intruder in the Dust*, which describes the capture of a fugitive who has jumped into a river. In isolation it is excellent – but, remember, a whole book has been written in this eye-blinding, mind-stunning incantation:

> . . . he saw the old man jump feet first off the bank and with no splash, no disturbance of any sort, continue right on not through the bland surface but past it as if he had jumped not into anything but past the edge of a cliff or a window-sill and then stopping, half-disappeared as suddenly with no shock or jolt; just fixed and immobile as if his legs had been cut off at the loins by

one swing of a scythe, leaving his trunk sitting upright on the bland, depthless milklike sand.

'All right, boys,' old Gowrie cried, brisk and carrying: 'Here he is. I'm standing on him.'

And one twin got the rope bridle from the mule and the leather one and the saddle girth from the mare, and using the shovels like axes the Negroes hacked willow branches while the rest of them dragged up other brush and poles and whatever else they could reach or find or free and now both twins and the two Negroes, their empty shoes sitting on the bank, were down in the sand too and steadily there came down from the hills the ceaseless strong murmur of the pines but no other sound yet although he strained his ears listening in both directions along the road, not for the dignity of death because death has no dignity, but at least for the decorum of it: some little at least of that decorum which should be every man's helpless right until the carrion he leaves can be hidden from the ridicule and the shame, the body coming out now feet first, gallowsed up and out of the inscrutable suck to the heave of the crude tackle then free of the sand with a faint smacking plop like the sound of lips perhaps in sleep and in the bland surface nothing: a faint wimple wrinkled already fading then gone like the end of a faint secret fading smile, and then on the bank now while they stood about and over it and he was listening harder than ever now with something of the murderer's own frantic urgency both ways along the road though there was still nothing. . . .

Faulkner clutches at every sight and suggestion with the avidity of suspicion and even mania, and all manias create monotony. This is true even of the mania for domestic realism in Defoe. But in that passage Faulkner is simultaneously conveying the effect of the event on a boy's mind – for the story is seen through the eyes of a boy. Faulkner's ambition is visually poetic and he is attempting the instantaneous delivery of a total experience. In all his novels, he is trying to give each instant of experience in depth, to put not only physical life as it is seen directly on the page, but all the historical and imaginative allusions of a culture at the same time. And to the eye alone. If the reader is stunned by the slow deliberate blow, that is precisely the effect Faulkner is seeking, for we do, in fact, live stunned and stupefied by the totality of our experience and our present position in our own life story is simply the little clearing we have cut and the devious fading path we have left behind us, in the jungle. Order, or at any rate pattern, is that which comes *afterwards* to this romantic novelist who begins in the middle of the mind. He is a man outside the imposed, clarifying authority of some established system of values. We do not really know the beginning of Faulkner's stories until we have reached the end, till we have worked our way out of the jungle.

Faulkner's method of story-telling requires no justification: it has the conundrum quality of a pattern, and intricate patterns are as interesting as elaborate plots. He is a superb creator of episode – the opening train scene in *Soldiers' Pay*, the comic brothel scenes in *Sanctuary*, the account of the raid on the Federal breakfast table in the opening chapters of *Sartoris* – and when he creates passing character, the awful politician Snopes for example, the ink bites. But the true justification of the method is that it creates the South in depth as, I think, no other part of America has been created by a novelist since the time of *Huckleberry Finn*. American novelists have composed reports, records, chronicles of other regions, but the impression is of life in some passing, cynical, littered encampment; Faulkner, on the other hand, seems to be engaged in a compulsive task, as if he had undertaken awkwardly the building of a culture out of its ruins, as a one-man mission. And perhaps, because of its social tragedy, its knowledge of ruin and decadence, the guilt felt because of its crimes against the Negro, the South is America's richest artistic soil.

Faulkner has the ubiquity of the reporter who knows the corruption of a town or a region inside out. He has also the moodiness of the man of letters. His capacity to catch mood is apparent in *Soldiers' Pay* when he placed a dying, speechless, returned soldier in the midst of his story and played the reviving post-war world of 1918 around him, as it moved into jazz and bootlegging. His lyrical power in that book is mannered, but his mannerisms represent a passionate attempt to burn the scene into our senses for ever. He is excellent at crowded scenes; in social life, in dances, court house gatherings, riots, train journeys, Saturday night streets, where a sinister action winds separately in and out among the wanderings of people. He is a novelist of journeys. He is no great hand, indeed he is painfully stiff, in describing the inner life of sensitive people; and he is too concerned with the visual scene for the crucial business of creating large characters. Even his distinctive people are minor figures, and this suggests sterility of imagination. But he is remarkable in grasping the essential fragment, the live coal which keeps a life going, so that we are aware of living among the unconscious motives of people and of knowing how they will act. His men are rarely friends, his women nearly always enemies except for idealised creatures like Mrs Powers in *Soldiers' Pay*. He is especially good at shallow young women, whom he hates and exposes, but whose points and vanity attract him. His weakest characters are the rhetorical cynics whose Shakespearian tone adds a vague oratorical fog to the tale; but this strange mixture of artifice and realism is his native mixture. In all his people, except the figures of pure evil like Popeye, he is sifting until he comes down to the infinitesimal deposit of humanity. His brutality is frightening because it is sardonic and always has a theatrical twist – one thinks of the man, running with a petrol can at a lynching, who gets himself blown up by mistake.

Faulkner's sense of human pain and the damage done to people, their blank cruelties and the disguised suffering which they have accepted as part of the furniture of life, comes from a maturity rare in American novels; and he has shown here the power to grow out of the bitterness and cynicism and bragging sentimentalities which Hemingway never advanced from. In the didactic novels of his later period there is no uplift. He inculcates the rudiments of humanity, by cunning and the correcting of observation. If the boy in *Intruder in the Dust* is likely to side with the accused Negro, it is because he has learned to test his experience and to listen to his sensibility. He will always remember what the smell of the Negro really is after being wrapped in the old Negress's quilt in her cabin: it is the smell of poverty.

I do not know whether these merits could have made Faulkner a great novelist, but they make him a source. Rancorous and obsessive, he has carried his quarrel with his region very wide, like some preacher chased out of town. And, what subjects – the English novelist will sigh – he has to hand. What advantages a lawless society brings to the writer.

(1962)

HENRY JAMES

The Last Letters

In the final volume of Leon Edel's exemplary selection of 'Henry James Letters' we find two contrasting views of letter writing. If letters have real charm, James said, they are the most delightful of written things. He is the majestic bumblebee of that art, pollinating his friendships with his speculations and his intimacies. But, thanking that voluminous novelist Mrs Humphry Ward for 'ploughing' through 'The Golden Bowl' and praising it, he groans on her behalf. Looking at the pile of unanswered letters on his own desk, always late with his replies, and knowing that he will have to sit up long past midnight to deal with them, the toiling novelist says:

> The letters of life, in general, become more and more its *poison*, moreover, surely – and are a matter against which, for myself, my heart is rapidly casing itself in impenetrable steel. One must at last go in, absolutely, for life-saving (the 'life' being our own); and they are verily life-wrecking.

They are at odds with his principle that 'art' – the art of his fictions – 'makes life'. If, as it seems to Mr Edel, the letters of this volume may be the best James wrote – less formal, less distant, more candid, affectionate, and even passionate – this is because in middle life his character has altered. The sleepy erotic and physical impulses of his nature have been awakened late, but not 'too late', as Strether felt in *The Ambassadors*.

There is indeed more openness in James's personality. Edmund Wilson noted it. In the early volumes, the brisk, even pushing American Puritan has come to Europe to discover and conquer. He is the eager annalist of his adventure in a ripe civilisation and, above all, of its manners and social history. The classic American obligation 'to keep in touch' – to leave no social stone unturned, and to report back to his gifted family – excites him and makes him cogent and amusing. He is won over imaginatively to the extent of hating what he called 'American simplicity' and, of course, by the 'sense of the past'; but he retains, especially in offhand London, his love of what he called (in one of his novels) the beautiful American 'fuss'. We have seen him, in the earlier letters, giving up magical Rome and his nostalgias for Paris in favour of 'odious' London and the comforts of the English language; because the city was livable, you became accepted as a character in a society of characters, to whom being what they were (or pretended to be) was a kind of mundane religion. London, especially after the Oscar Wilde trial, was no longer Victorian and was knowing about family secrets: Edwardian manners had contrived discreet, ironic formulas for 'speaking out', though not in front of the children.

For Mr Edel, the change in James's character starts first of all after the personal shock of his humiliating failure in the theatre. He had been jeered by the unsparing Cockney gallery. Sick of dining out, the engaging bachelor who knew everyone went briefly to Italy, where (heaven knows) life is lived out on every yard of pavement, and then returned to 'chuck' London for Lamb House in Rye, where there was no wear and tear, to write his last novels. And to brood on a startling Italian experience. In Italy, in his fifties, he had fallen in love – a 'first love', too – with the handsome young Norwegian-American sculptor Hendrik Andersen. Innocent of physical love (it is supposed), James had discovered what many had suspected: his nature was homosexual. As a novelist and a man, he had been a neutral observer of love, seeing it through a veil of interests and manners: he had not know the body's craving for physical touch, the prompting of the blood. Now to Andersen he will write, in this volume, of 'a caress of your hand'; he will admit, as Mr Edel says, 'the body's insistence on an active tenderness'. The passionate letters to Andersen leave no question of James's helpless physical attraction – if nothing more – to a young man whom he thought godlike but who was not a great sculptor (as James soon saw) and who had shrewdly sought out the famous novelist largely to push his own career. James invited him to live and work in the studio of his house at Rye. The young man came for a matter of days and then went his way, and after that was evasive and negligent. James now had the wretched experience of the 'too late'. A fitful correspondence goes on. In 1902 (when he is fifty-eight), he writes to comfort the young man, who has lost a brother:

Now, at least, my weak arms still can feel you close. . . I've gone through Death, and Death, enough in my long life, to know how all that we *are*, all that we *have*, all that is best of us within, our genius, our imagination, our passion, our whole personal being, become then but aides and channels and open gates to suffering, to being flooded. But, it is better so. Let yourself go and *live*, even as a lacerated, mutilated lover . . . Beautiful and unspeakable your account of relation to Andreas. Sacred and beyond tears. How I wish I had known him, admirable, loveable boy – but you make me: I *do*. Well, he is *all* yours now: he lives in you and out of all pain.

This is the letter of an awakened and tender man, no longer withdrawn. James returned to Rome only once after this; correspondence flags. Replying to a 'missive', he writes with affection for the man but with candour about his work:

Your production *is* prodigious and heroic and very beautiful and interesting to me – so much so that, dearest Hendrik, I affectionately and heartily declare, even while seeing less than ever where this colossal multiplication of divinely naked and intimately associated gentlemen and ladies, flaunting their bellies and bottoms and their other private affairs, in the face of day, is going, on any *American* possibility, to land you. I won't attempt to go into this last question now – you know already how it perplexes and even not a little distresses me.

In another letter, he complains that Hendrik appears not to differentiate sufficiently between the gentlemen and the ladies, notably in the case of his last ballerina, who is insufficient in hip 'or to speak plainly, Bottom. She hasn't *much* more of that than her husband.' He would wish the faces of the sculptures were not so 'blank and stony' and without individuality. He hopes against hope that he and Hendrik may meet again, and says he will be 'cast down' if they don't.

It is surprising that the avid reader of Flaubert, of the Balzac of the *Contes Drôlatiques*, even of Turgenev's *First Love*, should have known the sexual impulse (so far as we can tell) only through the printed page – not that this has ever been a guiltless indulgence, as everyone knows. What impresses us is the effect of the Andersen affair on the novelist. He has had – as, indeed, his father had had – a 'vastation', if of a different order.

The spell of the letters really lies in their idiosyncrasy. They are communings with himself as much as with his friends. They are also talking letters. They are written in his dictating period, and he writes as one listening to his own voice as it leads him on, watching his words float on the air, and delighting in the studied mischief of his hesitations and parentheses. He always evokes the friend to whom he is writing. His enormous privacy flowers. His lonely room fills up with voices; he carries his friends down the happily rambling stream of consciousness. He is full of affection and news. With almost socialite cunning, he has placed himself not far from Folkestone, the cross-Channel port: in turn the spider and the fly – catching or caught by his American friends as they come chattering in from the Continent or depart to it. 'Life-wrecking', of course – life being 'art'. He amuses his friends with literary prattling. About Kipling – who is not far off – James reports once feeling that he had the seeds of an English Balzac in him. But 'I have quite given that up in proportion as he has come steadily from the less simple in subject to the more simple, – from the Anglo-Indians to the natives, from the natives to the Tommies, from the Tommies to the quadrupeds, from the quadrupeds to the fish, and from the fish to the engines and screws.'

As Mr Edel says, James himself had his own mania for minutiae. From other mysterious rumblings sudden moral definitions shoot out. Remembering that 'dear man' George Meredith: 'Still, it abides with us, I think, that [he] was an admirable spirit even if not an *entire* mind. . . . The fantastic and the mannered in him were as nothing, I think, to the intimately sane and straight.' In his remarks about George Sand he stages a prolonged alarm. 'Dear old George' is 'more prodigious the nearer one gets to her.' He remembers Nohant:

> What a crew, what *mœurs*, what habits, what conditions and relations every way – and what an altogether mighty and marvellous George! – not diminished by all the greasiness and smelliness in which she made herself (and *so* many other persons!) at home. Poor gentlemanly, crucified Chopin! – not naturally at home in grease.

And then he goes off at a tangent into something we have all noticed about the French and their 'precisions' and formulations on the subject of *amour* – and, indeed, everything else. One feels, he writes,

> that Providence laid up for the French such a store of remark, in advance and, as it were, should the worst befall, that their conduct and *mœurs*, coming *after* had positively to justify and do honor to the whole collection of formulae, phrases and, as I say, glibnesses – so that as there were at any rate such things there for them to inevitably *say*, why not simply *do* all the things that would give them a *rapport* and a sense?

These words about George Sand come from a letter to Edith Wharton, the great friend of his last years – they met in 1903. Before his own visit to America in 1904, he urged her not to miss 'the

American Subject' – 'Profit, be warned, by my awful example of exile and ignorance. . . . *Do New York!*'

All James's friendships were caring and generous. Edith Wharton is notoriously in trouble with her marriage and her defiance of society. Like James, she has been through the mill of injured innocence. He advises her, wisely, 'Only sit tight yourself *and go through the movements of life*. . . . Live it all through, every inch of it.' He is admiring or concerned about her work. But she is enormously rich, and he will frankly write to other friends that she is 'pampered' and 'facilitated'. (Just as he had mockingly described Isabella Stewart Gardner years before, arriving from Brussels 'charged with the spoils of the Flemish school' – 'I must rush off, help her to disembark, see all her Van Eycks and Rubenses through the Customs.') What are letters without malice and the grotesque? Edith Wharton, dear as she is, has to pay the price when she turns up with her 'crew' and her splendacious car so fatally near Folkestone. He loves to glide around in that car – but the price! Writing to Howard Sturgis, he starts by calling her 'the Firebird' and is soon calling her the 'Angel of Devastation'. She becomes

like an extravagant dandy who sends thirty shirts to the wash where you and I (forgive, dear Howard, the collocation!) send one; or indeed even worse – since our Firebird dirties her days (pardon again the image!) at a rate that no laundry will stand; and in fact doesn't seem to believe in the washing, and still less in the ironing – though she does, rather inconsistently in the 'mangling'! – of any of her material of life. Well, let us hope that the Divine Chemisier will always keep her supplied straight and to sufficiency with the intimate article in which he deals!

This passage, I suppose, must be put to the debit account of *The Golden Bowl*. James had the Edwardian habit of irony at the expense of the heroic, beautiful, and sublime. He loved rolling his eyes as the preposterous came into his mind.

In serious matters, in sorrows, in the sad concerns of his family, especially, he is deeply tender, wise, and concerned. He is a great praiser and healer, the care showing as much in his sentences as in his feelings. When the 1914 war comes and he has to see the collapse of the civilisation he has been celebrating, he sees it in terms of the human agonies of his friends; also, he feels an obligation to his adopted country. The illnesses that are crippling him turn him into a figure almost spectral and alone. He is dying. We come to the strange record of his powerful ramblings from his deathbed. They were recorded and are, in their way, grandiose. In his disarray, he appears to think of himself and his family as Napoleonic. He evokes his brother William and sister-in-law Alice as Imperial figures. He issues commands for the decoration of the palaces of the Tuileries and the Louvre. In a letter to his brother and sister-in-law he signs himself Napoléone – the Corsican spelling. Delusions of grandeur in a broken mind? I think not. The old man is remembering vivid *données* from childhood: perhaps fragments left in the memory when the family was taken to Paris by his father and had that first, blinding sight of the Napoleonic spoils in the Louvre, when James first saw 'the imperial eagle'. He murmurs clearly:

The Bonapartes have a kind of bronze distinction that extends to their finger-tips and is a great source of charm in the women. Therefore they don't have to swagger after the fact; fortune has placed them too high. . . . There have been great families of tricksters and conjurors; so why not this one, and so pleasant withal? Our admirable father keeps up the pitch.

The dying man has pride in the distinction of the family from which his own imaginative genius sprang. He dies protesting his own triumphant 'sense of the past' halfway through a war that is destroying it. His words are an artist's last fling. One says, 'Yes, he is entitled to this madness': his novels, even these letters, are what so fascinated him – the spoils.

(1984)

NATHANAEL WEST

Miss Lonelyhearts

Nathanael West is one of the novelists of the breakdown of the American dream in the Thirties. His real name was Nathan Weinstein, he moved in fashionable literary society, became a script writer in Hollywood after the success of *Miss Lonelyhearts* and was killed in a motor accident at the age of forty. Two of his novels, *Miss Lonelyhearts* – which is very well known – and *The Day of the Locust*, show that a very original talent was cut short. He was preoccupied with hysteria as the price paid for accepting the sentimentalities of the national dream. He feared hysteria in himself, he was morbidly conscious of it in his people; he was attracted and repelled by its false dreams as one might be by a more poisonous way of mixing gin. West did not feel that life was tragic, for the sense of tragedy was lost in the moral collapse of the period he lived in. Like Chekhov – but only in this respect – he was appalled by the banality of urban civilisation. Instead of being tragic, life was terrible, meaningless and without dignity. Mr Alan Ross, in a warm, if sometimes difficult, introduction to a volume containing all four of West's novels, makes this point and suggests that while the English writers of the Thirties reached their conclusions 'through a series of well-bred intellectual convictions', Americans like West were thrown helplessly among the brute economic facts. For them the experience was emotional and even theatrically so, because hysterical violence is very near the surface in American life.

West's resources were Art – he learned from the surrealists – and compassion. Except in his satire, *A Cool Million*, which is an American *Candide* done in the manner of a parody too obvious and prolonged, he was not a political writer in the literal sense. He explored the illness behind the political situation. Human beings have always fought misery with dreams, Miss Lonelyhearts observes; the dream and its ignoble deceits, the panic, anger and frustration these deceits expose, gave him his material. In *The Day of the Locust*, his mature novel, it is the boredom exposed by the failure of the Californian dream of an earthly Paradise that puts an expression of hate and destructiveness on the faces of the weary middle-aged population who have retired to Los Angeles. As they pour in to gape at the stars arriving for some world première, they have the look of lynchers. Lynch, in fact, they do, and for no reason.

This does not convey that West is a comic writer. He has freakishness, wit and a taste for the absurd from the surrealists, also their sophistication in parody and styles, but moved quickly away from their gratuitous and perverse humour. He became comic and humane. *Miss Lonelyhearts* is a potent and orderly distillation of all the attitudes to human suffering. Miss Lonelyhearts himself is the drunken writer of an advice column in a newspaper who begins running it as a joke, a sort of sobbing *Americana*, and ends by becoming overwhelmed by the weight of human misery and by his inability to do anything about it. The office gambits sicken him. Christ, Art, the Karamazov line, the Value of Suffering, back to Nature, on to Hedonism and so on have been taped long ago by Shrike, the editor with the deadpan face, an expert in 'how to play it'. Shrike is one of West's many attacks on the dream-generators of the mass-media – an attack in the sense of being one of those unholy recognitions that lie at the centre of the comic view of life:

'I am a great saint,' Shrike cried. 'I can walk on my own water. Haven't you heard of Shrike's passion in the Luncheonette, or the Agony in the Soda Fountain? Then I compared the wounds in Christ's body to the mouths of a miraculous purse in which we deposit the small change of our sins. It is an excellent conceit. But now let us consider the holes in our own bodies and into what these congenital wounds open. Under the skin of a man is a wondrous jungle where veins like lush tropical growths hang along overripe organs and weed-like entrails writhe in squirming tangles of red and yellow. In this jungle, flitting from rock grey lungs to golden intestines, from liver to lights and back to liver again, lives a bird called the soul.'

In the vulgar, exhausted way of the mass media, deadpan Shrike is an aesthete. His jaunty little face looks like a paralysed scream of fright. His remarks are pictorial, but without relation to any meaning. Miss Lonelyhearts is muddled by Shrike's cleverness. He would like to be able to believe in the efficacy of Christ, but the name for him has become another word for hysteria, 'a snake whose scales are tiny mirrors in which the dead world takes on a semblance of life'. He plowters through a series of alcoholic bouts, tries to seduce Shrike's

cold and salacious wife, gets into fights in speakeasies, terrorises and
tries to torture an old man in a public lavatory; for Miss Lonelyhearts has strong sadistic fantasies, his pity has a strain of cruelty in it
and he has begun to hate the sufferers who have the tempting horror
of freaks. He is seduced by the nymphomaniac wife of a cripple, tries
illness, love on a farm. These struggles are fuddled but heroic; he
feels his 'great heart' is a bomb that 'will wreck the world without
rocking it'. In the end he has a vision of the love of Christ and rushes
to tell his friend the cripple about it; but the cripple shoots him in a fit
of jealousy. Christ may not be hysteria, but he is a tale told by an
idiot.

This might have been a slushy book, the derelict lot behind James
Barrie's hoardings. It is, instead, a selection of hard, diamond-fine
miniatures, a true American fable. West writes very much by the eye
and his use of poetic images has a precision which consciously
sustains his preoccupation with the human being's infatuation with
his dream and inner story. (All his people are spiders living in the
webs they spin out of their minds.) Leaves on trees are like thousands
of little shields, a woman's breasts are like 'pink-tipped thumbs', a
thrush sings like a 'flute choked with saliva', a cripple limps along
'making waste motions, like those of a partially destroyed insect'. If
we call *Miss Lonelyhearts* a minor star it is because we feel that the
Art is stronger than the passion; that, indeed Miss Lonelyhearts
himself is capable only of pathos. His advice to the nymphomaniac
who is torturing her husband, to 'let him win once', is just wise old
owlishness; her happiness is to accuse and torture, his to drag his
loaded foot. West has not considered that human beings overwhelmingly prefer suffering to happiness and that their sobbing letters are
part of the sense of the role or drama that keeps them going. Still, as a
performance, *Miss Lonelyhearts* is very nearly faultless.

The Day of the Locust is an advance from fable and from
fragments of people, to the courageous full statement of the novel. I
say 'courageous' because in this kind of transition the writer has to
risk showing the weakness of his hand. The artificial lights of the
freak show are off in this book and we see human absurdity as
something normal. This is a novel about Hollywood. West worked
in the hum of the American dream generators and he chose those
people who have done more for American culture than their coevals
in Europe have done for theirs: the casualties, the wrecks, the
failures, the seedy and the fakes. They are the people to whom the

leisureless yea-sayers have said 'No'. The observer is a painter from the East who is dreaming up what sounds like a very bad picture, a sort of Belshazzar's Feast. (He is a vestige of West, the aesthete.) He has fallen for Faye, a day-dreaming creature who secretly earns money as a call-girl for a 'cultured' brothel, and who hopes, like others in the novel, to get into pictures. She lives among a ramshackle group which includes old stage hangers-on, a ferocious dwarf, a woman who is grooming her son to be a wonder-child of the screen, an absurd, fairly genuine cowboy extra and a pathetic hotel clerk from the Middle West. Faye is carefully observed. She is the complete day-dreamer, insulated to such an extent by the faculty that it acts as an effective alternative to innocence; she is sexually provoking, cold, little-minded and cruel, but puts gaiety into the roles she takes on and has the survival power of a cork in a storm. If Los Angeles were destroyed by fire she would easily survive, not because she is hard but because she is flimsy. Already, in *Miss Lonelyhearts*, West had been a delicate student of the American bitch.

The Hollywood novel is mature because the compassion has no theatrical pressure; because now West is blocking in a sizable society, and because his gift for inventing extraordinary scenes has expanded. The novel is dramatised – in Henry James's sense of the word – in every detail, so that each line adds a new glint to the action. His sadistic streak comes out in an astonishing description of an illegal cockfight in a desert lot. His comic powers fill out in the scenes with the angry dwarf and in the pages where the hero gets lost in a film Battle of Waterloo. The psychological entangling is brought to an appalling climax when Faye leaves her exhausted hotel clerk for a Mexican and this leads on to the great final staging of the world première, where riot and lynching are sparked off by the wonder boy of the screen and the hate behind the Californian myth comes out:

> Once there, they discover that sunshine is not enough. They get tired of oranges, even of avocado pears and passion fruit. Nothing happens. They haven't the mental equipment for leisure, the money nor the physical equipment for pleasure. . . Their boredom becomes more and more terrible. They realise that they have been tricked and burn with resentment. Every day of their lives they read the newspapers and go to the movies. Both feed them on lynchings, murder, sex crimes, explosions, wrecks, love nests, fires, miracles, revolutions, war. This daily diet makes sophisticates of them. The sun is a joke. Oranges can't titillate their jaded palates. Nothing can be violent enough to make taut their slack minds and bodies.

It was a warning against Fascism; it makes the witch-hunt understandable; by extension, it is a statement about the nearness of violence in American life.

The Day of the Locust has the defect of insufficient ambition. It calls for a larger treatment and we have a slight suspicion that the painter-observer is slumming. And West had not the breath for full-length works. Script-writing snaps up the clever. His important contribution to the American novel was his polished comedy, which he displayed with the variety of a master and on many levels. If his talent was not sufficiently appreciated in the moral Thirties, it was because comedy as a world in itself and as a firm rejection of the respected was not understood. West had something of Europe in him, where it is no crime to know too much.

(1962)

The Con-man's Shadow

Humorists have a hard life. As a matter of habit the reader comes round to saying, 'I don't think he's funny any more', the point being that life is so unfunny that the pace gets hotter with every joke. There is the inborn feeling that the humorist is a temporary fellow. A jester must not be allowed to approach the norm. He has to divert you from the intolerable or make you digest it. The difficulty is that while stomach-ache becomes funnier the worse it gets, the stomach-ache genre becomes standardised. In her introduction to *The Most of S. J. Perelman* Dorothy Parker says of humorists in general that they find a little formula and 'milk it till it moos with pain'. Her list is rather more American than European: 'the tyrannical offspring, the illiterate business associate (American), the whooping devil-may-care spinster, the man trying to do a bit of carpentry and the virtuous criticisms of the little wife, mainly European.' The virtuous wife in America is outsize: she arrives home grandiose, in mink, to take hell out of the husband who has burned the dinner. As S. J. Perelman, or rather his stand-in Prebbleman, remarks of his Xanthippe, she has the classical, martyred look of someone who would be 'a wow as St Joan at a Little Theatre.'

The one or two English humorists I have met have been sad men, anxious of eye, hag-ridden by efficiency of mind, mechanically ulcerated and teetering on the edge of religious conversion or the hospital. Their writings have usually contradicted this impression. The English thin man has a fat man inside him, a creature dilatory, sedentary and nourishing his joke, often over-nourishing it. Our humorists have mostly been juicy men dwelling in the belly of society; or, if this was not possible for them, have become mad cherubs like Carroll or Lear. The one general characteristic of the English humorists, good or bad, is that they are at home, dreaming private follies or shut up under lock and key in the attic, but still in the family. There is a profound satisfaction in the perils of the public face. Even if the family rejects, the pubs and clubs accept. The clubs, alas, in the older generation, have been a disaster for English humour; there it falls into persiflage. The best Americans escape this. Homelessness and the nomadic – as Miss Constance Rourke instructed us in her classic work on *American Humour* – are basic to the American tradition. So is overstatement, that Elizabethan gift which we carelessly exported lock, stock and barrel to America. So is the monologue which has been left, by us, to the Irish – see Beckett and Joyce. Our humorists – even Saki and Anstey – have had good digestions, the joke with them being that they knew that they bloody well *had* to digest what was given to them and put a peculiar face on it. Less subjected to the pressures of a dense society, Americans have had the freedom to send up howls of enjoyable pain at the raw muck set before them and instead of being digressive they have put a poker face on their duodenums. The elongated joke has been important to both traditions, but this has worked to the advantage of the American humorist who relies so much on monologue; the European cult of conversation may inspire refinement in comedy but is likely to comb all the nits out of the hair. The American monologue leaves the nits in. It can also dip into myth and, to be endurable, this has to be enlivened by image and pungency of language. In England, since the decline of the joke of middle-class periphrasis, we are only just beginning to explore exaggeration again; and at the very moment when American humour shows some signs of becoming middle-class, the sick joke being fundamentally suburban.

The huge advantage of American humour, as one sees it in S. J. Perelman, is in the punishment of character and the use of language. Unlike Thurber who has been much admired by us, Perelman is not an understater who suddenly throws out an almost spiritual blossom. He drops ash into the dessert. Perelman either grew up with burlesque or soon got caught up in it. Immediate action is his need. An idea has to seize him. His very best things have come out of grotesque experiences in Hollywood; or when, not having enough time to read Palgrave's *Golden Treasury*, he has had to feed on the advertising columns of glossy papers. One gets the impression that English humorists snub the commercials, whereas an American like Perelman regards them as part of the general awful meal that makes us what we don't want other people to be. Having acquired a stomach of zinc, he knows it's his duty to swallow the poison, like someone who feels it a duty to see what cyanide does to the system. As a character, he is a harassed detective, stuck in some lobby, chain-smoking, pedantic, always in disguise, with the air of one about to follow footprints and tracking something down. He is Groucho Marx's more sensitive alter ego, the con-man's shadow. What one owes to the other, apart from cigars, may be conjectured from Groucho's letters – especially those to Kurnitz – which are very funny about Hollywood. The T. S. Eliot letters suffer, on both sides, from the paralysis which occurs when a highest common factor meets a lowest common denominator and both are awed. On the evidence, Perelman's life has been passed in film studios, dressing rooms, cigar stores, hotels, tailors, barbers, steak grottoes and in bad journeys on inferior shipping lines to the phoney Orient. He will be caught – trying to hide behind *Time* or *Harper's Bazaar* – by acquaintances with names like Spontoon, Henbane, Follansbee and Crump who, spotting his lonely but springy figure, have treated him like flypaper and have buzzed in an ear made for higher things. He has been the sort of man who having, for the moment, to identify himself with a No 1 Stripteaseuse who has married a young Maharajah, can say that 'although she had little need of paper work in her line of business', she is obliged to be 'the only ecdysiast on record with a Zoroastrian amanuensis'. The phrase is her agent's. She breaks it down into the following:

A skinny little man with a big bugle on which one flange has a diamond the size of your pinkie welded into it. He has a shift embroided with rubies and around his neck five strands of pearls like Mary Garden or Schumann-Heink in the Victor Book of Opera.

Flustered by the pass he makes at her after this aesthetic impression, she asks what about his family in Cawnpore. 'Don't you,' she asks, 'have any wives?' It is at the centre of this tradition of American humour to build up a rococo fantasy and then slap its face with a wet towel. Mr Perelman has that art. Many a gorgeous balloon goes 'pop' at the touch of his cigar tip. Occasionally, under the name of Prebbleman, he is at home, usually minding something in the oven and waiting for his Joan of Arc to come back, rather late, in something new and blinding, and full of complaint. He defends himself: 'I haven't the faintest clue to what you're foompheting about.' Wherever else he may fail it is not in adding a valuable word to the gag book. And he is soon off to a sentimental reunion of the old alumni of Dropsical High. There the old folk are 'acquiring a skinful' wearing paper hats, clutching phials of adrenalin, nitroglycerin and other restoratives.

Again the puncturing anti-climax: 'I give them a wide berth because they may topple on to me during a seizure and wrinkle my suit.' The noise is deafening. In it one hears 'the clash of bridge work and the drum fire crackle of arteries snapping like pipe stems'; the chief speaker, recovering from his third stroke, has a voice that 'ripples from his tongue as if strained across an entire creek of gravel'.

Perelman's speciality, like O. Henry's and Mark Twain's, is Fraud. He looks at the landscape and it is gashed and bill-boarded with the poetic news that here someone made a killing and cleared out quickly. The inner life of a grey Puritan culture is dramatic, gaudy and violent; fraud, in the sense of the double-think, double appearance or fact and the image that palms them off, is basic. The tall story, wearisome in Europe, so that a Münchausen is a bore and a meaningless liar who wastes your time, has a more nourishing role in the American tradition. Fantasy – in English comics – has a different part to play. The distinction is suggested by comparing the extravagances of, say, Dickens with those of the O. Henry, Twain and Perelman school. The speeches of Mrs Gamp or Mr Pecksniff are, in essence, soliloquies that fountain out of their inner lives. They tell us less about the scene in which they live than about the privacies of their minds and of their history. The flights of a Carroll, a Lear, a Beerbohm, an Anstey or a Wodehouse reject the oppressive scene around them and assert the rights of private vision in a culture which has generally been obsessed – as John Stuart Mill said – with the necessity of a social discipline. The exaggerations of the American humorists have a different impulse. If you look at their greedy use of the grotesque, you see that they are guzzling impedimenta and namable products. You hardly see the people there but you see American paraphernalia; their metaphors take you on to the joints or to what is happening semi-legally on the sidewalk. Chicken Inspector No 23 Perelman of the Fraud Squad surveys the field of conspicuous waste, the biggest fraud of the lot, with a buyer's hypnotised eye. He is the un-innocent abroad; at his best in the subjects of showbiz, he is a tangy raconteur, though I find him less speedy when he turns his idea into a script with dialogue. This is odd since he has been one of the finest script writers in the funny business; indeed, remembering the Marx Brothers, a genius. He is above all a voice, a brisk and cigary voice, that keeps up with his feet as he scampers, head-down upon the trail; in his own words 'button-cute, rapier-keen and pauper poor' and having 'one of those rare mouths in which butter has never melted'. He has a nose for non-news. For a long time the English humorists have suffered from having achieved the funny man's dream; they have either gone straight for the information or have succumbed to the prosaic beauty of their own utterance. They are 'facetious' without being Boswell. Mr Perelman is not entirely free of the English vice. I have caught him adding an unnecessary, 'I said with hauteur' or 'I said with dignity'. This weakness he may have picked up on his annual visits to those fake cathedral closes of ours in Savile Row. (The metaphor is his.) But he does not wear thin. There are four or five narky things in the present book which are as good as anything in *Crazy Like a Fox*.

(1967)

Sofa and Cheroot

When we ask ourselves what the heroes of novels did with themselves in their spare time, a hundred to a hundred and fifty years ago, there can be no hesitation in the answer. Novel after novel confirms it, from *Tom Brown at Oxford* back to Fielding and Smollett: they stretched themselves on a sofa, lit a cheroot and picked up again *The Adventures of Gil Blas*. Once more they were on the road with that hopeful young valet from the Asturias as he went from town to town in Old Castile in the reign of Philip IV, always involved in the love affairs and the money secrets of his employers, until, a model of Self-Help, he enters the valet-keeping classes himself and becomes secretary to the Prime Minister. Say your prayers (his loving parents advised him when he set out for the University of Salamanca which he never reached, at least not to become a student), avoid bad company, and above all keep your fingers out of other people's property. Gil Blas ignored this good advice from the beginning and returned home at last to a benign retirement as a rich man and a noble. Not exactly a sinner, not exactly virtuous, Gil Blas is a kind of public statue to what we would call the main chance and to what the Spaniards call *conformidad* or accepting the world for what it is and being no better than your neighbour.

English taste has always been responsive to Le Sage; his influence on English writers and his vogue were far greater among us than they were in France. Defoe probably read him; Smollett translated and copied him. Le Sage became the intermediary between ourselves and that raw, farcical, sour, bitter picaresque literature of Spain which, for some reason, has always taken the English fancy. Gil Blas took the strong meat of the rogues' tales and made it palatable for us. He put a few clothes on the awful, goose-fleshed and pimpled carnality of Spanish realism, disguised starvation as commercial anxiety, filled the coarse vacuum, which the blatant passions of the Spaniards create around them, with the rustle and crackle of intrigue. We who live in the north feel that no man has the right to be so utterly stripped of illusions as the Spaniard seems to be; Gil Blas covered that blank and too virile nakedness, not indeed with illusions, but with a degree of elegance. It was necessary. For though the picaresque novel appealed to that practical, empirical, rule-of-thumb strain in the English mind, to that strong instinct of sympathy we have for an ingenious success story – and all picaresque novels are really unholy success stories – we have not the nervous system to stand some of the things the Spaniards can stand. What is *Lazarillo de Tormes*, the most famous of the picaresque novels, but the subject of starvation treated as farce? We could never make jokes about starvation.

Compared to the real Spanish thing, *Gil Blas* is a concoction which lacks the native vividness. It belongs to the middle period of picaresque literature when the rogue has become a good deal of the puritan. Historically this transition is extraordinarily interesting. One could not have a clearer example of the way in which the form and matter of literature are gradually fashioned by economic change in society. The literature of roguery which Le Sage burgled for the compilation of *Gil Blas* is the fruit of that economic anarchy which early capitalism introduced into Spanish life. In England the typical character of the period is the puritan; in Spain his opposite number is the man who has to live by his wits. A system has broken down, amid imperialist war and civil revolt, poverty has become general among those who rely on honest labour. There is only one way for the energetic to get their living. They can rush to the cities and especially to the Court and help themselves to the conquered wealth of the New World, to that wealth or new money which has brought poverty to the rest of the population by destroying the value of the old money. I am not sure how far economists would confirm the generalisation, but it seems that Spain used foreign conquest and the gold of the New World to stave off the introduction of private capitalism, and the parallel with Nazi policy is close. At any rate, instead of the successful trader, Spain produces the trader frustrated, in other words, the rogue.

They are, of course, both aspects of the same kind of man, and that is one of the reasons why Defoe and English literature got so much out of the picaresque novel, so that it is hard to distinguish between Defoe's diligent nonconformists and his ingenious cheats and gold-diggers. Gil Blas himself represents the mingling of the types. He is not many hours on the road before he is adroitly flattered and cheated. It is the first lesson of the young and trusting go-getter in the ways of the world. Until he gets to Madrid his career is one long list of disasters. He is captured by robbers, robbed by cocottes in the jewel racket. The hopeful young man on the road to an estimable career at the university is soon nothing but a beggar and is well on the way to becoming a knave by the time he sets up in partnership with a provincial quack doctor. Madrid really saves him from the louder kinds of crime. Intrigue is, he learns, far more remunerative. He goes from one household to another as a valet, filling his pockets as he goes. The knave has given place to the young man with an eye for a good situation and whose chief social ambition is to become a *señorito* or *petit maître*, extravagantly dressed and practising the gaudy manners of the innumerable imitators of the aristocracy. No one is more the new bourgeois than Gil Blas – especially in his great scorn for the bourgeois. And there is something very oily about him. How careful he is to worm his way into his master's confidence so that he may become a secretary and rake off small commissions or in the hope that he will be left something in the old man's will! Much later, by his attention to duty, he becomes a secretary to a Minister, and sells offices and pockets bribes. What of it? – he is no worse, he says, than the Minister himself, or the heir to the throne who has dirty money dealings all round, or those old ladies who pose as aristocrats in order to palm off their daughters on wealthy lovers. There is a sentence describing an old actress which puts Gil Blas's ambition in a nutshell. She was 'Une de ces héroïnes de galanterie qui savent plaire jusque dans leur vieillesse et qui meurent chargées des depouilles de deux ou trois générations'.

'To be loaded with the spoils' – that is very different from the fate of the real *picaro* of the earlier dispensation, and Gil Blas is not entirely cynical about it. 'After all' (he seems to say, his eyes sharp with that frantic anxiety which still exercises Spaniards when there is a question of money), 'after all, I worked for it, didn't I? I served my master's interest? I'm a *sort* of honest man.' And when he decides to keep a valet of his own and interviews the applicants, there is a charm in the way he rejects the one who has a pious face and picks out one who has been a bit of a twister too.

The character of Gil Blas himself could hardly be the attraction of Le Sage's book, and indeed he is little more than a lay figure. The pleasures of picaresque literature are like the pleasures of travel.

There is continuous movement, variety of people, change of scene. The assumption that secret self-interest, secret passions, are the main motives in human conduct does not enlarge the sensibility – Le Sage came before the sensibility of the eighteenth century awakened – but it sharpens the wits, fertilises invention and enlarges gaiety. But again, the book is poor in individual characters. One must get out of one's head all expectation of a gallery of living portraits. Le Sage belonged to the earlier tradition of Molière and Jonson and fore-shadowed creations like Jonathan Wild: his people are types, endeared to us because they are familiar and perennial. You get the quack, the quarrelling doctors fighting over the body of the patient, the efficient robber, the impotent old man and his young mistress, the blue-stocking, the elderly virgin on the verge of wantonness, the man of honour, the jealous man, the poet, the actress, the courtier. Each is presented vivaciously, with an eye for self-deception and the bizarre. The story of the Bishop of Granada has become the proverbial fable of the vanity of authors. And that scene in the Escorial when the Prime Minister, in order to impress the King and the Court, takes his secretary and papers out into the garden and pretends to be dictating though he is really gossiping, is delicious debunking of that rising type – the big business man.

The pleasure of *Gil Blas* is that it just goes on and on in that clear, exact, flowing style which assimilates the sordid, the worldly, or the fantastic romance with easy precision, unstrained and unperturbed. It is the pleasure of the perfect echo, the echo of a whole literature and of a period. You are usually smiling, sometimes you even laugh out loud; then boredom comes as one incident clutches the heels of another and drags it down. No one can read the novel of adventure for adventure's sake to the end; and yet, put *Gil Blas* down for a while, and you take it up again. It is like a drug. Self-interest, the dry eye, the low opinion, the changing scene, the ingenuity of success, the hard grin of the man of the world – those touch something in our natures which, for all our romanticism and our idealism, have a weakness for the *modus vivendi*. The puritan and the rogue join hands.

(1942)

HONORÉ DE BALZAC

La Cousine Bette

Those who admired the careful dramatisation of Balzac's *Cousin Bette* must have noted that television is always at home with the novels of the nineteenth century. These novels are bold and orderly in structure; the descriptive passages, often boring to the reader are valuable to producers; the moral drama can be gutted. Easy to do Balzac and Henry James; impossible to handle *To the Lighthouse* without upsetting sacred technical habits. There was a repressed dramatist in most of the nineteenth-century novelists whose theatrical impulses had to be steam-rolled into narrative prose because the novel had replaced theatre as the dominant literary form. So, given taste and tact, the script-writer has found it simple to extract the drama without seriously gutting the book. But if we assume that only a few of the viewers have read or will ever read *Cousin Bette* the question is: what will they have missed?

The voice of the author, of course, and in Balzac's work this is a tremendous loss. It was – as many of his contemporaries thought – a rather loud, pushing, incessant voice; though others found that its powers of story-telling, wit and fantasy, and its energy, imposed an irresistible spell. The voice of Balzac performs. It changes like an actor's. It is sanguine, sceptical, sensible in a blunt way, ready with the rash generalisation, the journalistic caricature; it easily contorts the larynx in passages of lurid melodrama and absurd hyperbole, and yet passes without a blush to asides that may be caustic, shameless or tender. It is a voice bursting with a non-stop interest in whatever his eye catches and the guesses of his own genius. Above all it is personally intrusive: Balzac bustles in among his characters and stops the action to explain to their faces that they are specimens taken out of a natural history of society; and performs the double feat of classifying their social type and of allegorising their inner lives. Balzac, without his 'Voici pourquoi ...' – the famous

explanatory phrase that comes out at all turning points of his story –
would lose all *his* point.

Cousin Bette and its companion piece *Cousin Pons* stand a little
outside the planned scheme of the *Comédie Humaine*. They
represent an astonishing renewal of his genius, at the penultimate
crisis of his life. His mortal illness had begun to get its grip on him;
the hopes of marriage to Madame Hanska had been set back once
more; he had plunged maniacally into larger debts as he speculated
with her money in railway shares; with something like insanity, he
was spending fortunes on antiques – the subject of *Cousin Pons*. He
felt the competition of Eugène Sue as a rising popular novelist, and he
suddenly found the energy to break new ground. Or rather, the
energy to go back to unfinished work and to see it in the light of a new
vision. In three years, at the age of fifty-one, he would be dead. These
two novels represent what every artist hopes to achieve: a revival and
crowning of the imagination. One can believe they contain a personal assertion. *Cousin Bette* is the study of a poor relation's jealousy
turning into a will to revenge that seeks to destroy a whole family. To
achieve this Bette has to see that the elderly Baron Hulot – her rich
cousin's husband – is put in the way of ruining himself and the family
by pouring out his fortune and indeed robbing government funds, in
order to keep a courtesan. The ruin is accomplished. A virtuous wife
is reduced to misery. Bette, the 'monstrous virgin', is triumphant.
Certainly, before the end of the story, the family is reunited, at any
rate until the last page but one. The courtesan dies a horrible death,
Bette dies, the wife herself dies; but the Baron, senile but still sexually
insatiable, lives on. A villain? No; deplorable, out of control, a victim
of history, always engaging, almost decent, but one endowed – if that
is the word – with an animality he cannot contain. The Baron is far
from being Balzac, but he does seem to be a Balzacian protest on
behalf of the revived life-force in Balzac, a protest against approaching extinction.

There is another, less speculative point to make when we consider
the expansion of Balzac's creative ingenuity in this novel: he moved
his story forward and nearer than had been his habit, to the time of
writing. In 'modernising' – that is to say in moving further away
from the Napoleonic shadow and figures of the Regency except to
mock them – and turning to the domestic complacencies of the reign
of Louis Philippe, he refreshed himself. Adeline is the Baron's
virtuous Catholic wife, but her virtue is timorous, Crevel is the

parvenu shopkeeper who had once worked for Birotteau, the per-fumer who wrecked himself by speculation in property. Crevel is too cunning for that. He suddenly wants to be a gentleman. He accepts that, at his age, love costs 30,000 francs a year. He plunges for Madame Marneffe because he imagines she is 'a lady' and can teach him fashionable manners. So she can, but maliciously: he wants to be 'Regency' and she well knows that is out of date. He also wants a revenge at Hulot's expense because Hulot is a Baron. Madame Marneffe knows that the new early-Victorian morality requires moral, indeed remorseful religious airs from its courtesans; and Crevel justifies keeping her by telling himself that, as a widower, he is still respectable because of his passionate affection for his daughter. When he is desperate for money, Hulot turns to the new colonial booty in Algeria – another morally topical theme. Hulot had been a good husband when he was a Napoleonic soldier, but after Napoleon's fall he is without serious occupation beyond a nominal job in the bureaucracy. He has lost the dignity of a profession. Idleness, in short, leads him to the pursuit of women. So the disquisitional Balzac who hands out shrewd, journalistic statements on the servant problem, the need for married women to keep their husbands by becoming the wife-mistress, the difference between artists and would-be artists, creates the new age of domesticity and corruption. The descriptions of furniture which have caused many groans among Balzac's readers, now become malign and interesting. The furniture of Crevel has failed to climb as fast as its owner:

The candelabra, the fire-dogs, the fender, the chandelier, the clock, were all in the most unmeaning style of scroll-work; the round table, a fixture in the middle of the room, was a mosaic of fragments of Italian and antique marble, brought from Rome where these dissected maps are made of mineralogical specimens – for all the world like tailor's patterns ... The bedroom, smart with chintz, also opened out of the drawing room. Mahogany in all its glory infested the dining room, and Swiss views, gorgeously framed, graced the panels. Crevel, who hoped to travel in Switzerland, had set his heart on possessing the scenery in painting until the time should come when he might see it in reality ... Everything was as spick and span as the beetles in an entomological case.

The differences between the furnishings at Madame Marneffe's love-nest and at Josépha's – the opera singer – are sharply marked; also the cost, of course. When Adeline calls nervously on Josépha to see if his ex-mistress knows where the Baron has fled after his downfall, the scene is masterly, for although genuinely moved by Adeline's

misery, the actress cannot resist playing contrition and kindness as a
new role with the skill of an artist:

Like those worthy folk who take men of genius to be a sort of monsters,
eating and drinking, walking unlike other people, the Baroness had hoped to
see Josépha the opera singer, the witch, the amorous and amusing courtesan:
she saw a calm and well-mannered woman, with the dignity of talent, the
simplicity of an actress who knows herself to be at night a queen, and also,
better than all, a woman of the town whose eyes, attitude and demeanour
paid full and ungrudging homage to the virtuous wife, the *mater dolorosa* of
the sacred hymn . . .

She made a charming bouquet for her 'as the Madonna is crowned in
Italy'. Yet this respectable Josépha had thrown Hulot out noisily for
a richer lover years before, and had called him an 'old popgun' when
he crawled back to her for help. And when she heard the enormity of
his behaviour she had cried out: 'Well, I admire that. It's a general
flare-up! It is Sardanapalus! Splendid, thoroughly complete . . . I tell
you I like a spendthrift, like you, crazy over a woman . . .' for, she
says, *he* has ruined only those who belonged to him, whereas the
calculating bankers, speculating in railways, are ruining hundreds of
families every day. We see, after such scenes, the pathetic inadequacy
of Adeline's cry to her husband when he comes home to confess; 'Let
me try to be an amusement to you'. The cry is all the more heart-
rending for being ridiculous: the passive, mundane characters have
not the imagination to grasp the force or the artistry of the obsessed.

   With his rather endearing pretentiousness Balzac thought of his
story as a tragedy in the manner of Racine. He certainly overdoes the
'sulphurous' and 'infernal' when he describes Bette's diabolical
jealousy. He is even absurd about it in his melodramatic way: virgins
are monsters in their desire for power and vengeance. The only
acceptable virgin is the Virgin Mary and for a moment, it looks as
though he is going to dash off a sermonette on the subject. If he did
he, luckily, cut it. (He was getting his own back – it is thought – on
Madame Hanska's Aunt Rosalie, who was succeeding only too well
in delaying his marriage.) He half convinces us that jealousy so long
repressed will certainly be appalling when it turns to action; what is
hard to believe is that it will be consistent and continuous in its
plotting. But Cousin Bette is a peasant and, as he says, the passions of
peasants last for life; they are ruled by a single idea. And Balzac –
often blamed for not being subtle as a psychologist – was surely
brilliant in one respect: he perceived that plotters like Bette will work

in secret through a third party, like Madame Marneffe, and all the more passionately because the relationship is a good deal erotic.

Balzac can be relied on to rescue himself from total melodrama by his curiosity about the recesses of human nature: the impartial doctor supplants the declamatory actor. The story is indeed no tragedy by Racine. It contains several comedies that flow from one to the other and set one another off. The relationship of Hulot and Crevel makes a farce by Molière, as Balzac well knew. There is an ostensible moral lesson, but in fact no one is shown to be perfect – not even, as he said, the virtuous. His texture is rich if coarse in the weaving because he is an endless questioner, insensitive but hurrying to the next turn of the screw so that we forget to question him. One gets attached to his comic pretensions, as when he shows off about painting and sculpture and furniture or about literature – Bette, he says, could have been an Iago or even Richard III – not to mention his entomology, phrenology, his animal magnetism, his weakness for a word like 'sublime' – a cant word of the period – and for phrases like 'incredible perfection'. Balzac was a greedy man. As he revised his proofs a dozen times, throwing in more and more, he could not resist swelling his invention and yet also refining it. But when he wrote *Cousin Bette* and its companion *Cousin Pons* he was able to rise above the disastrous confusion of his private desires and attain a kind of serenity as a gourmand artist. He often spoke of the artist's right to revenge. In this effusive pessimist the idea of vengeance was obsessional. *Cousin Bette* is about nothing else.

(1973)

And Lelia

The spell imposed by George Sand on European and Russian readers and critics in the nineteenth century is understandable; her people and landscapes are silhouettes seen in streams of sheet lightning. For ourselves, what has been left is her notorious life story and the throbbing of her powerful temperament. Yet Balzac, Dostoevsky and – of all people – Matthew Arnold admired her as a novelist. Proust admired her sinuous and gliding prose and Flaubert her exotic imagination. There she was pouring out ink in her sixty novels, her enormous autobiography, her works of travel and her thousands of letters; a thinking bosom and one who overpowered her young lovers; all sibyl, teacher, a Romantic, and, in the end, a respectable Victorian moralist.

There were hostile voices of course. As Curtis Cate reminds us in his exhaustive biography published four years ago, Baudelaire burst out with an attack on what had most allured her admirers:

She has always been a moralist. Only, previously she had indulged in anti-morality. She has thus never been an artist. She has the famous flowing style dear to the bourgeois. She is stupid, she is ponderous, she is long-winded: she has in moral judgments the same depth of judgment and the same delicacy of feeling as concierges and kept women.

(These last two words are wildly wrong: one thing she certainly was not was a pampered courtesan. She spent the large sums of money she earned extravagantly and a large part in charity.) Shuddering at her candour Henry James was closer to her in his judgement on her talents. Her novels, he said, had turned faint,

as if the image projected, not intense, not absolutely concrete – failed to reach completely the mind's eye. . . The wonderful change of expression is not really a remedy for the lack of intensity, but rather an aggravation of it through a sort of suffusion of the whole thing by the voice and speech of the author. . . . [There is] a little too much of the feeling of going up in a balloon. We are borne by a fresh cool current and the car delightfully dangles, but as

we peep over the sides we see things – as we usually know them – at a
dreadful drop beneath.

The woman who was known for her gifts as a silent listener took to
the upper air when she shut herself up at night and became garrulous
in ink.

Now, it is evident, an attempt to draw the general reader back to
George Sand is under way. The most obvious reason for this is
opportunism of the women's liberation kind, where she is bound to
be a disappointment to those who look for a guru. A disconcerting
sibyl she may have been; as a priestess she hedged. The Saint-
Simonians were discouraged when they tried to turn her into the Mrs
Eddy of free love. A more interesting lure to contemporary taste is
suggested by Diane Johnson in her introduction to the novelist's
edifying Gothic romance, *Mauprat*, written in the 1830s. Mrs
Johnson says that if George Sand's temperament was too strong for
her writing, temperament was her subject as an artist: '. . . readers
have come to hold in new high regard the truths of the imagination,
the romantic principle, the idea that the passionate artist had access
to truths and secrets of human nature more interesting than mere
dramas of social arrival.'

Gothic melodrama is back with us, if in dank condition, 'for
reasons best understood today in terms of psychology, but understood very well by George Sand in universal terms.' (The universal is
the trouble.) It is true, at any rate, that the Romantics – especially
those of the second wave, the *Hernani* generation – set the artist
apart as the supreme seer in society; and that for all their extravagance of feeling and even because of it, they were excellent pre-
Freudian psychologists. Their very violence is a prediction and their
inflation of the ballooning self makes it dramatic and macroscopic.
We have to add that she is shamelessly autobiographical. The love
affair of the week, month or year, along with mysticism, socialism
and The People was transposed into the novel that promptly followed; she spoke of herself as 'the consumer' of men and women too,
and the men often turned out to be projections of herself. The
passions of her characters, their powerful jealousies, their alterna-
tions of exaltation and gloom, were her own. She was half Literature.

Her finer powers emerged when her fame as a novelist declined,
above all in her *Histoire de ma vie*, in her lively travel writing and her
letters. In her letters there is no need of Gothic castles or dreadful
ravines: her mundane experience was extraordinary enough in itself.

As a traveller she had eyes, ears and verve. The short pastoral novels *La mare au diable* (*The Haunted Pool*) or *François le Champi* (*The Country Waif*) are serene masterpieces drawn from her childhood and her love of nature, which awakened her senses as they awakened Colette's. She was close to the peasants of Nohant. The self is in these tales, but it is recollected or transposed in tranquillity – in her own early life she had known what it was to be a waif, albeit a very fortunate one. These works have never lost their quiet, simple, truth-telling power and we understand why Turgenev, Henry James, and, later, Malraux praised them.

George Sand was the child of one of Napoleon's well-born officers. He was a descendant of the great Maréchal de Saxe and therefore, on the wrong side of the blanket, of the King of Poland. Her mother was a plebeian woman, the hot-tempered daughter of a Paris innkeeper and bird fancier. The inner class conflict enriched both George Sand's exuberant imagination and those sympathies with the poor which took her into radical politics; strangely like Tolstoy – but without his guilt or torment – she turned to presenting the peasantry not as quaint folk or a gospel, but as sentient, expressive beings. She listened to the curious Berrichon dialect and translated it, without folkish affectations or condescensions, into a truthful expression of plain human feeling. She had the humility and concern to discard dramatic earnestness without losing her psychological acumen or her art as a story teller who keeps her people in focus as the tradition of Pastoral does: very often her best work is a gloss on traditional forms.

In the feminist foreground of the present revival is *Lélia*, the confessional novel which she wrote at the age of twenty-nine in 1833 after the rebellion against her marriage, the break with Jules Sandeau, and the disastrous attempts to obtain sexual pleasure from an expert like Mérimée, or from any other man as far as we know. Chopin said she loved extremely but was incapable of making love. Partly because of its attacks on the Church and the marriage system, the male hold on property and the double standard, partly because of its erotic revelation and the rumour of a lesbian attachment to the actress Marie Dorval, the book itself was attacked for outrageous and morbid candour. Lélia is intended to be a Romantic heroine, a doomed but indomitable soul, one pursuing a mystical quest for spiritual love. She is beautiful, intellectual, independent, yet tormented by a sensuality that is nevertheless incapable of sexual happiness.

She cannot be a nun like Santa Teresa nor can she be a courtesan or married woman. The dreams of a poetically exalted adolescence have divorced the heart from the body. Literature has paralysed her. She says of a lover:

When I was near him I felt a sort of strange and delirious greed which, taking its source from the keenest powers of my intelligence, could not be satisfied by any carnal embrace. I felt my bosom devoured by an inextinguishable fire, and his kisses shed no relief. I pressed him in my arms with a superhuman force, and fell next to him exhausted, discouraged at having no possible way to convey to him my passion. With me desire was an ardour of the soul that paralysed the power of the senses before it awakened them. It was a savage fury that seized my brain and concentrated itself there exclusively. My blood froze, impotent and poor, before the immense soaring of my will . . .

When he was drowsy, satisfied, and at rest, I would lie motionless beside him. I passed many hours watching him sleep. He seemed so handsome to me! There was so much force and grandeur on his peaceful brow. Next to him my heart palpitated violently. Waves of blood mounted to my face. Then unbearable tremblings passed through my limbs. I seemed to experience again the excitation of physical love and the increasing turmoil of desire. I was violently tempted to awaken him, to hold him in my arms, and to ask for his caresses from which I hadn't yet known how to profit. But I resisted these deceiving entreaties of my suffering because I well knew it wasn't in his power to calm me.

The stone images of Catholic 'palaces of worship' give no comfort, for her imagination responds chiefly to the figurations of medieval nightmare: scaly serpents, hideous lizards, agonised chimeras and emblems of sin, illusion and suffering. Sublimation has two faces:

When the red rays of the setting sun played on their forms, I seemed to see their flanks swell, their spiny fins dilate, their faces contract into new tortures . . . While I contemplated these bodies engulfed in masses of stone, which the hand of neither man nor time had been able to dislodge, I identified myself with these images of eternal struggle between suffering and necessity, between rage and impotence.

The nightmares of the unconscious haunt the aspirant. And we are warned that when spring comes to stir the senses, all attempt to deny the calyx or the bud, by the study of botany, or to turn to science, will not annul the ferment of the imagination. As always in George Sand, poetic observation and imagery is rather fine: but the inevitable tutorial follows.

I take these passages from Maria Espinosa's translation. She has worked on the 1833 edition which George Sand toned down three years later. This early edition has not been done into English until now, and the version is remarkable for coming very close to the

resonant vocabulary and its extraordinary physical images. If there is
a loss it is because English easily droops into a near-evangelical tune;
our language is not made for operatic precisions and we have a
limited tradition of authorised hyperbole. Abstractions lose the
intellectual formality that has an exact ring in French.

It is important to remember, also, that George Sand's prose feeds
on a sensibility to music which dated from her childhood: she was
alert to all sounds in nature and to all delicacies and sonorities of
voice and instrument. (Her novels might be described as irresistible
overtures to improbable operas which are – as they proceed –
disordered by her didactic compulsion.) *Lélia*, I think, rises above
this, because it is so personal and arbitrary in its succession of sounds
and voices, and we are bounced into accepting the hyperbole as we
would be if it were sung, though we may be secretly bored by the
prolonging of the moans.

In *Lélia* we listen to five voices: there is the voice of Sténio, the
young poet lover whom Lélia freezes with Platonic love: she is an
exalted *allumeuse*; there is Trenmor, the elderly penitent gambler
and stoic – her analysis of the gambler's temperament is the best
thing in the book: George Sand was at heart a gambler – there is
Magnus, the fanatic priest who is made mad by the suppression of his
sexual desires and who sees Lélia as a she-devil; there is Pulchérie,
Lélia's sister, a genial courtesan living for sexual pleasure; and Lélia
herself, defeated by her sexual coldness, horrified by the marriage
bed, the mocker of a stagnant society, religion and the flesh. She is
sick with self-love and her desires approach the incestuous: she seeks
weak men who cannot master her, to whom she can be either a
dominating mother, sister or nurse.

In chorus these voices sing out the arguments for and against
spiritual love. As in opera, the plot is preposterous and scenes are
extravagant and end without warning. Pulchérie introduces a pagan
and worldly note and also – it must be said – the relief of more than a
touch of nature. She reminds the miserable Lélia of a charming
incident in their childhood when the beauty of Lélia troubled her as
they lay sleeping on the mossy bank dear to Romantic fiction.
Pulchérie says:

Your thick, black hair clung to your face, and the close curls tightened as if a
feeling of life had clenched them next to your neck, which was velvet with
shadow and sweat. I passed my fingers through your hair. It seemed to
squeeze and draw me toward you . . . In all your features, in your position, in

your appearance, which was more rigid than mine, in the deeper tint of your complexion, and especially in that fierce, cold expression on your face as you slept, there was something masculine and strong which nearly prevented me from recognising you. I found that you resembled the handsome young man with the black hair of whom I had just dreamed. Trembling, I kissed your arm. Then you opened your eyes, and your gaze penetrated me with shame . . . But, Lélia, no impure thought had even presented itself to me. How had it happened? I knew nothing. I received from nature and from God my first lesson in love, my first sensation of desire.

The scenes of Lélia's despair take place inevitably in an abandoned monastery, with its *débris* that suggest the horrors of death and the futility of existence. Lélia says: 'At times I tried to find release by crying out my suffering and anger. The birds of the night flew away terrified or answered me with savage wailings.' (Nature always responds to George Sand.) 'The noise echoed from vault to vault, breaking against those shaky ruins; and the gravel that slid from the rooftops seemed to presage the fall of the edifice on my head.' That gravel, it must be said, is excellent observation. Her comment is typically orchestral:

Oh, I would have wished it were so! I redoubled my cries, and those walls echoed my voice with a more terrible and heartrending sound. They [the ruins] seemed inhabited by legions of the damned, eager to respond and unite with me in blasphemy.

These terrible nights were followed by days of bleak stupor.

A scene of Oriental luxury was indispensable to the Romantics: the looting of Egypt was Napoleon's great gift to literature. There is the fantastic ball given by Prince Bambuccj in which lovers can disappear into boudoirs and artificial caves as busily as bees. The trumpets, one must say, acclaim the triumphs of fornication; they are gorgeously brazen in the lascivious scene; the perfumes are insidious. Pulchérie and Lélia are masked and Lélia plots to pass off Pulchérie as herself so that Sténio is deceived into thinking his cold mistress has relented. He awakens and is shattered by the deceit. He stands at the window of the palace and hears the voice of Lélia mocking him – in a somewhat classy way – from a pretty boat that floats by in the Asiatic lagoon. This is an operatic scene of a high order. Calamity, of course. Having tasted flesh, Sténio becomes a drunken debauchee and eventually commits suicide. If he starts, in real life, as the innocent Jules Sandeau, he ends as the drunken Musset. Magnus, the mad priest, is now sure that Lélia is possessed by a devil and strangles her.

With a rosary, of course. One recalls that Lélia has had fantasies of strangulation.

Lélia is a series of those self-dramatisations that break off as mood follows mood. She asks what God intended for men and women: whether he intended them to meet briefly and leave each other at once, for otherwise the sexes would destroy each other; whether the hypocrisy of a bourgeois society is the enemy; whether intellectual vision must be abnormal; whether poetry and religion corrupt. All the voices are George Sand herself – and very aware, as she frankly said, that she belonged to a generation which, for the moment, was consciously out to shock. What she did not expect was laughter. She had little sense of humour.

One can see how much of the book comes out of Hoffmann and even more precisely from Balzac's equally chaotic and melodramatic *La Peau de chagrin*. Lélia, it has often been noted, is the female Raphael de Valentin. Both writers feel the expanding energies of the new century; both have the confident impulse toward the Absolute and to Omniscience; but hers is the kind of imagination and intellect that breaks off before suggesting a whole. Balzac and Sand were both absorbed by an imaginative greed; they worked themselves to the bone, partly because they were like that, partly because they created debts and openly sought a vast public. Their rhetoric was a nostalgia for the lost Napoleonic glory.

How thoroughly she toiled in her social-problem novels! The tedious *Compagnon du Tour de France* is a garrulous study of the early trade unions, a politically pious book, enlivened by her strong visual sense. In the far more sympathetic *Mauprat* she goes to the heart of her life-long debt to Rousseau: the young brutal Mauprat who belongs to the brigand and mafioso branch of an aristocratic family rescues the aristocratic heroine from his gang – but with the intention of raping her on the quiet. She frustrates the attempt and is shown redeeming her brute: to love he must pass through a long psychological re-education. This is achieved but not entirely in a sentimental way; both he and the women are hot-tempered, sulky and sensitive to points of honour.

George Sand herself did not think we should be punished for our sins or our grave faults of character, but that we were called upon to learn from them: they were – *grâce à* Rousseau – opportunities for interesting self-education and reform. She is not a doctrinaire like Gorki in his Communist phase. Her advantage as a woman is that she is a psychologist who gives hostilities their emotional due: they are indications of the individual's right to his temperament. She may have been a domineering, ruthless woman and very cunning and double-minded with it, but there is scarcely a book that is not redeemed by her perceptions, small though they may be.

She understands the rich very well – 'There are hours of impunity in château life' – and she thinks of the poor as individuals but flinches from them as a case. Two words recur continually in her works: 'delirium', which may be ecstatic, bad, or, more interestingly, a psychological outlet; and 'boredom' – energy and desire had been exhausted. One can see that she is woman but not Woman. The little fable of *François de Champi* shows that she used every minute of her life; for not only was she in a fortunate sense a waif, as I have said, but an enlightened waif; and we note that when François grows up he marries the widow who has been a mother to him. Most of George Sand's men were waifs in one way or another; the Higher Incest was to be their salvation. Women were the real power figures, whereas men were consumable. She liked to pilfer their brains.

She certainly sought only gifted men who were usually sick and with whom she could assume the more powerful role of mother and nurse. Chopin was her 'child'. Sandeau was her 'little brother'. What about Michel de Bourges, her proletarian lawyer and Christian Communist, who almost converted her to the need for violent revolution and the guillotine? Here was a virile man, and he could offer oratory, notoriety, and powerful embraces, but he too was in bad health; she became frenzied – but was it the frenzy she desired? It may have been. She defiantly walked the streets of his native town in trousers and smoking her pipe, enjoyed the scandal, and caused scenes between him, his wife and his fat mistress. He was a tyrant, and one might think this was what she sought. Not at all. *She* could not dominate *him*; despite her passion for him, which drove her to ride for miles at night for a short, Chatterley-like tryst, he could not subdue the strongest thing in her – her intellect.

Michel de Bourges was responsible for her wordy novels of social revolt, but he could not break her opposition to the utilitarian view of art. Like all the Romantics, she believed in the vision of the artist as the unique and decisive spiritual force in society. He might dismiss all this as a self-regarding bourgeois delusion, but she would not yield. All the same, she wrote propaganda for the republican cause in 1848, and when the reaction came she handed out money to the hunted proletarian poets and took advantage of acquaintance with Louis Napoleon to get her friends and fellow-writers out of jail. In Nohant, she was a scandal because of her lovers. The villagers imagined orgies when the young men came and went. After 1848, she was a political scandal. The obsequious villagers touched their caps but sneered behind her back. This did not disturb her. She was a country girl at heart and knew that revolution was an urban industrial notion; in the countryside it meant nothing. And, in fact, the country crowd, particularly the women, took her side when the husband she had deserted made two savage and incompetent efforts in court to get Nohant from her.

This episode is thoroughly gone into by Mr Cate. It is important, for it brings out where she stood – or wobbled – on the crucial question of marriage and free love. The two court actions have the inevitable air of comedy: Michel de Bourges was her lover and her advocate, yet she had to appear respectable and demure. No trousers and no pipe now; she appeared in shawl and bonnet. An absurd but useful opportunity occurred for her to ascend astutely into the upper air when questions of adultery and free love were brought up. Those exalted ladies of the Saint-Simonian persuasion came to address her as a priestess. They invited her to become a 'mother' of the Saint-Simonian 'family', or phalanstery, and even sent a load of hand-made presents, which included shoes, trousers, waistcoats, collars, one watercolour and a riding crop. In reply, she recommended them to practice the ancient morality of faithful marriage for 'being the most difficult, [it] is certainly the finest', though she would not blame those who shook themselves free of tyranny, which was the product of a false society. The fact is that for her, as for her fellow-Romantics, the just society already existed metaphysically, and that in this sense she was chaste. And she was no fool. She *was* temporarily chaste with her lawyer, but at home, at Nohant, she kept another pretender, whom she was maddening with the kisses of platonic affection. This was Charles Didier, a Genevan, and Mr Cate differs from André Maurois's judgement in his opinion of his character. How far they went, no one knows; to judge by his tortured 'Journal', Didier himself seems unsure. All he could report was hugs that seem maternal. It is nearly impossible to translate the language of the Romantics, but in reply to one of his injured letters George Sand is masterly. She could easily squash rancour:

You don't love, all I can do is love. Friendship for you is a contract with clauses for the well-combined advantage of both parties, for me it is sympathy, embrace, identity, it is the complete adoption of the qualities and faults of the person one feels to be one's friend . . . You attribute to me . . . a calculated dryness, how shall I put it? – something worse, a kind of prostitution of the heart, full of baseness, egotism, falseness, you make me out to be a kind of platonic slut . . . My misfortune is to throw myself wholeheartedly at each fine soul I encounter . . . What I took for a noble soul is a gloomy, sickly suspicious soul that has lost the ability to believe and thus to love.

Honesty or sophistry? Goodness knows. Better to call it incantation. Didier was soon forgotten. The loss of Michel de Bourges looked fatal to her reason, but she was quickly, so to say, back in the saddle. An amusing actor arrived, and there was soon a troupe of young men, all hoping to be the favourite.

And, distributing her kisses, back to her room she went for her nightly five- or six-hour stint on the next novel. The blood – her own and that of others – was turned into ink. We remember the cold words of Solange, the daughter who was no less wilful than herself: 'It would take a shrewd fellow to unravel the character of my mother.'

(1980)

A Swiss Novel

The difficulty, in thinking about *Adolphe*, is to lay the ghost of Constant. One is listening to Mozart against a disruptive mutter of music-hall which has got on to almost the same wavelength. But this happens with all the Romantics; their passionate exaltation of the first person singular is aimed at the solitary *cri de cœur* but it leaves one with a confusing impression of duet, in which life, with its subversive pair of hands, is vamping in jaunty undertone the unofficial version. Beside the broken heart of the imagined Ellenore, healed at last by death, stands Madame de Staël, in the full real flesh of her obstreperous possessiveness with no sign of mortality on her. She is off to Germany to write a damned good book. And as Adolphe, free at last, contemplates with horror the wilderness of his liberty, up bobs Constant, explanatory about his secret marriage, still hopelessly susceptible, still with a dozen duels before him on account of ladies' faces and with one leg out of the nuptial couch at the thought of the rather acid enticements of Madame Recamier. It is distressing that the man should obtrude so persistently on his own confessions.

One of the earliest psychological novelists, Constant is enmeshed in ambiguity. He is more than the surgeon of the heart; he is more than the poet of masochism. *Adolphe* is not the tragedy of unequal love created out of the comedy of his chronic amorousness: it is the tragedy of the imagination itself and rendered in words as melodiously and mathematically clear as the phrases of a Mozart quartet. One understands as one reads *Adolphe* why the tears streamed down Constant's face and why his voice choked when he read his book. But he did weep rather a lot. He went weeping about the courts of Europe with it – taking his precautions. Would Madame de Staël object to this line? Had he sufficiently toned down the money difficulties? (One would like to write the financial side of

Adolphe, but that kind of thing was left to the vulgar Balzac.) Had he beaten up his literary omelette so well that none of his wives and mistresses could put out a finger and exclaim, Lo! here, or Lo! there? He was very anxious and very evasive. Never can autobiography – disguised though it was – have emerged from the facts with such a creeping and peeping. There was even a special preface for the English edition, in which, knowing his England, he declared *Adolphe* was a cautionary tale to warn us of the wretchedness of love which tries to live outside the necessary conventions of society. There is a sort of sincerity in this, of course; Constant had the bullied free-lover's sneaking regard for marriage as a kind of patent medicine. The dictatorship of Napoleon and the despotism of Madame de Staël had given him a hunger for the constitutional. But for one who thought nobly of the soul he is – well, shall we say, practical?

One looks up from the music of *Adolphe*, from the cool dissertation of that unfaltering violin, to the noble head of his portrait. At Holland House, when they watched him, aware that they were being entertained by one of the most intelligent scandals of exiled Europe, they must have noticed that he had none of the frank charlatanry of the Romantics. A dignified and even debonair forty, he was sensitive, witty and vivacious. The nose suggests firmness and probity. And yet one can understand that Constant was considered a shade tough. One detects the buried outline of the original human monkey under the half-smile of the small courtier. In the pose and in the eyes there is something of the mandrill's mask, something of that animal's vanity and temper. So gentle – and yet Ellenore and Madame de Staël, violent themselves, complain of the rasp of his tongue. The mouth is almost beautiful, a talker's mouth caught with the perpetual epigram, but it lifts at the corner with an upward twist of slyness. It hints at the hard malice of the inhibited. One does not altogether trust Constant even before one has read *Adolphe*. One foresees the danger of a cleverness which is indecisive, the peril of an elusiveness which is captivating but never revealing.

What is lacking in the portrait is any sign of the morbid apathy of his nature. M. Gustav Rudler, the most searching editor of *Adolphe*, says Constant lived in a sort of apathy which 'made crises of passion an essential need'. A cat-and-dog life with all those mistresses, duels with young Englishmen – he was still at it in his crippled old age, being carried to the ground to fire from his chair – a wicked senility at the gaming tables. 'I leave myself to Chance,' Constant wrote, 'I go where it puts me and stay there until it sweeps me away again.' Brilliant and unrevealing in conversation, he buries his serious opinions which he can contemplate only when he is alone. And then the temperature is so cool that the sensibility is still thwarted and unmelted. He lives listlessly and constrained. This is Byronism once more, the beginning of the malady of the age; but Byronism turned analytical, without the guts, without also the hocus-pocus. His world weariness has no sense of theatre; it is not so highly coloured; it is the fatigue which makes for the abstract mind and not for poetic journalism, the sickness of the *âmes sèches*.

'Je ne puis que vous plaindre', the father of Adolphe writes when he observes that, as he expected, the young man's determination to break with Ellenore is going to weaken. 'Je ne puis que vous plaindre de ce qu'avec votre esprit d'indépendance, vous faites toujours ce que vous ne voulez pas.' But lovers of independence are like that; the love of liberty is more easily come by than the will to ensure it. Constant was inured to despotism; society conspired with Madame de Staël to reduce his will. Adolphe and Constant together both lament their lack of career. And if one can think of the writer of a masterpiece as a failure, the *âme sèche* of Constant was not the sole or even the chief cause of his disorientation. It is true that Madame de Staël's party was the wrong one to belong to; but it was anyway hopeless for Constant to be a liberal democrat, full of the ideas of the Edinburgh Whigs, under an unconstitutional regime; and one can only sympathise with him when, shut out of public life where he could excel, and kept in the backwaters of scholarship and dalliance by the Napoleonic dictatorship, he should find this backwater dominated by a female of the Napoleonic species. One hesitates, of course, to call any place that Madame de Staël inhabited a backwater. Maelstrom comes nearer to her disposition. 'Storm' was his word for her (modified to *bel orage* in *Adolphe*); warming up to 'earthquake' and settling finally on 'volcano'. And not extinct, either, like that crater to which Chateaubriand's René climbed, in a famous passage, to weep for the mere matter of an hour or two. The real Romantics were men of theatrical moments; a borrower like Constant had to endure the years. He was ten years among the explosions of Madame de Staël, and even Napoleon, it is said, could not withhold a breath of congratulation when he heard she had gone to Italy where the volcano, as he pointed out, is natural to the scenery.

Constant's own solution was simply liberal constitutionalism.

Marriage, he seems to suggest, was devised by society precisely for this kind of malady, i.e. the fatigue of the imagination, the discovery that when you possessed your mistress you did not love her. Cynical – but the idea had been in his mind since he was a boy of thirteen. He seems to have thought that even Madame the Volcano in full eruption would become amenable after standing at the altar. He was obeying the instinct of the male who, drowning in the passion he has unwittingly roused, seeks to appease the storm by throwing off his lifebelt: 'Scène épouvantable avec Madame de Staël. J'annonce une rupture décisive. Deuxième scène. Fureur, reconciliation impossible, départ difficile. Il faut me marier.'

'Départ difficile' – that sums up the diminuendo of human love. And even when it was not 'épouvantable' it went on quietly nagging: 'Minette est de mauvaise humeur, parceque je ne veux pas veiller le soir. Il est clair que je serai forcé de me marier pour pouvoir me coucher de bonne heure.'

Well, he had two good goes at it and marriage was not a success.

Adolphe is the intellectual in love, beginning it all out of *amour propre* and some fashionable imitation, creating love out of his head, rejoicing in the mind's freedom, and horrified to find that the heart desires slavery. The beauty of the book is that the theme is lived and not argued; not indeed lived with the accidental paraphernalia or even the embellishment with which life mercifully obscures fundamental human problems, but with the austere serenity of abstraction. There is a little of the Romantic foliage taken from the literature of the time – the presentiments, the solitary walks, the wintry landscape and some notes in the deathbed scene are *de rigueur* – but he is not lyrical, nor does he go back to the urbane generalities of the pure eighteenth-century manner. He is something new. The lives of the lovers are singled out like two trees in the winter, their branches articulated in exact and delicate skeleton against a clear and cloudless sky.

He was restless, it was noted. He could not keep still when he was in a room. The imagination is the most quickly wearied of our faculties; it craves for more and more stimulus. After its ecstasies it leaves a void; hollowness and listlessness lie like ashes after it has burned. Presently sentiment rewarms them and the tepid souls like Constant begin to live on the imagination's memories. They are not memories of real things; but a mistress abandoned twenty years ago begins to be clothed in a glamour which, mathematically speaking, is twice the glamour of a mistress abandoned ten years ago; and twenty times the attraction of one he happens to be living with at the moment. She, poor wretch, has to deal with him, stark naked. It is a familiar perversity. The oldest of Constant's ladies, now old enough to be his grandmother, seems almost proper for the magic state of marriageability. Alas, he had left it too late. She was dead. How far back would Constant's memories have to go before he hit upon the ultimate and assuaging woman?

At that question, out of malice to all, one wants to transplant him. One always wants to do this with the early liberals. One wants to show them where it was all leading, this exaltation of life, liberty and the pursuit of autobiography. Since that time there has been only one period in which the intellectuals have had it all their own way; when imagination and experiment were to be canonised, where liberty made its last if desiccated whoopee. One leads him into the Bloomsbury of the Twenties. The Lawrence wave catches him, as Chateaubriand and *Corinne* caught him before. Presently he is thrown among the psychoanalysts. They seize him and one hears (as he describes the ever-enriching associations of his memory) the inevitable question: 'When did you last see your mother?' He has to confess he cannot remember: it was his father who had bothered him; *she* had died at his birth. And then one hears the shrill, scientific howl as Constant at last hears the cause of his trouble, the seat of that sullen will-lessness. It was the charm of living 130 years ago that the psychological novelists did not have to know what their own trouble was.

(1939)

Playing Stendhal

'I would be rather taken for a chameleon than for an ox': one of Stendhal's pungent remarks, uttered, no doubt, in some Paris salon where he was, as usual, posing, and where his scornful wit was making its random hits. Someone who heard the phrase noted that the stocky, rather overdressed and ugly, timid man had made a studied effort to pass as 'an ungraspable, conjectural figure'. In early portraits he looks bluff, even doggish. Silvestro Valeri's picture of him in consular uniform in 1835 gives him a bitter mouth.

A great talker, something of a coxcomb, yet also a dreaming, drastic adolescent when he was a young man, at heart a solitary, Stendhal certainly played studied roles, as later generations know from his letters and his journals. They are so full of strategies that his continuously autobiographical writings give him the air of a man writing a manual in the art of seduction. He set out at an early age to scrutinise his character, to experiment with it and remake it. He was, in one sense, an artifice. Born bourgeois, he sought to break with his class and to become an aristocrat, even to the length of intriguing for a baronry; at heart he was a man of superior sensibility and feeling, a mixture of artist and man of the world.

He had felt the release of the Revolution, the elation of the Napoleonic glory, and the disillusion of Napoleon's eclipse and saw himself as one caught in 'an age of transition', between two dispensations – the classical worldliness of the eighteenth century and the romantic energies of the nineteenth – an outsider in both or, as he put his ideal, an exceptional soul, one of 'the happy few'.

As everyone knows, to his contemporaries he was an eccentric. The nature of his genius as a novelist was not understood until after his death when he was eventually recognised as a precursor of the psychological novelists Proust, Henry James, Gide, and even, today, of Joyce and the novel 'without a centre'. Julien Sorel and Fabrice seem to us to have uncertain temperaments close to our own. In one of the many good essays on Stendhal written in the last few years Robert M. Adams, for example, says:

Perhaps the most enchanting yet terrifying thing about the heroes of Stendhal's novels is that they define themselves provisionally, in conflicts of thought and action, in negations; without enemies, they are almost without natures and wither away, like Fabrice when deprived of danger.

The biographer of Stendhal faces tantalising competition in the autobiographer. The unfinished *Vie de Henri Brulard*, published after his death, is one of the finest terse and ruthless autobiographies ever written, reckless or careless as it may be in its detail. The indefatigable Beylists seem to have traced every moment of a man who was always on the move. They know, within a day or two, how long he spent with his many mistresses, every person he met, and where he lodged. One of his stormier mistresses hid him in the cellar of her château, out of fear of her violent husband. That was a coup.

A plain narrative of his life is as diverting as any picaresque novel. But as Robert Alter in his new biography says, as others have done before him, the life is so entwined with his work as a writer that the significance is lost without a critical attempt to interpret it. There is hardly a scene in his novels without its echo of inner or active experience. This is true but I fear one more portentous psychoanalytical analysis of the Oedipal aspects of his character or another obfuscating examination of myths and symbols suggested by towers, the Alpine summits, prison, the hermitage, and the mire of vulgar life. Mr Alter is tactful about these inescapable matters. He is a perceptive biographer, sensible, fresh, fairly free of academic jargon – though he is overfond of that newish academic technological cliché 'stance' and there is the horrible package word 'complementarity'.

In his lively narrative Mr Alter is good on the natures of the women Stendhal successfully or unsuccessfully pursued in the cause of what he called his profession: 'the study of the human heart'. He is sound about the novelist's changes of character, mind, and feeling in each important phase of his life. He does not miss Stendhal's surprising efficiency as an administrative officer in Napoleon's army in Germany and Russia, and is very good on the influence of his journalistic habits, including his plagiarisms, on his practice as a great novelist. If Stendhal's own character is provisional, like that of outstanding characters in his novels, we see how important improvisation was – as important as his powers of minute scrutiny were to his work. As a man he is separated from observing his dreams and sensual desires by an almost military concern for strategies and inventing obstacles. The obstacle provokes the psychologist. In life his stratagems often misfire, in love and politics: in art – as he would say, the thing that alone can make experience 'real' – they lead to the rewards of reverie he had caught from Rousseau.

Stendhal's finest work was written late because, as he said, he lived first. He was a refractory son, careless of education. He broke with his father and sought the important influence of his well-placed relations in Paris. He was not as uncouth an outsider as the half-self he projected in Julien Sorel – but he strikes one as standing in his own light and naïve. He was after a comfortable job and rising fortune so that he could dress well, conquer women, and devote himself to playwriting and literature. He was conscientious in his boring offices and fixed in his mistaken belief that he was a playwright: it took him years to see that Napoleonic times did not provide the stable society, set manners and morality on which eighteenth-century comedy depended.

Luckily the romantic young man got into Napoleon's army in Milan and he found in Italy a spiritual home. Like the pushing young Boswell in London, he found actresses and opera singers who so often played the parts of great ladies were surrogates for aristocratic women in Society; but the calculating and timid Stendhal was given to something like seizures of romantic feeling which dissolved in tears, before the moment of achievement. He was driven to brothels. In Paris he did not impress his benefactors, but at last he did manage to cadge his way into administrative rank in Napoleon's Russian adventure, though not as a fighting soldier. He was again efficient but spent his time toiling at his impossible play, and reading. He saw Moscow burn, managed barely to survive the appalling retreat, and lost for good the illusion of Napoleonic glory which so deeply affected his generation. This is all well known. More interesting is Mr Alter's comment:

Whatever Beyle actually saw [he was not yet disguised as Stendhal] of cowardice, crudity, savage egoism in the masses of men fleeing across the frozen Russian countryside conveyed to him an abysmal vision of human nature (parallel in a way to what many sensitive writers experienced in World War I) for which the polished precision and the cool confidence of the language of the *Philosophes* were somehow beside the point.

The idea of a rational control over personal relationships was chimerical. After the Russian experience where he had been flung into the mire,

Beyle would tend to place himself as much as he could within the civilised, protected perimeter of that symbolic clean well-lighted place . . . the ball-room of a high culture that knew how to translate desire into a perfectly choreographed pattern of repeated fulfilment.

This is the point where Stendhal's doctrine of 'the happy few' was shaped.

The next point at which Mr Alter does well is on Stendhal's attitude to women as it appears in that eccentric essay 'De l'Amour'. He was a feminist and, being an Anglophile who had read of Bentham, he held that to deprive women of education 'deprives society of half its potential for intellectual achievement'. The argument was not original, but Stendhal made it witty as he drifted from theory to anecdote. His work is (Mr Alter notes) free of the female stereotypes – the patient sufferer, the gentle paragon of redemptive virtue – which were found later in the novels of Balzac, Dickens, and Dostoevsky. The memorable women in Stendhal's novels have the 'same qualities of energy, wilfulness, self-dramatising extravagance, physical daring, and intelligence' that are present in his male heroes.

On the puzzling idea of 'crystallisation' which 'De l'Amour' advances, and which we could perhaps call the igniting power of 'idealisation', Mr Alter notes the importance of Stendhal's change of heart about the merits of Don Juan and Werther. Don Juan had been his guide as a youth, first as the eighteenth century's adaptation of the myth in Valmont of *Les Liaisons dangereuses*. In maturity he changed his mind. Don Juan paid too high a price for his useful virtues of daring, resource, and wit, and Stendhal turned to the nineteenth century and Werther, 'who opened the soul to all the arts, to all the soft and romantic impressions.' Mr Alter writes, 'The plots of his two greatest novels are a kind of derailing of Don Juanism and the discovery of a Wertherian dénouement.' There is a romantic withdrawal from the world. Don Juan kills love.

We come closer to the writer at his desk when we turn to the origins and side effects of Stendhal's habit of borrowing and impro- visation. Despite his class – perhaps because of his rejection of it – Stendhal was so at odds with the education he had that he was, like so many other great writers, really self-taught and therefore, for all his enormous reading, a guesser who relied on dash, impulse, and wit.

He became a very clever and readable journalist, notably as a correspondent of the *Edinburgh Review*, for that paid well; at times he lifted other people's ideas as it suited him and notoriously lifted the text of other people's work. He had two hundred pseudonyms and these, if they protected him politically – for the Austrian police kept an eye on him in Italy – they also covered his plagiarism. This, as Mr Alter says, is deplorable and uncovers the marked strain of opportunism in his character. But if he was guilty of this, what at once strikes one in his works of travel is the presence of his person, his sharpness of sight and ear, the sound of the journalist's voice, disputing, asserting, generalising. He loves pungent anecdote, he catches character and dialogue. Mr Alter quotes one passage which has all the anecdotal undertone of *La Chartreuse de Parme*:

We were told the touching anecdote of Colonel Romanelli who killed himself in Naples because the Duchess C had left him. 'I could easily kill my rival,' he said to his servant, 'but that would distress the Duchess too much.'

Fabrice has a very similar reflection when he steals a horse from a stranger who he thinks threatens his life as he escapes across the Swiss frontier.

The plain writing that winds back and forth in time as it runs through the mind enables Stendhal when he moves into longer analyses of feeling to be crisp and exact – to see Count Mosca moving from day to night about his house tormented by jealousy yet coming slowly upon the proper strategy to adopt. Yes, we say, that is what jealousy is like, it moves from hour to hour, from room to room. The plain style is essentially conventional, but when rapture has to be evoked it comes spontaneously. In one sense his novels are as declamatory and yet as flat as opera. More important, in the great novels, the talker makes no bones about the point of view: he can be the narrator outside the character and yet drop into direct dialogue and slip into words of interior monologue between utterance and thought so easily that we hardly notice it. What we do notice is that the people have become, as in life, many-dimensional: they seem to be singing and moving in Mozartian arias among themselves.

Where did he acquire this fluency and domination? His adoration of operatic music plays its part. But strangely, from Fielding in *Tom*

Jones, a novelist who, as Mr Alter says, invents 'a genial expatiating narrator who casts a finely woven net of cultural, social, and political commentary over the narrated events; enriches our perception of the characters through a shifting play of ironies.' Stendhal wrote in the margin of *Lucien Leuwen*, after rereading *Le Rouge et le noir*: 'true but dry. One must adopt a more ornate, less dry style, witty and gay, not like the *Tom Jones* of 1750, but as the same Fielding would be in 1834.' There is an additional reason for the speed he puts into his circuitous inspections and the dominance of the conversational style: he dictated his work; his hand could not be deciphered. After the five weeks in which he is said to have 'written' *La Chartreuse de Parme* his amanuensis must have been a wreck.

It seems to me that Mr Alter's interpretation weakens at one critical point: the significance of *Armance*, Stendhal's first novel written in his forties. The subject is surmised sexual impotence. It was a fashionable subject borrowed from another novelist. (That, by the way, is all we mean when we say he lacked invention: in the borrowed subject he acquired the necessary freedom which enables the novelist to invent a deepened self and to pour in random echoes of his own experience.) It is agreed that Stendhal was far from impotent despite his fascination with the experience of fiasco. In the *Promenades dans Rome*, and in his own peculiar mixture of French and English, he had written: '*Enfin Dominique regarde* love as a *lion terrible* only at forty-seven.' But in the far more detailed and searching examination of *Armance* by Martin Turnell (*The Novel in France*, 1951) one understands that Armance is the first of Stendhal's 'outsiders' whose singularity points less to a sexual or social context than to a haunting psychological and moral dilemma: the conflict between misanthropy, duty, and sensibility. And Turnell's writing is superior to Mr Alter's.

Mr Alter is more acceptable on that other difficult unfinished novel *Lucien Leuwen*, which becomes tedious and breaks in two: the subject of French bourgeois politics killed Stendhal's Italian brio and blurred his real powers of self-invention. The portraits from provincial life are nevertheless very freezing examples of his ideal of 'exact chemistry'. Mr Alter does his best with *Lamiel*. Here Stendhal was nonplussed by his real-life model: she was to be a female Julien Sorel who lived for active political conspiracy and danger – things which had an uncomfortable bearing on the pursuit of happiness and the rewards of reverie. Perhaps he was too old and too embittered and melancholy in his humiliating role as a mere consul in Civitavecchia to 'see' this book. He went to Paris briefly and died of a stroke as he came out of the office of the foreign ministry. A year before, maintaining his irony as an enigma, he had said: 'I find that there is nothing ridiculous in dying in the street, so long as one does not do it deliberately.'

(1979)

MARCEL PROUST

Proustifications

As a young letter writer Proust is already talking himself into what would eventually become autobiography as a continuing art. There will be no stopping the rush. He is about seventeen, still at the Lycée Condorcet —

> Forgive my handwriting, my style, my spelling. I don't dare re-read myself. When I write at breakneck speed. I know I shouldn't. But I have so much to say. It comes pouring out of me.

He is sending a younger friend one or two tips about half a dozen of the teachers he will have to face and issuing a warning:

> Well, I beg you — for your own sake — don't do what I did, don't proselytise your teachers. I could do it, thanks to an infinitely liberal and charming man, Gaucher [he had lately died]. I wrote papers that weren't at all like school exercises. The result was that two months later a dozen imbeciles were writing in decadent style, that Cucheval thought me a troublemaker, that I set the whole class about the ears, and that some of my classmates came to regard me as a poseur. Luckily it only lasted for two months, but a month ago Cucheval said: 'He'll pass, because he was only clowning, but fifteen will fail because of him.' They will want to cure you. Your comrades will think you're crazy or feeble-minded. . . . If it hadn't been for Gaucher, I'd have been torn to pieces.

What is he up to? His friends called it Proustification. Earlier we've seen him dazzling his adored grandmother with phrases swearing 'by Artemis the white goddess and by Pluto of the fiery eyes', paraphrasing Musset — it will please her generation — and 'consoling his woes' with 'the divine melodies of Massenet and Gounod'. He will soon be sagely worshipping Anatole France from whom he seems to have learned what was to fertilise him as a novelist: that each human being is made up of many selves. He is classicist, romantic, and exotic at will. In his introduction to Philip Kolb's selection of the early letters from the Plon edition, written before Proust remembered tasting the madeleine, J. M. Cocking remarks that Proustifying is a flexing of the linguistic muscles by a youth of enormous reading who seems to know more about literature and the arts than can be good for any novelist to know. He is experimenting not only with the actual use of words, but with thought, too. He is attempting to analyse and understand his own spontaneity, his cascading hyperbole, his out-rageous flights of social flattery as exercises of the 'imagination and sensibility'.

Later Proust called that divine pair 'the two ignorant Muses which require no cultivation'. The young man fears the dilettante in himself, but that will not prevent him from going all-out for the flowery manners of the *belle époque* and their sinuous pursuit of paradox. (Here Ralph Manheim's translation is excellent.) What an up-to-the-minute chaos the young Proust is. He is drunk on Emer-son, for example, as he was to be on Ruskin, having glided over the moral content of these misty figures, yet (as Mr Cocking shrewdly says) Proust was a sort of transcendentalist without belief in any definable metaphysic. He transcends in person. The *sound* of the music was enough. Music, as we soon see in his letters, was the art apart. He reproached one of his early lovers for having a literary view of it.

The letters are also a kind of open, floating notebook in which he hopes to delight his correspondent, not only by the sight of his passing selves, but by his fascination with theirs. The letters are also displays. He is passionate in those written to his mother and his grandmother, but to others, men or women, he can be bold. To Mme. Emile Straus, the family friend who seems to have been one of the models for the Duchesse de Guermantes, he risks saying:

At first, you see, I thought you loved only beautiful things and that you understood them very well – but then I saw you care nothing for them – later I thought you loved people, but I see that you care nothing for them. I believe that you love only a certain mode of life which brings out not so much your intelligence as your wit, not so much your wit as your tact, not so much your tact as your dress. A person who more than anything else loves this mode of life – and who charms. And because you charm, do not rejoice and suppose that I love you less. . .

To practice writing love letters, as Balzac said, improves a writer's style. But Proust's turn out also to be a store of fragments that will find their way, years ahead, in *A la recherche*. Proustian detectives have noticed that the nose of the Marquis de Cambremer (in *Cities of the Plain*) – the nose being 'the organ in which stupidity is most readily displayed' and which in this instance was moujik-like and suggested an artifact imported from the Urals – was noticed years before in 1903 and is therefore evidence of the victory of *Time Regained*. The nose transcends.

The young climber is a romantic snob and a moralist as he notes class habits. Unlike the admired Balzac he is uninterested in social forces. At one of Mme. Alphonse Daudet's parties, he notes (sadly) the 'frightful materialism, so surprising in "intellectuals". They account for character and genius by physical habits or race.' Mme. Daudet was 'bourgeois' and had no manners, not even bad ones. 'From the viewpoint of art, to be so lacking in self-mastery, so incapable of playing a part, is abominable.' As for the aristocracy – pre-Napoleonic, of course,

they certainly have their faults, but show a true superiority when thanks to their mastery of good manners and easy charm they are able to affect the most exquisite affability for five minutes, or feign sympathy and brother-hood for an hour. And the Jews . . . have the same quality though in another way, a kind of charitable self-esteem, a cordiality without pride, which is infinitely precious.

By this time he has become the journalist writing the witty sketches for *Le Banquet* that will become *Les Plaisirs et les jours*. He has met and flattered the fantastic Montesquiou and has been caught out mimicking his stormy voice and mannerisms. Montesquiou is no fool. The youngster is put in his place. The count tells him 'he does not need a travelling salesman for his own wit.'

Presently Proust's adored mother steps in and puts the young butterfly on to a more serious task. She does a rough translation of Ruskin's *Bible of Amiens* to help him and makes him work on it. A grind. His English is not good, yet he does claim to have read *Praeterita*, which, on reflection, might come too close to his relations with his mother. But what a stroke of genius on her part: the influence of Ruskin's metaphors, his labyrinthine sentences, his imaginative flights, and his melodious pedantries will be so beguiling that years will pass before he notices the intransigent and Protestant moralist. Marie Nordlinger, the young English scholar and minor poetess, comes over to help him. In return he is moved to become her critic. We see that the word 'memory' is already planted in his mind.

Don't complain of not having *learned*. Strictly speaking, no knowledge is involved, for there is none outside the mysterious associations effected by our memory and the tact which our invention acquires in its approach to words. Knowledge, in the sense of something which exists ready-made outside us and which we can learn as in the Sciences – is meaningless in art. On the contrary, it is only when the scientific relationships between words have vanished from our minds and they have taken on a life in which the chemical elements are forgotten in a new individuality, that technique, the tact which knows their repugnances, flatters their desires, knows their beauty, plays on their forms, matches their affinities, can begin. And that can happen only when a human being is a human being and ceases to be so much carbon, so much phosphorus, etc.

He worked on *The Bible of Amiens* for four years. There were many mistakes, but some were due to the irreducible obscurity of the text. It turns out that his translation of *Sesame and Lilies* was excellent. About this time he seems to have been bowled over by *Middlemarch*. He sees that translation is not his real work. He writes to Antoine Bibesco:

It's enough to arouse my thirst for creation, without of course slaking it in the least. Now that for the first time since my long torpor I have looked inward and examined my thoughts, I feel all the insignificance of my life; a thousand characters for novels, a thousand ideas urge me to give them body, like the shades in the *Odyssey* who plead with Ulysses to give them a little blood to drink to bring them back to life and whom the hero brushes aside with his sword. I have awakened the sleeping bee and I feel its cruel sting far more than its helpless wings. I had enslaved my intelligence to my peace of mind. . . So many things are weighing on me! when my mind is wholly taken up with you. I never cease to think of you, and when I write to you I keep talking about myself.

Ruskin dragged on and on. We pick our way forward to see Proust at odds with his invalid life, his travels, his appetite for society, and his absorption in the intrigues, jealousies, suspicions, and almost comic fusses of his homosexual love affairs. His love for Antoine Bibesco is a strange mingling of adoration and the strategies and practical pedantries of jealousy. We laugh at the comic word *tombeau* – 'silent tomb' – which occurs even in telegrams as a warning to 'keep this to yourself'. This is Albertine without the tedium. The letters written by the sick writer about a proposed journey to Constantinople, the where, how, and when of it, the changes of mind, the splitting of hairs are fuss raised to the point of sublimity, yet to be taken seriously. Proust is a tyrant in love. He is frank. One never desires to fight off an affection, yet 'You know in me, no affection can withstand absence.' On the other hand, 'Some affections go on too long. They must be dropped before they become too important.' 'A year or a year and a half is the term beyond which affection or, I should say, infections, abate and die away.' The bother is that discarded lovers may 'register an upswing,' some 'bring on a slump'. The more serious trouble is that Ruskin has slumped. So no trip to Constantinople. He will finish with a hysterical joke: 'I shall not see the Golden Horn, a thought which gives me palpitations.'

The 'real work' is presumably *Jean Santeuil*, the 'straight' autobiographical novel which he came to see was following the pedestrian course of voluntary memory. (The madeleine has not yet been tasted.) His father dies and he is caught by grief and guilt at being the invalid son who has caused nothing but sorrow to his parents. We read his pathetic, self-pitying outbursts against his mother, which begin fiercely and end in the miserable fretfulness of a baby.

The selection inevitably ends too soon, that is to say years before *A la recherche* begins. For the moment we seem to be in the midst of an enormous web of glittering intrigue in which Proust clings to his friends and rules them by his demands and charm.

For the reader the letters improve as Proust approaches his discovery of what he must do. His health is worse, he is already forced into the necessary solitude, but his Proustifications are calmed by his sense of serious purpose. At two key points we have seen the thinking political moralist strongly appear: scathingly on the scandal of the Dreyfus case; with wisdom in his reaction to the anticlerical ban on teaching by the religious orders. What he fears in both cases is the perversion of justice, the loss of the lasting images of a civilisation. He is both Catholic and Jew. Looking back on the letters to his mother one realises the enormous, protective, nourishing influences his grave and gifted family had on his conscience and on his formation as both man and artist.

(1983)

Albert Camus

Albert Camus is one of those writers who are idolised in their lifetime and then are trapped by their legend. Now he is neglected in France, though he is still admired in Great Britain and the United States. He was entangled in the fierce and barren quarrels about political and moral commitment during and after the Second World War, and allowed himself to appear as a hero of the Resistance from the beginning, though in fact he did not join it until eight months before the Liberation. He came to be thought of as a 'lay saint' and as 'the moral conscience of his generation'. His famous novel *L'Étranger* (*The Outsider*) seemed to put the bleak halo of existentialism above his head, although, as he said and Sartre feelingly agreed, he was no existentialist. His world-famous novel *La Peste* (*The Plague*) passed as an allegory of the Nazi Occupation. He, indeed, said it was, and most readers of the time thought so, too. We can now see that the matter was more complex. In time, the hero from Algiers who believed in justice and assimilation for the poor Arabs disconcerted his admirers by siding with the *pieds noirs* against Algerian freedom. Camus was really a kind of liberal who had a lifelong horror of bloodshed, terrorism, and war. To the next generation of French writers, for whom the doctrine of political commitment has burned itself out, Camus has some interest because of his experiments in multiple narration and language. A new critical biography – *Camus*, by Patrick McCarthy – attempts to sort out facts from prejudice. For McCarthy, Camus was no 'saint' (though many saints have been as ambiguous and as devious as he was); a poor philosopher and no political thinker, his temperament being religious but not god-seeking; a wooden playwright and a fine novelist. It strikes me that Camus's real distinction is that of the mythologising autobi-ographer, the essayist and probing talker; that the man himself is more interesting than his legend. In personal life, he had a spell that was half physical. Compared with the immensely well-educated, upper-middle-class Sartre, Camus is the proletarian and near-auto-didact – part journalist, part artist, and, above all, the uprooted colonist, on his own. He was also an instinctive actor who was a collector of roles. McCarthy concludes:

> Camus's life was almost the opposite of what it seemed to his con-temporaries: a long, losing battle against wars and terrorists, tuberculosis and fame. French Algeria, which had offered him instincts, passions and happiness, however tangled with poverty and prejudice, almost destroyed him along with itself.

The tuberculosis seems to have been responsible for his euphoric excesses, his sexual promiscuity, his gallows humour, and his obses-sion with death.

Camus was the son of an Algerian labourer of French descent who was killed in the 1914 war. The son had not known him. He *did* know that his father had been obliged to see a man guillotined, and that stuck in the mind of father and son. The mother was a charwoman of Minorcan descent, one of the thousands of poor workers of mixed Mediterranean races in the Algerian colony – a real *pied noir*. Camus was very proud of his Spanish connection, and as he grew up he cultivated the impassive Spanish pride and macho bearing. (However, note that the Minorcans were not Spanish but energetic Catalans.) The mother brought up her son in the slums of Belcourt, outside Algiers. She was simple and illiterate and was known for her stunned silences. The household, Camus said, was a speechless solitude. He saw her silence as an act of revolt against her life. Close to the home was the Arab slum, more wretched than their own. Camus said there were no words of affection between mother and son; he simply worshipped her. She became mythical in his eyes. It does not seem that McCarthy goes too far when he remarks that 'their bond lay in their joint indifference, the badge of the suffering and the knowledge that they shared.' Camus spoke of inheriting a 'profound indifference which is like a natural infirmity.' Eventually, as McCarthy points out, 'her suffering assumed a religious form. Her stoicism was not merely a rebellion; it was an ascetic rejection of the things of this world.' 'A God is present in her,' Camus wrote when he was young. This God, McCarthy says, was 'remote and uncaring' yet was the source of Camus's own 'strong, ever-frustrated religious impulse'.

McCarthy is excellent on the Algerian boyhood and, indeed, on the history of French rule in Algeria. The colony had something of the quality of a frontier or pioneer state. The colonists had the colonial 'chip', the colonial loneliness and violence, the colonial fear of the conquered Arabs. Algiers was a city where robbery, murder, and death were brutally familiar. At the carnival, it was normal that one float should contain a man stretched out in a coffin, acting the corpse. The colony

drew on cultures which had known centuries of bloodshed and had turned fighting into a ritual. . . But the main cause of violence lay, inevitably, in the colonial situation, in that secret, unavowed fear. Algeria was becoming [in Camus's boyhood] ever more a frontier country because the European population was retreating into the coastal cities.

Camus was the complete wandering street kid, the tough and personable young proletarian, always ready to fend off a blow, fanatical about soccer and swimming and bodily fitness. The solid, communal ethos of the working class was to remain with him all his life, even after his two middle-class marriages and his final wealth. It was soon clear to his alarmed mother that he was a passionate reader and very intelligent. He was helped by a remarkable schoolmaster who was a dogged philosopher and a minor writer. The boy easily got through the lycée; he read Nietzsche and Dostoevsky, and at the university he distinguished himself by his thesis on St Augustine. But the soccer and the swimming went on, the lonely wanderings in the countryside and the low quarters of Algiers, and presently the easy sexual encounters on the idyllic Mediterranean beaches with the girls from the cigarette factories. He saw himself as the impassive Spanish Don Juan to whom girls and women flocked. He turned to journalism and was also soon working with poor theatrical groups; and, with his chosen friends, was for a time involved in Communist politics. It was natural to be a left-winger and to feel that something ought to be done about the Arabs who were the victims of the rich French farmers and entrepreneurs. He read and argued about the mixed cultures of the Mediterranean. He deplored the ruthless Roman influence that had prevailed rather than the Greek sense of limits and 'nothing too much'. Algeria was mindless, exploited by France, and was barbarous, but the barbarity was of nature and could be called primitive and innocent. His senses responded to the harsh mountain landscape, the stony plateau, and the desert that was another sea; to the clear sunlight, the brassy heat, and the seductive silence of the evenings. The deep sense of 'indifference' in him responded to the indifference of nature, but not in a Northern, Wordsworthian way: there was nothing 'deeply interfused' here. Each stone or tree was an object: his visual sense of the 'things' of landscape is intense in all his writing. Mortality was a presence as unanswerable as rock. His work as a journalist would eventually lead him to lapse sometimes into rhetoric and sentimentality, but his best manner is plain, detached, lonely, and laconic: abruptly lyrical and briefly sensuous. There is a sentence in his *Notebooks* – 'One of our contemporaries is cured of his torments by contemplating a landscape' – that marks his identification with his country. What are those torments? Not of conscience or poverty alone. At the age of sixteen, he had become tubercular. The disease never left him; it is at the heart of his 'indifference', and the almost too vivid sense of the instants of hope.

A large part of McCarthy's book is given to the stormy story of Camus's career as a polemical journalist, first in Algiers and then in Paris during the German Occupation. One marvels that, coughing out his lungs, Camus was able to work and quarrel so hard and carry on with his compulsive drinking and his part as habitual seducer – who tried desperately to save his first wife, a morphia addict; who loved his much-tried second wife and their children, and was capable of tortuous passion in his liaison with the Spanish-refugee actress Maria Casarès. In love, Camus was a gambler but (as McCarthy says) a prudent one.

I find McCarthy helpful about *The Outsider*, *The Myth of Sisyphus*, *The Rebel*, and *The Fall*, and especially *The Plague*. Defoe's *Journal of the Plague Year* was, of course, the literary source of *The Plague*. In Defoe, the storyteller is omniscient. In Camus, the real narrator is concealed in the voices of Oran, the city of the plague; the use of many narrators is a success because it 'flaunts' the limits of the people's understanding and says 'less' to suggest mysteriously 'more'. 'Anonymity' and 'amputation' remain, McCarthy writes, 'the watchwords of Camus' art'. The aim is to offer a collective view and to make it more positive than a single narrator can; the remote, invisible 'narrator who puzzles' is, to McCarthy, a 'thoroughly modern achievement'. It seems to derive from Camus's inheritance of the communal mind. Only short passages of his journalistic rhetoric break the spell for a moment. Outside of his political polemical writing or works like *The Rebel*, which are rather lumbered up with research (which is, in fact, sketchy), Camus is a natural personal essayist.

McCarthy thinks the last book, *The Fall*, is a far better book than *The Plague*. *The Fall* was written in defiance of the writer's block that paralysed Camus's imagination during the Algerian conflict, and at a time when he had no hope of recovering his health. The remedy for the artist was to transfigure his evil by attacking himself. Simone de Beauvoir thought that the story was a confession of a hidden guilt – the guilt that the Don Juan, the habitual seducer, felt toward his wife. It is true that in his *Notebooks*, which I find very revealing, he does groan and lacerate himself on this score. But *The Fall* goes far beyond the personal. Camus was a great mimic and talker, and in this tale he magnifies these gifts: the verbosity of a hypocrite at the confessional. Camus has a strong sense of the French classical tradition, and McCarthy says that Clamence, the penitent lawyer, 'is a pessimistic moralist in the long French tradition that goes back to La Rochefoucauld and La Bruyère. Like them, he attributes all man's actions to egoism.' Clamence feels himself justified by his resemblance to all mankind. But Camus undercuts the language of Clamence with the irony that is the classical French gift. McCarthy's final word is that 'despite the lack of redemption' *The Fall* is a piece of religious writing about man's fallen state: 'It is a superb novel written from the viewpoint of a world without men.' Clamence is indeed as isolated as Tartuffe. By a stroke of genius, Camus sets the confession not in the clear light of Algeria but in the deceiving fogs of Amsterdam, with its concentric circles of canals, which are the inescapable circles of Hell. The place is 'hemmed in by fogs, cold lands, and the sea steaming like a wet wash'. Holland is a country where 'everything is horizontal, no relief; space is colourless, and life dead. Is it not universal obliteration, everlasting nothingness made visible? No human beings, above all, no human beings! You and I alone facing the planet at last deserted!' With an awful glee, the penitent lawyer, who has himself committed a crime that will implicate anyone so foolish as to discover it, talks his way into moral complacency by incriminating mankind. What an irony that 'the outsider' of Algiers should turn up as 'the insider' in Amsterdam!

(1982)

Camille Pissarro

The exhibition which celebrates the 150th anniversary of Pissarro's birth has now travelled from London to Paris and is soon to arrive in Boston, and three stout, handsomely illustrated and scholarly volumes are here to inform a layman like myself. They also test and enlarge our response to a restless and prolific artist of very complex character. The introductory essay to the general catalogue by John Rewald is a rhetorical attempt to revive the history of the long battle between the Impressionists and the Salon. He appeals to Nietzsche and grinds his teeth at the name of Gérôme. Two other contributors, Richard Brettell and Françoise Cachin, are more inquiring and more nourishing. The Ashmolean volume reproduces an enormous number of Pissarro's drawings and working sketches; we see Pissarro's foundations as a graphic artist who came to painting late. And Ralph E. Shikes and Paula Harper are very searching and enlightening on the relation of the life and work.

A literary person, venturing to write on a delightful art, can, at any rate, be fortified by some words of Walter Sickert – I take them from Françoise Cachin – partly because Walter Sickert was a painter who was also dashing and got to the heart of the matter in print; partly because he liked to make the then unfashionable assertion that he was a literary painter, which was almost true: 'Pissarro . . . remains the painter for those who look at, rather than for those who read about, painting.'

We have read; but we have also looked, and Pissarro does take one clean through the surface of his pictures into their depth and architecture. Sickert's word, 'remains', has exactly the overtone of ambiguity to which we respond. Pissarro does distinctly 'remain' in our visual sense and minds. Other Impressionists give us sensations of evanescence and the dance of suffused light; Pissarro seems to convey the haunting permanence of an hour that has been lost.

The distinguished writers who rallied to the Impressionists were, like ourselves, in the usual literary difficulty of seeing the ostensible subject as 'the hero' of the painting whether it is person, action, or landscape; we are also apt to see analogies between the manner of prose and paint, each arrangement of brush strokes being a possible phrase. For us the famous 'Young Girl with a Stick' is 'the dawn of adolescence'. George Moore was lyrical about those dream-like apples that would 'never fall'. Hostile critics who were bored by Pissarro's fields of cabbages and who called him 'a market gardener' got the tart reply that the Gothic artists were bold enough to use the humble cabbage and the artichoke as ornaments in their cathedrals.

As a firm atheistical materialist Pissarro hated being credited with penetrating 'the soul of nature', but none of our literary tribe went so far as Zola, in his later years, when he inflated Cézanne in 'L'Oeuvre' and turned the painter's life into a typical Zola-esque melodrama. For myself I am tempted to see Pissarro and other Impressionists as artists who retrieve that forgotten storyless hour of the day in which the clock has beautifully stopped. One of the merits of Ralph E. Shikes and Paula Harper's *Pissarro: His Life and Work* is the following statement that puts the hour back into paint – look again at the early and Courbet-like *Côte du Jallais near Pontoise*:

It is often perceived that Pissarro was consistently interested in firmly structured compositions, in itself a visual statement of permanence. His perspectives imply a single, fixed viewpoint; if the world of nature is in flux, the one who views it is stable. Monet, by contrast, in many of his last paintings, dissolves the viewer into the scene; there are few reference points that relate to space on a human scale or gravity as a human experience. But Pissarro constantly reasserts the fact of humankind interacting with the natural world both in his subjects and in his insistence on a logically constructed space seen from a still point.

Yet there was a transformed prose in Pissarro's mind; it lay in his political convictions. He had read Property-is-Theft Proudhon, Elisée Reclus, and Kropotkin. He was called 'the poet-logician' by Gauguin. Like more than one of the Impressionists, but more lastingly and even in a practical way, he was imbued with the innocent millenarian dream of Anarchism. He had an active hatred of the centralised bourgeois state. Vague though the dream was – and he was never able to define what he precisely meant by it beyond talking about the joyful liberation of perpetual creative work that would insulate us from the sorrows of life – the dream gave a grace to his sense of the need for social justice. His anarchism was not sentiment: it is related to his particular kind of humanism, an earnest of manna for the humble worker at a period when Guizot was telling everyone to 'get rich'; it was also perhaps a spur to his changes of style and the eagerness to try new means. Yet also, in some intimate way, it was connected with what he called, with some irony, his 'Creole passivity' or foreignness; in the sense that Chekhov was a passive artist, i.e. one who chooses to be hidden in his work.

It is clear that Pissarro, who appeared simple to the point of sanctity, was a deeply complex man. Some believed he was naïve and self-taught: he was not. Far from being a peasant, he was distinctly a bourgeois and had little in common with the peasants he lived among in the valleys of the Seine and Oise. He rarely individualised the peasant. His revolt against the bourgeois was (he always said) a personal family affair but not violent as Cézanne's was in his relation to *his* banker father.

Pissarro's own upbringing had anomalies. Born in 1830 in the Danish island of St Thomas in the West Indies, he was a child of one of the Sephardic families of part French and part Portuguese Jews who had emigrated to the island because it had become the most prosperous entrepôt for trade in the days of sail. His parents were successful general shopkeepers, mainly in cloth. Money-making (as Trollope said when he went to St Thomas) was the sole preoccupation of the colonial population, and the strong Jewish colony benefited from the religious tolerance of the Danes.

The colonial wealth had also drawn a shrewd itinerant Danish painter, Fritz Melbye, who did well out of the European demand for exotic topographical landscapes, and it was he who noticed and first tutored the young Pissarro's remarkable and lasting graphic talent there, and indeed made possible his eventual freedom from the detestable fate of keeping shop.

Pissarro had two particular gifts: intense concentration in sketching the humble mestizos and Indians, and an eye for intimate rather than panoramic landscape – as one can see in the exhaustive store of drawings in the Ashmolean collection. He had also power as a colourist. One picture, 'Carnival Dance', has the verve of Goya in his *maja* period. (This picture was done when he and Melbye went to Venezuela.) What really released him from his years in the shop was an economic crisis: the sudden change from sail to steam which killed the St Thomas trade. The crowded Pissarro family returned to their relations in France in 1855 and were prosperous enough to live in Rue de la Pompe in Passy. At the age of eleven Camille had been sent to school in Paris, as was common for colonial boys. But now he was in France for good to study Courbet and get the friendship of Corot, but bringing with him his 'Creole passivity' which for him meant, by a paradox, a dedicated and intellectual absorption in work. He had in mind a revaluation and revival of the French landscape tradition which was at first stimulated by the then unfashionable Barbizon School. He had also arrived in the Paris of Napoleon III and Baron Haussmann and the triumph of the bourgeois reaction.

Pissarro's was the classic rejection of the bourgeois ethos by a dissident son. He went so far as to quarrel with his dominant mother, a woman given to hysteria, because of his liaison (which eventually became a much opposed civil marriage) with the family servant. He went off to live close to rural poverty in Pontoise and then Eragny, painting peasants at work in the fields; moving to the logical link of the peasant with the market, on to the appearance of the factory in the rural scene, and to daily labour on the docks of Rouen.

All the critics in the present volumes point out that Pissarro was not really close to peasant life – even his wife, a country girl whose family had a little land of their own, 'came to have marked bourgeois leanings.' He rarely notes the harshness of field labour. He can even be said to have generalised those awkward bodies as they bend to the pattern of work.

Richard Brettell's long essay on each phase of Pissarro's art says his upbringing in a Jewish bourgeois family 'did little to equip him to understand or sympathise automatically with the peasantry,' and if he made obvious gestures to Millet he in fact reversed Millet's tendency to 'aggrandise' the peasant monumentally. Yet, although in many pictures his peasants are seen pausing or resting in the private satisfactions of being simply alive, there are many others who are the half anonymous shapes of a team enclosed in the geometric trance of a habitual drama. I am thinking of *The Harvest* (1882) and *The Gleaners* (1889). The superb apple gatherers *are* working, but their work is stylised, almost arrested; and from the arms of the figures reaching up to the tree one gets the sensation of a moment slowed down, explored, even enlarged and enriched as if caught, as Brettell says, in a pavane in which the grasses, the trees, the flowers and fruit, the light and shadow of the hour have merged with the bodies of the gatherers in a conspiracy of nature with man; yet without any intrusive suggestion of allegory. We are in that '*plein air*' which annoyed the Salon.

The critic Mirbeau put Pissarro's manner in excellent words: 'Even when he paints figures in scenes of rustic life, man is always seen in perspective in the vast terrestrial harmony like a human plant.' On the other hand, as Brettell says in another connection, Pissarro's innate sense of social history emerges in his market pictures, where the figures *are* individual, talking shapes:

These pictures suggest that it was the economic inter-relationship between the fields and the town which fascinated Pissarro and that for him the life of the peasant was not a seasonal cycle of sowing and harvesting, but rather one of events that ended with the market. . . . These images form the necessary bridge between 'la vie agreste' and 'la vie bourgeoise,' and complement Pissarro's landscapes with factories.

The peasant turns into 'the *petit commerçant*.' (However, *The Harvest* does seem to contradict this theory.) I incline to the belief that what drew Pissarro and others to the country factory was the novel arrangement of shapes that had to be assimilated to the rural scene and even tamed. Industrialism came late to rural France. There is nothing Satanic in the well-known chimneys of the factory near Pontoise. Satan comes later in Pissarro's political cartoons.

Like all important artists Pissarro feared to repeat himself. A painter's painter, he was preoccupied with experiment in style and means to the point of anxiety and restlessness. There is an exchange of influences in his responses to Cézanne, Monet, Degas, Gauguin, and Seurat particularly. To some contemporaries, most of whom became famous before he did, his changes of style marked him as a conservative who had become derivative and undecided in his objectives. Modern critics like Rewald and Brettell reject this view and see the intellectual vitality of a man re-making himself.

The passion for increasing the difficulty year by year was indeed innate from the beginning. If there *is* self-doubt it is of the studied fertilising kind; if there is anxiety it is the anxiety of an ambition which had to endure many harsh setbacks. Monet and the others became successful long before he did, partly because they were consistent and also – Shikes and Harper say – because Monet was a man of spontaneous passion and immediate conviction, if in the end he repeated himself, whereas Pissarro sought renewal in the temptation to see reality through many windows, and yet wavered because he was essentially a 'balanced thinker'.

Yet the contradictions in his character, the pervasive strength of his philosophy, the simplicity of his life, do not affect the serenity of his work, whether he is painter, etcher, or lithographer, whether he is painting on window blinds or designing fans to make money. Brought up in a crowded family, he turned by nature to begetting a crowded family of his own; no solitary artist he – rather the pedagogic patriarch who, to his wife's despair, was determined to turn the whole family into painters. The primacy of art which he firmly believed in had to carry the Pissarro tribe with it. The family became a kind of school, even a cooperative.

He could not bear the quarrels of the Impressionists: he was the pacifying friend with the long white beard of '*le bon Dieu*' and the beautifully modulated voice; in old age as ardent as a young man. One gets a very amusing guess at his character from a comical incident in his warm friendship with Gauguin, to whom he was a father figure. Gauguin claimed to be able to analyse character from handwriting and his report, of course, tells as much about Gauguin as it does of his victim. Gauguin said, as most people did, that Pissarro was 'simple and frank' but added that he was 'not very diplomatic,' 'more poet than logician'; had 'great ambition,' 'stubbornness and softness mixed'; was 'enthusiastic' yet 'mistrustful,' 'egotistical and a little cold'; wrote in 'graceful letters'; was a 'little eccentric'. It was rather silly of Gauguin, who was rich and a wild spender, to say that Pissarro was 'parsimonious' and 'money hungry'. He was often driven to borrow money, but he was a firm repayer of debts.

The one serious crisis in Pissarro's painting life occurred when he turned, almost against his nature, to neo-Impressionism under the influence of Seurat and pointillism. Under that influence some think his scenes became static and flat, so that for all the skill in perspective we are not borne into them. The scientific theory has displaced the human. His natural mode prevented him from continuing in this manner for long. And there is something almost droll in the seriousness with which the painter thought the solution to his torment was to put the pointillist dots further apart, so as to leave some larger gap for reflection, or the human throb; thus destroying the point of pointillism and the exhilaration of its blinding chemical noonday glitter. (Pissarro had always held that the noonday sun neutralised colour and Seurat had outbid Pissarro's doctrine.)

For a period the demand for his work collapsed; his self-confidence was baffled. In his depression he turned to suspicion. Perhaps – he wrote to his niece Esther who lived in England – his failure

was a matter of race. Until now, no Jew has made art here, or rather no Jew has searched to make a disinterested and truly *felt* art. I believe that this could be one of the causes of my bad luck – I am too serious to please the masses and I don't partake enough of the exotic tradition to be appreciated by the dilettantes.

Although, as Shikes and Harper say, anti-Semitism was common in France, there is no evidence that Pissarro suffered because of it, despite his public defence of Zola and his own political cartoons. He had indeed more to fear personally when the militant anarchists turned to violence and President Carnot was murdered. For Pissarro terrorism was a betrayal of the Anarchist dream. In old age his imagination made one of its magnificent leaps when he painted his extraordinary Parisian panoramas – the Place du Théâtre Français, for example – in which he looked at Paris from a high window and tipped the city almost on end with powerful effect.

There is much more to be got out of these immensely informative volumes than I have space or judgment to suggest, for Pissarro grows as an artist and a man as the reader looks and reads and looks again. There is one curious period in his later years, however, that still puzzles me: his people are rarely seen enjoying careless pleasure, except in some very late drawings when he attempts *baigneuses* as if he recalled Cézanne. It is true that it was difficult for him to get models for the nude in the country, and that he found contemporary nudes lubricious. His figures may be shown undressing to go to bed or even washing, by domestic habit; then suddenly we have a few surprising drawings of a naked country bather confronting geese in a pond, and in another a group of women wrestling and larking in the water or sprawling as they gossip on the bank. The bodies are plain enough but we have what seems to me the first sight of laughter. He had refused earlier to paint the cheerful bourgeois weekend holiday on the Seine, but now he catches the wanton country women. They are very individual. The poet-logician lets himself go, as he had done once, many years before, in his pictures of the carnival dance in Venezuela.

(1981)

Goya

The Spanish Civil War was felt to offer both a prophetic meaning to the art of Goya and an irresistible chance to Marxist critics. The most remarkable of these was Francis Klingender, whose *Goya in the Democratic Tradition* (1948) is still important. Klingender was a sociologist but, as the son of a painter and sculptor, had a spontaneous feeling for the diffused responses of art. His subject was the effect of society and history on the artist. For example, Goya's mysterious breakdown in 1792–3, at the age of forty-six, which left him stone-deaf for the rest of his life, was seen as a reaction to a personal conflict in which he was caught: between the need for conformity and the instinct of revolt. Later criticism suggests that Goya's social attitudes as a man and an artist who had grown up in the Enlightenment were more ambiguous and ultimately more pessimistic than Klingender thought. Thirty years on, in *Goya: The Origins of the Modern Temper in Art*, the art historian Fred Licht is rather less tendentious in his approach. Although Licht shares much with Klingender, he is closer to the autonomy of the artist's imagination; he sees Goya as a precursor of the development of painting in the 'modern epoch', until the present day, and one who has a special meaning for us in our disorientation in the continuing wars, revolutions, and atrocious persecutions of our time. (After 1790, the long classical tradition – and its market – collapsed.) For myself – whose approach to Spanish art, society, and history is that of the addicted amateur – Licht's book is a refreshing corrective. His erudition is rich and allusive. He looks minutely at the pictures, his argument is arresting, and the many illustrations – although they are in black-and-white, and most are small in size – are placed at exactly the pages in the text where his interpretations can be tested. One ought not to go to the Prado without him.

The son of a gilder, of modest family, Goya was a canny man of the

people, with a keen business eye for the right patron; he rose fast to
be a court painter. He had the art of survival in dangerous times and
all his life was skilful in covering his political moves and his troubles
with the Inquisition by holding a plausible alibi in reserve. He was
adroit with money and was blessed with the extraordinary Spanish
gift of prolific, and even inchoate, invention. He survived the
collapse of Habsburg feudalism, the savagery of invasion, and the
corruption of the Bourbon succession. A liberal, and no friend of
clericalism, he managed to keep his supremacy by, as it were, 'living
inside the whale'. Mr Licht says:

> Owing partly to his own character, owing perhaps also to his deeply
> rooted Spanish bias, he was the only artist to absorb the very principle of
> revolution and anarchy into his art . . . Goya was willing and able to express
> revolution in revolutionary terms. Living in a time that he perceived to be
> basically anarchic, he invented a language that conveyed the very principle
> of anarchy. Our baffled attitude towards a universe that grows more alien
> the more scientific data we accrue about its nature was already presaged in
> the images he created.

He goes on:

> Rejecting with equal force the faith in God of his ancestors and the faith in
> history and progress of his contemporaries, he set about to construct a new
> world built of the pieces and fragments of his knowledge, his intuition, and
> his invincible pride in being a man – no matter how reduced in stature.

Licht's point is that Goya is 'modern' because, with the collapse of
Christian and aesthetic values, he was left staring out of vacancy at
the plain facts before him, unembellished by mystical or traditional
consolation. His death scenes, for example, are final. The body loses
dignity. In sickness and in death, the soul dissolves among the
shadows of animal terror and is then extinct. The sick are in misery;
the dead are alone and unblessed. The blacks and greys in the
backgrounds of his maturing work suggest meaningless space. The
person, the thing can exist only for its own sake. Spanish painters,
like Spanish writers, have always been drawn to a realism that is
carnal, unflinching, and harsh. Spanish individualism finds it natural
to 'set figures as it were against each other'. There is a hostility to
Italian ornament and bravura. If there are scenes of butchery and
hangings, hackings-to-death in war, we are not given emotions by
Goya: the detached rendering of the sight evokes the scream inside
us, rouses our own fantasies, and makes us recognise that brutalities
rise from our own fears and the unseating of our reason. And here,

indeed, with a growing pessimism and detachment – perhaps, too, with Goya's haunted intuition of his own pathology, as some psychologists have suggested – Goya makes his famous utterance: that monsters arise in our minds when our reason sleeps (i.e. is forgotten or abandoned); we are then at the mercy of common superstitions or primitive fantasies, which may even become embodied.

Mr Licht follows Goya's growth as he passed the early neoclassical influences to the satirical 'Caprichos', the early portraits that have his undismayed eye for weakness of character, and the 'Disasters of War' (for some unknown reason, unpublished until well after his death) and is arresting, because he shows the artist impelled by his inner nature. In the 'Caprichos', Goya does not attempt to reform society, as the bourgeois Hogarth does; nor is he a Gillray, who distorts as he rages. Where I find Licht at his best is in things like the detailed discussion of that famous, insulting picture 'The Family of Carlos IV'. Even though we know of the decline of the passion for splendour as Spanish decadence moved toward its nadir, even if we recognise that Spanish individualism can assume an easy and proud indifference to shabbiness, and could do so especially in the nineteenth century, it is hard to imagine a royal family consenting to be portrayed in such homely disarray. Were they pretending – as Louis Philippe was to do in France – to be an ill-assorted bourgeois family? How did Goya nerve himself, as the court painter, to this performance? As Licht says, Goya may have been an impetuous man, tolerated as a 'character', but as a painter he was strictly disciplined, and careful in the preparation of his subject and its design. Velázquez and Rembrandt were his masters. He was immensely knowledgeable in European painting. So Licht turns for his explanation to the Velázquez of 'Las Meninas'. There are many portraits and drawings that show Goya's preoccupation with the double effect of mirrors and with what one may call the mirror's freezing or suspending a moment of life and splitting the personality. Goya's royal family were not standing before the painter in the manner of actors taking a curtain call; he was behind the straggling group and shows them standing slack yet bemused by themselves, in a mirror we cannot see. They have slowly slumped, as if entranced with themselves to the point of apathy: Goya 'has presented them as they saw themselves'. The only aspect of royalty on which they may be congratulating themselves is that they are human and need not appear to be royal. This, of course, suits Goya's love of experiment and the secretiveness of his insight. Here, by the trick of the mirror, is 'the thing itself'.

And here Licht turns back to the historical argument of his book. Goya is not caricaturing. He is looking at a group of shabby bodies that have lost faith in their role. History has made a king who cannot bear himself as a king: 'He doesn't know how to be himself because he doesn't know who he is.' The picture is 'a tragic comment on a condition of human life that is essentially modern'. It expresses man's lack of 'a higher ideal of himself, man's doubt in the signifi-cance of his destiny and in the guiding hand of an all-powerful divinity'. Once more: Goya 'presents us with a painting that no longer attempts to transcend or artfully simulate nature and that has no pretences beyond that of being an impassive reflection of *what is*'. That, Licht says, is the position of the artist in the 'modern epoch'. And he neatly quotes the well-known exchange of courtesies between a German official and Picasso in Paris during the Occupa-tion. Seeing a reproduction of Picasso's 'Guernica', the officer asked, 'Vous avez fait ça, n'est-ce pas?' To which Picasso replied, 'Non, monsieur, c'était vous.' The artist cannot be anything but a medium who signals 'recognitions of the world without being able to testify to their meaning'. The painter knows he has finished a work when he has 'painted himself out of it'. For Licht, the hermetic quality so frequent in modern painting dates from this picture.

The discussion of Goya's 'Third of May' takes an unexpected turn. We had been persuaded that as a painter, if not as a man, Goya was detached from the classical or religious statement of man's case, that he was neither a consoling nor an adjuring artist – he saw that he was alone, 'alienated', without an availing ethic. But here Goya 'for the last time . . . paints a picture that still bears a full didactic charge.' Licht adds, 'For the last time he tries to wake us from "the sleep of reason."' The figure who is screaming, his arms raised, before the firing squad as he stands among the dead bodies has what may be called a lay-Christliness, even the stigmata, but whereas in the pictures of Christian martyrdom the light of Heaven shines on the martyr, here the light comes from the utilitarian lamp on the ground which enables the firing squad to do its night work. '"The Third of May" is the first altar to the anonymous millions whose death is irrelevant,' Mr Licht writes. 'Anonymity becomes a condition of modern man.' And in his continuing examination of the structure of the picture Licht also notes that there is no space for the spectator in the picture except behind the French executioners: 'To survive is to be guilty of complicity' with them. For Licht, 'the heart-rending quality' of the defiance or the terror in the young man about to be shot 'lies partly in its being addressed not in the oratorical manner to a neutral audience or to God, but in the urgent and heedless intimacy that exists between the murderer and the murdered.' The word 'heedless' is striking, for it can be felt in a great number of Goya's paintings and groups of figures, even among the graceful. There is no other painter, I would say, who so completely gives one a clue to the anarchic egotism of his countrymen at the crisis of passion before that passion suddenly collapses into indifference or resignation. But let this literary generalisation pass. Goya does not deal in generalities. We make them. He does not.

Many important pages of this book are given to Goya's curious position in society and his intuitions about the new social condition of man. Mr Licht says – quite rightly, it seems to me – that it is a mistake to think of Goya as a partisan of any given system of political doctrine. On this matter, he shows how profoundly Goya differs from his French contemporary David:

David's great strength lay in his ardent desire to teach, in his passionate will to place art and the artist in an efficient, practical position within a rationally established governmental system. The painter must be in equal parts artists and responsible member of the body politic. Goya's position was far more equivocal. He, too, often wished to teach. But he taught a subject that he had apprehended either intuitively or by means of bitter personal experience . . . Goya teaches by arousing our sympathy and our curiosity . . . David the regicide, David the sincere republican was an enlightened, militant member of the middle classes.

Whereas Goya was closer to the worker and the artisan:

Men doing a job and doing it well, the dignity of workers caught in the performance of tasks that require mastery – these were the true themes of much of Goya's best later work.

In his etchings of the bullfight, the bullfighter is the 'artisan of courage'; like the artist, he finds 'the only fulfilment there is in modern life: the consolation of work freely accepted and perfectly done'. Here there is a very intelligent comparison of Wright of Derby's 'Iron Forge' and Goya's 'The Forge' – both powerful examples of physical action caught at its climax:

It was in work that [Goya] found the strongest intimation of the survival of man's dignity . . . It is his only painting that is an integral whole rather than a meaningful fragment torn out of an inscrutable context.

And then we come to portraits of working women, such as 'La Aguadora' – the water carrier, who was until very recent times a perennial Spanish figure. These women are more composed than the pretty figures of Murillo, the sentimentalist. More satisfying, to my mind, are Goya's late portraits of mature and sensuous women, and, indeed, of men. As he aged in politically risky times (if Licht is right), Goya became more attached to his few close Anglophile friends, and evaded the passing celebrities of aristocratic life.

A dozen suggestions have jumped to scholarly minds when faced by the almost inexplicable 'Black Paintings', which the seventy-five-year-old man painted on the walls of his little house outside Madrid. These paintings may be the expressions of a deep melancholia or of schizophrenia, but when Licht reminds us of Fuseli and of Franken-stein and the Gothic frenzy, and talks of them in relation to nightmares – such as the legend of the Witches' Sabbath – and then takes a leap forward to contemporary consciousness, we are ready to believe that the 'Black Paintings' may be concerned with 'the infectious nature of evil', the preoccupation with monstrosity, or the sense in which we may feel that the chaos of the unconscious is not an 'intruder' but the real, subverting inhabitant of the scene. What is most striking in these paintings is Goya's concern for the massive – perhaps because of fading sight. The pictures are 'primitive', but at the same time they evoke a particular sensation of horror about the future as an epic aroused by a past that has not been outgrown. There is also the possibility that they spring from private sources: the self-mockery of melancholic old age, the malicious jeering at dying faculties. It is said that the horrifying image of Saturn devouring one of his children was painted on the walls of Goya's dining room. When one recalls the bloody Crucifixions of classical Spanish paint-ing, especially those in which the subject is plainly treated as a divinely permitted murder, one realises that the 'Black Paintings' may belong to a tradition that events had revived. The sense of menace is like the menace of nightmare, which in real life is brief but here is spelled out as if the suspended moment had become flatly eternal. Unlike the Spaniards, other Europeans had to wait for the theatrical props of the Romantic movement – the hideous ravine, the abandoned monastery, the House of Usher – before they could face the nihilism that Goya seemed to be able to evoke at random in his fantasies, from whatever dark sources they came. It is only Licht's stimulating gift for eager cross-reference as a man soaked in his subject which prevents me (as an amateur Spanish hand) from pressing some evidently literary suggestions. He takes us back to the art gallery and brings the pictures into the double light of Goya's time and our own.

(1975)

VLADIMIR NABOKOV

The Supreme Fairy Tale

When a novelist takes to a bout of lecturing to university students he knows that for him it is sin to live by his mouth. He is throwing away his syntax and his prose; the charms of the impromptu will not work unless he has first gone through the drudgery of preparation. Without his habit of thorough preparation, his dash, his delight in mischief, prejudice, and the cheerfully perverse, Vladimir Nabokov's lectures would have been no more than pepper and salt. He was an extraordinary preparer. When he came to deliver his course on *Don Quixote* at Harvard in 1951–2 he had, for example, gone to the length of writing a summary of the events in this enormous novel, chapter by chapter, so making an invaluable crib. He wrote and rewrote his script, and at once destroyed its virginal look by covering it with corrections, possible asides, alternative paragraphs and optional quotations. He arrived at the lectern with a mass of possibilities.

In collating these martyred pages his present editors have had what must have been an exasperating task; but, for the lecturer himself, the mess was a guarantee of clarity and natural utterance. (There is nothing like a clean typescript for arresting thought and destroying personality.) Nabokov had a special talent for quotation: he knew that students, even those who are keen enough to read, will not have heard the 'tune' or real voice of the author's sentences; that reading aloud tests a style. Then, as a linguist, he had strong views about the merits of Cervantes's translators. He was equipped also for skirmishes with the well-known Spanish and foreign critics. He found the terse intelligence of Madariaga good, but he loathed the mellifluousness of the learned Aubrey Bell.

Nabokov was amusing on minor disputes too: he was irritated by Joseph Wood Krutch's claim that Don Quixote was always defeated in his battles. He went to the trouble of reckoning the score of victories and defeats and was delighted to find the score even. And to be sure his students had some idea of what a book of chivalry was, he supplied them with pages of Malory and *Amadis of Gaul*. Most of us have taken these romances as read. In short, I strongly recommend this edition of Nabokov's lectures as a practical guide to all incipient lecturers.

Nabokov cleared the ground aggressively at once with his usual *de haut en bas*:

We shall do our best to avoid the fatal error of looking for so-called 'real life' in novels. Let us not try and reconcile the fiction of facts with the facts of fiction . . . *Don Quixote* is a fairy tale, so is *Bleak House*, so is *Dead Souls*. *Madame Bovary* and *Anna Karenina* are supreme fairy tales. But without these fairy tales the world would not be real.

Don Quixote is seen as a fairy tale about a fairy tale. Not the greatest novel in the world but the supreme fairy tale. True, it is patchy in its narrative. Cervantes is patently improvising for a long time, without certainty of plan. On his dull days he is just filling in to keep the thing going. The stroke of genius is the invention of Don Quixote himself who imparts enormous and growing vitality to the book, so that his figure ends by looming 'wonderfully above the skyline of literature'; within twenty years of the publication of the first part, it started to fertilise other literatures, and went on doing so for centuries after it was written. Don Quixote became a universal myth. (And, one might add, has escaped the demise of, say, Don Juan, who has become suddenly unadaptable to our century.)

It is striking, Nabokov continues, that such a figure as Don Quixote should have risen serenely out of the knockabout roguery and low-life meanness of picaresque writing. (On the other hand, isn't there a gleam of light in *Lazarillo de Tormes*?) Distressed by his failure as a poet and playwright, Cervantes seems to have thrown himself on the mercy of an intuition which up until his fifties he neglected and despised. He seems to have been slow in seeing a plan; perhaps he intended no more than a short story. He was no good at landscape; he simply followed the painfully artificial tradition established by the Renaissance. Making landscape real and making it *work* for the story (Nabokov notes) did not appear until the nineteenth century.

What saved Cervantes was a gift that he may have learned as a playwright: the ingenious delight in all varieties of dialogue, high and low. Sancho Panza's proverbs Nabokov finds boring – in

translation – and one suspects he thinks the Russian peasant proverbs superior to the Spanish! The true spell of Cervantes is that he is a
natural magician in pure storytelling. He has no mission, no particular social conscience. He is no fiery adversary of social evil.
(However, what about those utterances in Part II, about the nature of
plain justice and good government? Are we to take these as no more
than the traditional Spanish complaint that 'good government' is
impossible in his country, an impossible dream?) About the cult of
chivalry:

Cervantes . . . does not really give a hoot whether or not books of chivalry
are popular in Spain; and, if popular, whether or not their influence is
pernicious. . . Although Cervantes makes a great show of being morally
concerned with these matters, the only thing about this chivalry or anti-
chivalry affair that interests him is firstly its most convenient use as a literary
device to propel, shift, and otherwise direct his story; and secondly its no less
convenient use as a righteous attitude, a purpose, a flutter of indignation
which in his pious, utilitarian, and dangerous day a writer had better take.

He had to keep a wary eye on the political and clerical authorities.
Equally there is no reason for believing he was either for or against
the great power of the Catholic Church. It seems that Nabokov
would have no time for the theory that the fun at the expense of the
romances of chivalry made *Don Quixote* the book that 'destroyed a
nation'.

As for the book being humane or humorous, Nabokov thinks it a
veritable encyclopedia of shocking cruelty and brutality, one of the
most barbarous books, in this respect, ever written. Its powers to
rouse belly laughs is vulgar and nauseating. Most popular humour is
brutal and perhaps arises from an attempt to forget the pain. The
tossing of Sancho in the blanket is unbearable – though is not
Sancho's own comment on not knowing where he was as he was
flung into the air an imaginative one? Even a comment on Quixot-
ism? Of course Nabokov is indignant at the appalling acts of political
cruelty of our own time. When his lecture moves on to Part II, in
which the 'civilised' dukes and duchesses invent degrading torments
for Don Quixote, Nabokov is as shocked as we are by sadism as an
ingenious or fashionable amusement. But he goes on:

Art has a way of transcending the boundaries of reason. . . This novel would
have died of the laughter its picaresque plot was meant to provoke had it not
contained passages that gently usher or sweep the reader into the dream
world of permanent and irrational art. . .

He is referring to the chapters in Part II when Don Quixote is alone after Sancho has got his promised island. Separated from each other they are unsustained by illusion, and a frightening element in their inner experience emerges, above all for Don Quixote:

Don Quixote . . . is the maker of his own glory, the only begetter of these marvels; and within his soul he carries the most dread enemy of the visionary: the snake of doubt, the coiled consciousness that his quest is an illusion.

He experiences not 'the dark night of the soul' (as one might expect especially from a Spanish writer) but something far more delicate. We see him alone in his room, listening to the singing of the duchess's maid in the patio. It is that sometimes childlike singing of a *soledad*. Here Nabokov himself is very perceptive:

The inward hint, the veiled suspicion that Dulcinea may not exist at all, is now brought to light by contrast with a real melody. . . He is deeply moved because at that moment all the innumerable adventures of a like sort – barred windows, gardens, music, and love-making – all he has read of in those now strangely true books of chivalry – come back to him with a new impact, his dreams mingling with reality, his dreams fertilising reality. . . But his innate modesty, his purity, the glorious chastity of a true knight-errant, all this proves stronger than his manly senses – and after listening to the song in the garden he bangs the window shut, and now even more gloomy than before, 'as if,' says Cervantes, 'some dire misfortune had befallen him,' he goes to bed. . . This is an admirable scene. . . Back to the torture house.

What is Nabokov's final judgment? That the book is more important in its eccentric diffusion than in its own intrinsic value. Sancho is a bore, his proverbs lose their piquancy in English, but he is most interesting when he himself catches the infection of enchantment. The Don, on the other hand, undergoes a multiplication. He is enlarged by the ingenuity and subtlety of his madness. He embodies the mystery of reality and illusion. He is courageous to a degree.

We are confronted by an interesting phenomenon: a literary hero losing gradually contact with the book that bore him; leaving his creator's desk and roaming space after roaming Spain. . . We do not laugh at him any longer. His blazon is pity, his banner is beauty. He stands for everything that is gentle, forlorn, pure, unselfish, and gallant. The parody has become a paragon.

The students who listened to Nabokov used Samuel Putnam's careful, slightly bland translation but also J. M. Cohen's, which Nabokov often preferred. If they were able to turn to the Spanish the students would have discovered the sustained and luminous irony of the style, irony enhancing the subtlety of experience without any cruelty or dryness. From Nabokov they would have got stimulus. Fascinated by structure in his own work, he was very interesting on the growing ingenuity of the book. The introduction of the imaginary Arab author and of the notorious false version which stirred Cervantes to rise to the height of his powers in Part II were complexities very much up Nabokov's street. The only protest I have concerns his offhand comment on the redoubling of illusions in the grand scene at Montesinos's cave. That famous episode may have started as 'another twist that Cervantes gives to the Enchanted Dulcinea theme in order to keep the reader entertained and Don Quixote busy.' But what a powerful, critical, and dramatic elaboration of the theme of illusion it is. It amounts to a sight of imagination imagining itself.

(1979)

A Portuguese Diplomat

Eça de Queiroz (1845–1900) is the Portuguese classic of the nineteenth century – not an Iberian Balzac, like Galdos but, rather, a moistened Stendhal, altogether more tender, and, despite his reformist opinions, without theories. He was a diplomat, something of a dandy and gourmet, whose career took him abroad in France, Britain, the Near East, Cuba and the United States, and he was responsive to the intellectual forces that were bringing the European novel to the height of its powers. The temptations of a light and elegant cosmopolitanism must have been strong, for he is above all a novelist of wit and style, and he was amused by the banalities of diplomatic conversation.

But the foreign experience usually serves to strengthen his roots in the Portuguese idiosyncrasy: under the lazy grace, there is the native bluntness and stoicism. A novel like *The Illustrious House of Ramires* is very rich, but it also contrives to be a positive and subtle unravelling of the Portuguese strand in the Iberian temperament. The soft, sensual yet violently alluring Atlantic light glides over his country and his writing, a light more variable and unpredictable than the Castilian; no one could be less 'Spanish' and more western European, yet strong in his native character.

The fear that one is going to be stuck in the quaint, exhaustive pieties of the *folklorico* and regional novel with its tedious local colour, its customs and costumes, soon goes at the sound of his misleadingly simple and sceptical voice. The Portuguese love to pretend to be diminutive in order to surprise by their toughness. Portuguese modesty and nostalgia are national – and devastating. In an introduction to an early short story, 'The Mandarin', he wrote a typically deceptive apology to its French publishers, in which he puts his case. 'Reality, analysis, experimentation or objective certainty,' he said, plague and baffle the Portuguese, who are either lyricists or satirists:

We dearly love to paint everything blue; a fine sentence will always please me more than an exact notion; the fabled Melusine, who devours human hearts, will always charm our incorrigible imagination more than the very human Marneffe, and we will always consider fantasy and eloquence the only true signs of a superior man. Were we to read Stendhal in Portuguese, we should never be able to enjoy him; what is considered exactitude with him, we should consider sterility. Exact ideas, expressed soberly and in proper form, hardly interest us at all; what charms us is excessive emotion expressed with unabashed plasticity of language.

Eça de Queiroz, we can be certain, did not commit the folly of reading Stendhal in Portuguese. The most exact of novelists, he read him in French, and the comedy is that he was very much a romantic Stendhalian – he was even a Consul-General – and in exactitude a Naturalist. Under the irony and the grace, there are precision and sudden outbursts of ecstasy and of flamboyant pride in a prose that coils along and then suddenly vibrates furiously when emotion breaks through, or bursts into unashamed burlesque.

He was an incessant polisher of his style. The following passage, from *The City and the Mountains*, shows his extraordinary power of letting rip and yet keeping his militant sense of comedy in command. His hero has just been thrown over by a cocotte in Paris. His first reaction is to go and eat an expensive meal of lobster and duck washed down by champagne and Burgundy; the second is to rush back to the girl's house, punching the cushions of the cab as he goes, for in the cushions he sees, in his fury, 'the huge bush of yellow hair in which my soul was lost one evening, fluttered and struggled for two months, and soiled itself for ever'. He fights the driver and the servants at the house, and then he goes off home, drunk and maddened:

Stretched out on the ancestral bed of Dom 'Galleon', with my boots on my pillow and my hat over my eyes, I laughed a sad laugh at this burlesque world. . . . Suddenly I felt a horrible anguish. It was She. It was Madame Colombe who appeared out of the flame of the candle, jumped on my bed, undid my waistcoat, sunk herself onto my breast, put her mouth to my heart, and began to suck my blood from it in long slow gulps. Certain of death now, I began to scream for my Aunt Vicencia; I hung from the bed to try to sink into my sepulchre which I dimly discerned beneath me on the carpet, through the final fog of death – a little round sepulchre, glazed and made of porcelain, with a handle. And over my own sepulchre, which so irreverently chose to resemble a chamberpot, I vomited the lobster, the duck, the

pimientos and the Burgundy. Then after a superhuman effort, with the roar
of a lion, feeling that not only my innards but my very soul were emptying
themselves in the process, I vomited up Madame Colombe herself . . . I put
my hat back over my eyes so as not to feel the rays of the sun. It was a new
Sun, a spiritual Sun which was rising over my life. I slept like a child softly
rocked in a cradle of wicker by my Guardian Angel.

This particular novel savages Paris as the height of city civilisation,
a wealthy Utopia; it argues for the return to nature in the Portuguese
valleys. Eça de Queiroz can still astonish us in this satire with his
catalogue of mechanical conveniences. They are remarkably topical.
(His theatre-telephone, for example, is our television or radio.) The
idea of a machine civilisation that has drained off the value of human
life recalls Forster's *The Machine Stops*. Maliciously Queiroz describes our childish delight in being ravished by a culture of affluence

or surfeit. He was in at the birth of boredom and conspicuous waste.
One brilliant fantasy of the hero is that he is living in a city where the
men and women are simply made of newspaper, where the houses
are made of books and pamphlets and the streets paved with them.
Change printed-matter to the McLuhanite Muzak culture of today,
and the satire is contemporary. The hero returns to the droll, bucolic
kindness of life in Portugal, in chapters that have the absurd beauty
of, say, Oblomov's dream.

The prose carries this novel along, but one has to admit there is a
slightly faded *fin de siècle* air about it. *The Illustrious House of
Ramires* is a much better rooted and more ambitious work.
Obviously his suggestion that the Portuguese are not experimental-
ists is a Portuguese joke, for the book is a novel within a novel, a
comedy of the relation of the unconscious with quotidian
experience. One is tricked at first into thinking one is caught up in a
rhetorical tale of chivalry *à la* Walter Scott; then one changes one's
mind and treats its high-flown historical side as one of those
Romances that addled the mind of Don Quixote; finally one
recognises this element as an important part of psychological insight.
What looks like old hat reveals its originality.

Ramires is an ineffectual and almost ruined aristocrat who is
rewriting the history of his Visigothic ancestors in order to raise his
own morale. It is an act of personal and political therapy. He is all for
liberal reform, but joins the party of Regenerators or traditionalists
whose idea is to bring back the days of Portugal's greatness. Ramires
revels in the battles, sieges and slaughterings of his famous family

and – while he is writing this vivid and bloody stuff – he is taking his mind off the humiliations of his own life. The heir of the Ramires is a dreamer. He is a muddler and his word is never to be relied on. He shuffles until finally he gets himself in the wrong. This is because he is timid and without self-confidence: he deceives a decent peasant over a contract and then, losing his self-control when the peasant protests, has him sent to prison on the pretext that the man tried to assault him. Then rage abates and he hurriedly gets the man out of prison.

Ramires has a long feud with a local philandering politician of the opposite party, because this man has jilted his sister; yet, he makes it up with the politician in order to get elected as a deputy – only to see that the politician does this only to be sure of seducing the sister. The price of political triumph is his sister's honour and happiness. How can he live with himself after that? Trapped continually by his pusillanimity, he tries to recover by writing one more chapter of his novel of chivalry, fleeing to an ideal picture of himself. What saves him – and this is typical of the irony of Queiroz – is his liability to insensate physical rage, always misplaced. He half kills a couple of ruffians on the road by horsewhipping them and, incidentally, gives a fantastically exaggerated account of the incident; but the event and the lie give him self-confidence. He is a hero at last! He begins to behave with a comic mixture of cunning and dignity. He saves his sister, becomes famous as a novelist, long-headedly makes a rich marriage, and tells the King of Portugal that he is an upstart. Total triumph of luck, accident, pride, impulse in a helplessly devious but erratically generous character loved by everyone. Tortured by uncertainty, carried away by idealism and feeling, a curious mixture of the heroic and the shady, he has become welded into a man.

And who is this man? He is not simply Ramires, the aristocrat. He is – Portugal itself: practical, stoical, shifty, its pride in its great past, its pride in pride itself raging inside like an unquenchable sadness. There is iron in the cosiness of Queiroz. He has the disguised militancy of the important comedians. His comic scenes are very fine, for there is always a serious or symbolical body to them. His sensuality is frank. His immense detail in the evocation of Portuguese life is always on the move; and the mixture of disingenuousness and genuine feeling in all his characters makes every incident piquant.

A match-making scene takes place in the boring yet macabre crypt where the ancestors of Ramires are buried. Ramires knows his ancestors would have killed his sister's lover; all *he* can do is to pray feverishly that her silly, jolly, cuckolded husband will never find out. Prudence and self-interest suggest caution; not mere caution but an anxious mixture of politeness, kindness, worldly-wisdom and a stern belief in dignity, if you can manage it, plus the reflection that even the most inexcusable adulteries may have a sad, precious core of feeling. Ramires is not a cynic; nor is Eça de Queiroz. He is saved from that by his lyrical love of life, his abandonment – for the moment – to the unpredictable sides of his nature; in other words, by his candour and innocence. His people live by their imagination from minute to minute. They are constantly impressionable; yet they never lose their grasp of the practical demands of their lives – the interests of land, money, illness, politics.

In the historical pages of Ramires's historical novel, there is a double note, romantic yet sardonic. The scenes are barbarous and bloody – they express the unconscious of Ramires, the dreams that obsess him and his nation – but the incidental commentary is as dry as anything in Stendhal. During a siege:

The bailiff waddled down the blackened, spiral stairway to the steps outside the keep. Two liegemen, their lances at their shoulders, returning from a round, were talking to the armourer who was painting the handles of new javelins yellow and scarlet and lining them up against the wall to dry.

Yet a few lines farther down, we shall see a father choose to see his son murdered, rather than surrender his honour. The violence of history bursts out in Ramires's own life in the horsewhipping scene I have mentioned earlier. The sensation – he finds – is sublime. But when Ramires gets home his surprise at the sight of real blood on his whip and clothes shatters him. He does not want to be as murderous as the knights of old. He is all for humanity and charity. He was simply trying to solve his psychological difficulty: that he had never, in anything until then, imposed his own will, but had yielded to the will of others who were simply corrupting him and leaving him to wake up to one more humiliation. It is a very contemporary theme.

The making of this novel and indeed all the others, is the restless mingling of poetry, sharp realism and wit. Queiroz is untouched by the drastic hatred of life that underlies Naturalism: he is sad rather than indignant that every human being is compromised; indeed this enables him to present his characters from several points of view and to explore the unexpectedness of human nature. The elements of self-surprise and self-imagination are strong; and his excellent prose glides through real experience and private dream in a manner that is leading on toward the achievements of Proust. His translators have done their difficult task pretty well: Roy Campbell being outstanding.

(1980)

A Brazilian

Few English readers had heard of Machado de Assis before 1953. His novel *Braz Cubas* was translated in that year by William Grossman, under the title of *Epitaph for a Small Winner*, forty-five years after his death. There was also a very good translation published in 1955, by E. Percy Ellis. Since then we have been able to read *Dom Casmurro*, a collection of stories called *The Psychiatrist*, and *Esau and Jacob*, which has awkward inflections of truck-driver's American in the dialogue. Assis is spoken of as Brazil's greatest novelist. He was born in 1839 and his work comes out of the period marked by the fall of the monarchy, the liberation of the slaves and the establishment of the Republic. He pre-dates the later European immigration which was to change the great cities of Brazil completely and introduce new Mediterranean and Teutonic strains into the Brazilian character.

Assis said that his simple novels were written 'in the ink of mirth and melancholy'. The simplicity is limpid and delightful, but it is a deceptive distillation. One is always doubtful about how to interpret the symbolism and allegory that underlie his strange love stories and his impressions of a wealthy society. The picture of Rio could not be more precise, yet people and city seem to be both physically there and not there. The actual life he evokes has gone, but it is reillumined or revived by his habit of seeing people as souls fluttering like leaves blown away by time. In this he is very modern: his individuals have the force of anonymities. His aim, in all his books, seems to be to rescue a present moment just before it sinks into the past or reaches into its future. He is a mixture of comedian, lyrical poet, psychological realist and utterly pessimistic philosopher. We abruptly fall into dust and that is the end. But it would be quite wrong to identify him with the sated bankers, politicians, sentimental roués and bookish diplomats who appear in the novels. His tone is far removed from the bitter-sweet mockery and urbane scepticism of, say, Anatole France; and it is free of that addiction to rhetorical French romanticism which influenced all South American literature during the nineteenth century. He eventually became an Anglophile.

Epitaph for a Small Winner was a conscious break with France. It is a lover's account of an affair with a friend's wife. The affair is broken – perhaps luckily – by circumstance and the writer concludes that there was a small surplus of fortune in his life: 'I had no progeny, I transmitted to no one the legacy of our misery.' To get a closer idea of Assis, one must think chiefly of Sterne, Swift and Stendhal. He is an exact, original, economical writer, who pushes the machinery of plot into the background. His short chapters might be a moralist's notes. Like Sterne, he is obsessed with Time, eccentric, even whimsical; like Stendhal, accurate and yet passionate; like Swift, occasionally savage. But the substance is Brazilian. It is not a matter of background, though there is the pleasure of catching sight of corners of Rio and Petropolis – the little St Germain up in the mountains where Court society used to go to get out of the damp heat. Some of the spirit caught by Assis still survives in Rio: under the gaiety there is something grave; under the corruption something delicate; under the fever something passive and contemplative. The Portuguese *saudade* can be felt within the violence; and a preoccupation with evasive manoeuvre, as it occurs in games or elaborate artificial comedy, is a constant recourse and solace, in every department of life. Like the Portuguese before Salazar, the Brazilians attempted to circumvent their own violence by playing comedies.

Assis' career could be seen as a triumph of miscegenation. He was born in one of the *favelas* or shack slums that are dumped on the hills in the very centre of Rio, the son of a mulatto house-painter and a Portuguese woman. She died and he had no education beyond what he picked up in an aristocratic house where his stepmother worked as a cook. He learned French from the local baker, got a job as a typesetter and eventually turned journalist. It is not surprising that he was sickly, epileptic and industrious and that one of his interests was insanity. Like many other Latin American writers, he supported himself by working in the civil service; but in his spare time he wrote thirty miscellaneous volumes and became President of the Brazilian Academy.

It is said that he is even more admired in Brazil for his short stories than for his novels and from the small selection called *The*

Psychiatrist, one can see why: here the dreamy monotone of his novels vanishes. From story to story the mood changes. He astonishes by passing from satire to artifice, from wit to the emotional weight of a tale like 'Midnight Mass' or to the terrible realism of 'Admiral's Night', a story of slave-hunting which could have come out of Flaubert. In a way, all the novels of Assis are constructed by a short story-teller's mind, for he is a vertical, condensing writer who slices through the upholstery of the realist novel into what is essential. He is a collector of the essences of whole lives and does not labour with chronology, jumping back or forward confidently in time as it pleases him. A man will be described simply as handsome or coarse, a woman as beautiful or plain; but he will plunge his hand into them and pull out the vitalising paradox of their inner lives, showing how they are themselves and the opposite of themselves and how they are in flux.

In *Esau and Jacob* there is a fine comic portrait of the pushing wife of a wobbly politician who has just lost his governorship. She is a woman who kisses her friends 'as if she wanted to eat them alive, to consume them, not with hate, to put them inside her, deep inside'. She revels in power and – a quality Assis admires in his women – is innocent of moral sense:

It was so good to arrive in the province, all announced, the visits aboard ship, the landing, the investitures, the officials' greetings. . . Even the vilification by the opposition was agreeable. To hear her husband called tyrant, when she knew he had a pigeon's heart, did her soul good. The thirst for blood that they attributed to him, when he did not even drink wine, the mailed fist of a man that was a kid glove, his immorality, barefaced effrontery, lack of honour, all the unjust strong names, she loved to read as if they were eternal truths – where were they now?

The grotesque, Assis says in one of his epigrams, is simply ferocity in disguise: but here the beauty of the grotesque comes from tolerance. Sometimes people are absurd, sometimes wicked, sometimes good. Timidity may lead to virtue, deception to love; our virtues are married to our vices. The politician's wife gets to work on her husband and skilfully persuades him to change parties. He is morally ruined but this stimulates his self-esteem. The pair simply become absurd. This particular chapter of comedy is very Stendhalian – say, from *Lucien Leuwen*.

Esau and Jacob is, on the face of it, a political allegory, observed by an old diplomat. He has been the unsuccessful lover of

Natividade, the wife of a rich banker, a lady given to a rather sadistic fidelity and to exaltation. She gives birth to identical twin boys and consults an old sorceress about their destiny. She is told they will become great men and will perpetually quarrel. And so they do. As they rise to greatness, one becomes a monarchist and defender of the old stable traditions, the other a republican and a believer in change and the future. They fall in love with the same girl, Flora, who can scarcely tell them apart and who, fatally unable to make up her mind about them, fades away and dies. (People die as inconsequently as they do in E. M. Forster.) The meaning of the allegory may be that Natividade is the old Brazil and that Flora is the girl of the new Brazil who cannot decide between the parties. But underlying this is another allegory. One young man looks to the Past, the other to the Future; the girl is the Present, puzzled by its own breathless evanescence, and doomed. All the people in Assis seem to be dissolving in time, directed by their Destiny – the old sorceress up in the *favela*.

The theme of *Esau and Jacob* is made for high-sounding dramatic treatment; but Assis disposes of that by his cool, almost disparaging tenderness as he watches reality and illusion change places. In *Dom Casmurro* we have another of his cheated lovers. A young seminarist has been vowed to the Church by his mother, but is released from his vow by a sophistry, so that he can marry a girl whom he adores and who patiently intrigues to get him. Their love affair and marriage are exquisitely described. But the shadow of the original sophistry is long. Dom Casmurro had made a friend at the seminary, and this friend becomes the father of the boy Dom Casmurro thinks his own. When the boy grows up, Dom Casmurro finds that he is haunted by this copy of his friend. All die, for the subject is illusion. The concern with exchanged identities and doubles – very much a theme of the Romantic movement – is not left on the level of irony or paradox: Assis follows it into our moral nature, into the double quality of our sensibility, and the uncertainty of what we are. We are the sport of nature, items in a game.

One sees how much Assis has in common with his contemporary, Pirandello. With the growth of agnosticism at the end of the nineteenth century, people played intellectually with the occult – one of the Assis bankers consults a spiritualist – and amused themselves with conundrums about illusion and reality, sanity and insanity. In *The Psychiatrist* a doctor puts the whole town into his asylum. But there is something heartless and brittle in Pirandello. The Brazilian is warmer, gentler. One does not feel about him, as about Pirandello, that intellect and feeling are separate. At his most airily speculative and oblique, Assis still contrives to give us the sense of a whole person, all of a love affair, a marriage, an illness, a career and a society, by looking at their fragments. There is a curious moment in the *Epitaph for a Small Winner* when we are told that the poor, wronged, unhappy woman who is used by the clandestine lovers as a screen for their affair was perhaps born to have just that role and use in their lives: the reflection is good, for if it conveys the egoism of the lovers, it also conveys the sense of unconscious participation which is the chief intuition of Assis as an artist, and which makes his creatures momentarily solid.

(1968)

ALEXANDER PUSHKIN

Stories

The reader who knows no Russian is cut off from Pushkin as a lyrical poet and yet can respond to a narrative poem like *Eugene Onegin* in, say, Sir Charles Johnston's recent Byronic version and to the volatile wordplay of Nabokov's translation. Like Byron, Pushkin is one of the world's greatest letter writers, open and impromptu in all his moods. He is the sunniest of devils. We can see from the narrative poems that he is the forerunner of the great Russian realists of the nineteenth century. Yes, he is the Russian Shakespeare or Cervantes. 'Not a giant' – as John Bayley defined him a few years ago in *Pushkin: A Comparative Commentary* – 'but a Proteus': like Shakespeare, presenting new forms with the laughing boldness of a Renaissance figure. In his translated fictions, especially those written between 1830 and 1837, when he was killed in a duel, we have the superb short stories 'The Queen of Spades', 'The Stationmaster', and 'The Undertaker', the unfinished and spirited 'Dubrovskii', and the gripping, if sometimes melodramatic, novella 'The Captain's Daughter'. They have delighted us, but have we understood what Pushkin was doing with their late eighteenth-century manner? First of all, his prose has struck us as formal and expository, as parts of Scott do. The bother is that the reader allows the Classics to stale in the memory. We respectfully fail to see the artist in the act of writing. One can easily be caught taking *The Queen of Spades* as a set piece by Mérimée or a conceit by Hoffmann, an ingeniously designed ornament. Yet it comes straight out of the Russia of Pushkin's time.

Two volumes by Paul Debreczeny – *Alexander Pushkin: Complete Prose Fiction* and *The Other Pushkin* – are a scholarly examination of the poet training himself to write prose. The *Complete Prose Fiction*, which Mr Debreczeny has edited and translated, contains some remarkable unfinished exercises. One, 'The Guests Were Arriving at the Dacha', is said to have given Tolstoy his start when writing *Anna Karenina*. This volume ends with notes for stories that were never written or took some other course. One is startling, because, as we are apt to say, it is 'so Russian': 'N. chooses Nevskii Avenue as his Confidant – he confides all his domestic troubles and family grievances to it. . . . They pity him. . . . He is satisfied.'

But this is by the way. Debreczeny's interest throughout these books is this: how scrupulously the poet trained himself to cut out the exotic images of poetry and write plain prose. 'A continuing tension between two trends – one toward a sparse, austere style, the other toward poetic techniques,' he says, 'produced the rich variety of Pushkin's prose fiction.' We are in the writer's workshop. The subject is not as academic as it sounds: the speed of Pushkin's narratives and the surprises of his changing tune give zest even to his formal writing. The poetry turns into élan. He is a cheerful pillager of styles, a parodist and an eager borrower of plots, a master of the sly art of frustrating the expectations of the unwary reader who is too excited to foresee the psychological design. Pushkin was deep in English, French, and German literature. He had read Voltaire, Rousseau, Stendhal's *Le Rouge et le Noir*, Hoffmann, Richardson, and Scott. He was an excellent critic. The tame love affair that is said to spoil 'Dubrovskii' may very well be an artful parody of the sentimental fiction imported from Europe. The penultimate scene of 'The Captain's Daughter' seems to have come from *The Heart of Midlothian*. Debreczeny is good on the tension and on the development of Pushkin's experiments, on the use of many voices breaking the surface of a story. Yet what Pushkin is really doing in his dramas and comedies is giving us the sensation, distinctive in the later Russian novelists, that 'the doors and windows of the human house are wide open': that if only one person lives there he is many inconsistent persons, or that more than one person tells the tale. Everything is, as Bayley suggested, provisional and open-ended. The dismissive endings of Pushkin's completed stories are ironical, and they are therefore still open, as art stops and life goes on. The impersonality is warm, if not altogether heartening. What everyone has noted is the tender or spontaneous tone of his famous letters, his extraordinary power of self-control. His wild or his worldly genius is governed by the skills of the craftsman who laboriously sharpened as he rewrote. We need not believe entirely the last phrases of Pushkin's exclamation 'I sing as a baker bakes, as a tailor sews, as Koslov writes, as a doctor kills – for money, money, money. Such am I in my

cynicism.' He was fly enough to see that the novel was the new and
popular thing; but, like Stendhal when he wrote *Le Rouge et le Noir*,
he made no concessions to popular taste. The laconic style, the
disabused and offhand wit unite the two novelists.

The *Complete Prose Fiction* opens with *The Tales of the Late Ivan
Petrovich Belkin,* done very much to the recipe of Scott's *Tales of My
Landlord*. Pushkin is the simple raconteur of another man's tales, a
man looking back on his time, and the dialogue is dull and largely
indirect and generalised, even though the stories amuse us. Pushkin's
early prose is still expository, and even scholarly. In fact, he had a
natural bent for exposition: his *History of Pugachev* is almost
official and neutral in manner, and was carefully reconstructed from
historical documents; yet out of this sprang 'The Captain's
Daughter', a Romantic and vivid story of spun-out suspense.
Debreczeny seems to me too much a structuralist in reading Oedipal
complexity into the tale. The ironical beginning – the wilful hero, a
young officer, and the morally rebuking family servant in their
journey through a blizzard to a military station on the frontier –
seems to promise the conventional theme of headstrong master and
testy servant. But it suddenly breaks with the eighteenth-century
tradition. By the time we get to the wretched fort where the young
man has been sent to be broken in, we are alarmed. The modest
commander at the absurd fort is a man risen from the ranks and too
self-effacing to drill his troops properly; his nice wife and their
daughter are charming – too charming for their dangerous life. The
young man is soon quarrelling with an unpleasant officer about the
commander's daughter. They all forget they are facing a savage
rebellion led by the primitive Pugachev and his tribesmen. Then
comes the attack and Pushkin's mastery of intrigue. The commander
has at any rate the wit to hide his daughter, an obvious prize. But
horror ensues. Pugachev captures the place, kills the commander's
wife, hangs the commander and a lieutenant, and *leaves them
hanging* in order to cow the villagers at the fort. The young officer
boldly demands a safe conduct for the girl. The crucial scene is the
meeting with Pugachev, who has him at his mercy. Pugachev is
suddenly obliging. Critics have found this unbelievable in a cruel and
savage leader. Why? So well is this incident managed that we are
convinced: the double self is not unknown. Then, the two men have
met before, in the blizzard, without knowing each other's names.
The young man had given Pugachev a hareskin coat. If we don't

accept this as a bond, surely it is plain that a daring rebel would admire a daring man, or a man of honour. Moreover, Pugachev has proclaimed himself King of Russia and can be expected to indulge the mercy of a king. Or maybe he is feeling the melancholy that has come after an easy victory. Perhaps in the self-command of the young man the rebel sees that his own successes with his ungovernable tribesmen will soon run out. Possibly he is a gambler vain of playing with risk. Pushkin is drawn to the mysteries of honour. Any one of these motives seems more than plausible. More serious is the criticism of the cruel and disgusting exposure of the bodies of the commander and his lieutenant. We have not seen them hanged, but worse – they are left obscenely hanging, and Pushkin does not miss a shocked glance at them. The sight indeed haunts the reader with a kind of shame at seeing it. Surely the contemporary reader in our far more cruel and violent times has seen or heard worse. But has the tone of the story been broken – a false note struck, not in life but in art? One Russian writer, the poet Marina Tsvetayeva (Mr Debreczeny tells us), has argued that we can accept the scene as children accept horror in a fairy tale. Pugachev, she says, 'is not an ordinary human being in our perception, but an incarnation of the evil of popular imagination, the wolf or robber of folklore.' And, in fact, a Russian of Pushkin's generation was closer to the figures and emotions of folklore than we are. The Flaubert of *Salammbô* would not have objected. Romanticism could not resist the macabre.

The unfinished 'Dubrovskii' is also a story of outlawry, which starts – almost as a document of social protest – with a quarrel between a villainous landowner and his humble, decent neighbour and turns into a tale of ingenious revenge and a charade of disguises. The helpless lover of justice, who has the oppressed peasants on his side, turns into an elusive Robin Hood, cleverly righting public wrongs. This story was founded on real court cases, and was no myth. Pushkin used all his skill in playing with it and then suddenly tired of his ingenuity.

The one certain triumph of the collection is, of course, 'The Queen of Spades'. It is hard to think of a short story so shapely, so diamond-like, a dire comedy so full and so ingeniously concentrated, and so morally convincing. The poet has written a sonnet – a series of interlocking sonnets – in prose. His tact is perfect. We are left astounded at 'the pack' of characters, the moments of Society life, phases of gambling fever, times of day and night that glitter beneath its deceiving surface. The weather itself is alive, and the story is as visual as a Vermeer. Moments are caught and held and pass, just as ordinary life passes, and now Pushkin becomes, at last, a connoisseur of the kind of natural talk that, like a played card, has a new meaning as it falls on the table. The superstition of the magic hand of three cards suggests a fairy tale, yet the real subject is the fever of greed. (Freud, Mr Debreczeny notes, said that gamblers seek self-destruction.) It is interesting that Hermann, the German gambler, is a little Napoleon in appearance, the very model of the upstart of enormous will: men of will are the most likely to become irrational. So the story is not artificial; nor is it a fantasy, asking us to suspend disbelief in magic. It is intensely real as a study of Petersburg types, and its predominant interest is psychological. Pushkin is a great painter of the miniature portrait that appears to be still and fixed yet becomes fiercely alive and moves, changes, and reveals what is hidden the closer we look. Pushkin, the craftsman-gambler, knew that the cards are not cards only but emblems of risk and passion. Like other things of Pushkin's, the story was not invented by him; such tales of magic sequences of cards go the rounds of those who are fevered by the game. Once more, the curt speed of Stendhal is seen in the writing. The German is a tedious little man, too cautious to play until he is equipped to cheat. No poet he. The old Countess, with her secret of the winning sequence and her history, is a superb creation. She is believable when she dies of sudden shock after the young gambler threatens her and begs for her secret, in the rightly famous bedroom scene. She simply dies, like a dropped card, in four simple lines. She is also believable after her death, when she 'walks' as a ghost. Her 'walk' is, of course, in the young German's guilty mind. It is a marvellous observation of Pushkin's that as an imagined ghost she is 'seen' still wearing her bedroom slippers and can slam a door loudly when she leaves. The very detail of the screens, the corridors, the staircase of her apartment dramatises the phases of the gambler's desperate secretiveness. Pushkin has learned how to make the detail of furniture and passages briefly work for him. His passing talk creates the crisis. If there is symbolism in it, it is beautifully concealed. I am not sure that it is safe for critics like Mr Debreczeny to dig it out; it is really an aspect of reverie. Again and again, as they looked at life, the Russian novelists thought the 'real' was not real until it was seen to be strange.

(1984)

MIKHAIL YUREVICH LERMONTOV

A Hero of Our Time

Mikhail Yurevich Lermontov was born in the year before Waterloo and was killed in a duel twenty-seven years later, a year after the publication of the novel which brought him fame throughout Europe. The extraordinary duel in the last chapter but one of *A Hero of Our Own Times* is said to have been exactly prophetic of the manner of his death. Lermontov had declared through his chief character that life was a bad imitation of a book; and the episode, if true, looks like some carefully planned Byronic legend.

A Hero of Our Own Times belongs to that small and elect group of novels which portray a great typical character who resumes the fashion and idiosyncrasy of a generation. Pechorin, the 'hero', is consciously a Russian Byron. He is cold, sensual, egoistical, elegant. He is neurotic, bored and doomed. Only one passion is unexhausted – and this is the making of him – the passion for personal freedom. He is the cold, experimental amorist celebrated by Pushkin (I quote from Oliver Elton's translation of *Eugeny Onegin*):

> Men once extolled cold-blooded raking
> As the true science of love-making:
> Your own trump everywhere you blew . . .
> Such grave and serious recreation
> Beseemed old monkeys, of those days. . .

Pechorin becomes the slave of perpetual travel, and finally fulfils himself not in love but in action. Byron goes to Greece. Pechorin becomes the soldier of the Caucasus who plays with life and death. He drives himself to the limit, whether it is in the duel on the edge of the precipice down which his absurd rival in love is thrown; or in the dramatic bet with Vulich where he draws a revolver and puts sixty roubles on the doctrine of predestination; or in the final episode when he goes in alone to collar the Cossack who has run amok. In its greater actors the Byronic pose of weariness is balanced by love of living dangerously in action, and here it is interesting to contrast the character of Constant's Adolphe with a man like Pechorin. Adolphe also is the imaginative man who loves from the head and then revenges himself secretively and cruelly upon the strong-minded woman who is devouring him and with whom he is afraid to break: Pechorin, more histrionic and less sensitive (more Byronic, in short), loves from the head also but takes special care to avoid strong-minded women. He possesses, but is not possessed. He prefers the weak and yielding who respond at once to cruelty and whom he can abandon quickly. Faced with the strong-minded, Pechorin becomes a man of action and makes his getaway. Readers of *A Hero of Our Own Times* will remember how Pechorin dealt with the determined duplicity of Taman, the smuggler's girl, when she took him out in her boat on a moonlight night. He threw her into the sea. What would not Adolphe have given for such decisiveness? What would he not have given for that Byronic ruthlessness in action, who knew only the cool vacillations of the mind? Of the two characters, Pechorin's is the more arrested and adolescent. He has not Adolphe's sensibility to the tragedy of the imagination. He does not suffer. Pechorin is sometimes a seventeen-year-old sentimentalist who blames the world:

> I have entered upon this life when I have already lived it in imagination, with the result that it has become tedious and vile to me. I am like a man who has been reading the bad imitation of a book with which he has been long familiar.

But perhaps the main difference between these lovers of freedom is merely one of age after all. Pechorin-Lermontov is young: Adolphe is the creation of an older man. Pechorin says: 'Now I only want to be loved, and that by a very few women. Sometimes (terrible thought) I feel as if a lasting tie would satisfy me.'

Adolphe would have been incapable of this naïve Byronic jauntiness; but he would have raised a sympathetic eyebrow at that first hint of nostalgia for respectable marriage.

This was not a solution which Russian literature was yet to permit its Pechorins. Press on to the middle of the century and we find Turgenev's Rudin, all Byronism spent, and with no exciting war of Russian Imperialism to occupy him, conducting an affair as heartless and disgraceful as Pechorin's affair with Princess Mary and very similar to it. But Rudin is reduced to the condition of an unheroic, rootless talker with no corresponding performance. Byronism, with its roots in the Napoleonic wars, was a fashion which fortunately could give the best of its followers something to do. For the maladjusted and the doomed there were duels; even better there was frontier war and the cause of Liberty. The poseur of Venice attained some dignity at Missolonghi: and the sentimentalist of the Caucasus, reviving new trouble with an old mistress, and in the midst of the old trouble with a new one, could feel the heady contagion of that half-savage passion for freedom with which his enemies, the Tartar tribesmen, were imbued.

Travel is one of the great rivals of women. The officers and visitors at the garrison town of Narzan spend their time drinking the waters, making love, scandal-mongering and playing cards; and into this gossiping frontier outpost Pechorin brings something like the preposterous coldness, austerity and violence of the mountain scene outside the town. The coach arrives, he yawns, stays a night, throws his diaries to a friend in lieu of a renewal of friendship and drives on, another Childe Harold on an eternal Grand Tour of the battle fronts. The *Hero* is not one of the calculated, constructed, and balanced books of maturity; its virtues and defects are all of youth. The book appears to pour out of the Caucasus itself. It is one of those Romantic novels in which a place and not a woman has suddenly crystallised a writer's experience and called out all his gifts. 'I was posting from Tiflis' – that opening sentence of Lermontov's classically nonchalant prose, takes the heart a stride forward at once. Like the traveller, we step out of ourselves into a new world. True, it is the fashionable step back to Rousseau, for the *Hero* is nothing if not modish; but who does not feel again with Lermontov, as he gazes at the ravines, breathes the rare, crisp, savage air and sees the golden dawn on the upper snows, who does not feel the force of the Romantic emotion? 'When we get close to Nature the soul sheds all that it has artificially acquired to be what it was in its prime and probably will be again some day.' One is captivated by such a nostalgia, by its youthful and natural idealism and by the artifice of its youthful melancholy.

The structure of the book is both ingenious and careless. Later novelists would have been tempted to a full-length portrait of Pechorin. Lermontov is episodic yet tells us all we need to know in a handful of exciting short stories. We first hear of Pechorin at two removes. The narrator meets a curt, humdrum officer who has known him and who tells the first story of Pechorin's capture and abandonment of Bela, the Tartar girl. Passion has ended in boredom.

In the next episode, when Pechorin meets again the officer who had helped him fight the girl's murderers, one sees the Byronic mask go up at the mere hint of the 'incident'. After that Pechorin himself describes his adventures in his diaries. They tell, with sadistic detachment, of how he is playing with the despair of an old mistress while planning to convert another woman's fear and hatred of him to love. He succeeds. Which is all Pechorin wants – a victory for his vanity. He explains this quite candidly to her. And he is candid not because he is an honest man but because, of course, he is interested only in himself. Equally coolly, he plans that the duel he fights with her lover shall take place on the famous precipice.

Pechorin's notions are not merely the melodramatic. He is the enemy of simple, highfalutin romanticism; his taste is for the reserved, the complex and extreme. The precipice is chosen, for example, as the right site of vengeance, because he has discovered that his opponent intends to fool him with blank cartridges. The opposing faction at Narzan has perceived that Pechorin's vulnerable point is his pride; knock the Byronic mask off his face and there will stand an empty actor. Lermontov is an expert in subtleties like this. In the final episode, when Vulich, the gambler, proposes to discover whether he is or is not fated to die that day, by putting a revolver to his head and pulling the trigger, the suicide is abortive. But Vulich does die that day, and in a most unexpected manner. The Calvinist doctrine of predestination in Byron's Aberdeen has become the almost exotic Oriental Kismet in Lermontov's Caucasus.

To the modern novelist, tired of the many and overdone conventions of the novel, the apparently loose and unconnected construction of *A Hero of Our Times* offers a suggestion. Lermontov's method is to thread together a string of short stories about a central character, using an inside and an outside point of view. But before he did this Lermontov had decided what were the important things in Pechorin's character. They were, as it happened, all aspects of Byronism. Mr Desmond MacCarthy has said in an essay on Pushkin, that from Byron and Pushkin 'men caught the infection of being defiantly themselves'; in so planning, however, they became other than themselves. They invented a simplified *persona*. It is this simplification of Pechorin's character which is exciting. The detailed realism of the modern novel tells us far too much, without defining the little that it is absolutely essential to know. In what modern novels are the main traits of a hero of *our* own times delineated? It is the measure of the failure of modern novelists that they have not observed and defined a characteristic man of these years; and the explanation of the failure is our lack of moral and political perceptiveness. Our novels would be shorter, more readable and more important if we had one or two more ideas about our times and far fewer characters.

(1942)

Dostoevsky's Wife

The story of Dostoevsky's extraordinary second marriage during which he wrote his greatest novels is a novel in itself. He was forty-five and a widower; his first marriage and his love affairs had been disastrous; he was bankrupt; he had assumed the heavy debts of his dead brother and responsibility for the family, also for the predatory and offensive son of his own first wife by a previous husband. Dostoevsky was ill and drowning in a sea of promissory notes, and had had to stop writing *Crime and Punishment* because he had been trapped by a publishing rascal into another novel. A penalty clause had been put into the contract which would bind his earnings to the man for nine years if he failed to deliver the book within four weeks. He was exhausted and ill, and he had no clear story in his head beyond his experiences as a ruined gambler tormented by a neurotic young mistress.

In his plight he was persuaded to call in a girl stenographer – a new career for women in the 1860s – and a plain, awed girl of twenty arrived. He stared at her with embarrassment and in silence for two days and then suddenly found he could dictate. The novel was *The Gambler*, it was finished within two days of the deadline, and, as the girl had sharply foreseen, the publisher had disappeared into the country in order to dodge delivery and close the trap. Dostoevsky was forced to go round from one police station to another in St Petersburg before he found an officer willing to give him a receipt for the manuscript. In the meantime the novelist had fallen in love with the stenographer – to whom he had nothing but his calamities to offer – and was astounded to find she had fallen in love with him.

Such young daydreamers as this Anna seemed to be do not usually last the course, but Anna did. The fact is that her obscure family and especially her father and herself were old admirers of Dostoevsky's work: he was a hero before she met him. She was no intellectual; her one pride was that she was the prize pupil of the stenography school. It is interesting that her mother came of stolid Swedish Lutheran stock and her father, who was a reading man, from the Ukraine: a uniting of efficiency and fantasy.

Anna inherited her mother's independence and her matter-of-fact temperament, and under the influence of the feminism of the Sixties (and in the manner of the Nihilists whom she defended, though she disapproved of their rude manners and their affectation of sloppy clothes) she believed a girl should earn her living. If she was literal-minded and frankly said she did not understand Dostoevsky's ideas, even when he tried to put them simply to her, she revered his work and gave him total devotion and family happiness for the fourteen years left to him. She saw at once that he had to have peace of mind for his work and that she must behave with total self-abnegation, even at the cost of her own feelings; yet if she might appear to him as one of his 'meek' characters, she was far from that.

It was soon evident to her that the immediate enemies of her marriage were the leechlike family and especially the arrogant stepson. They saw Anna as a frivolous young intruder who would take the bread out of their mouths. When she fought back they sneered and told her that the family – and not she – had the first claim on her husband's time and money. The course of the battle is set out in the *Reminiscences* which after Dostoevsky's death she tried to put together from the daily shorthand notes she made about every detail of their life together.

As Helen Muchnic says in her introduction to the present revised edition – the first appeared in 1925 edited by Leonid Grossman – it is a plain, straightforward, honest, and moving account of a happy if reckless marriage, a record tritely and exactly domestic. The tone is neither boastful nor fulsome. She says little or nothing about his work, and is unique in offering no theories about his genius. Dostoevsky appears as the childlike, toiling, anxious, and affectionate father who has to be protected from the world and whose inner tumults – his gambling for example – are understood without being censured. She is perhaps a little proud of his ludicrous jealousy. The brave, simple young adorer has written the only really intimate portrait of him that we have.

There is something more than his portrait and the joys and great sorrows and struggles of a marriage, the misery of the loss of two children. She evokes, without trying, what everyday Russian life in shabby districts was like, without dramatising it as the Russian realists do: the grey exposure to lies, meanness, trickery, cheating, and stealing, the dangers of the streets at night where violence and robbery were taken for granted, the rule of the pawnshop, the cult of begging, the flooding in of hungry hangers-on in every family, the fights with the landlords, the clumsy difficulties of getting about from one district to another, the damp, unhealthy climate of Petersburg which killed off the weak, the collusion of police with thieves. Her book makes one understand why Dostoevsky's novels are choked with people whose lives are hanging out on their tongues and whose only role seems to be to drag in others, living by custom at one another's expense. In his own flat the relatives swarmed in to borrow and be fed and to shout and cry in each others' faces by divine right. There is no privacy in Dostoevsky's novels and Anna had to fight for that above all, so that he could work.

And then, during the dragged-out and drunken jollities of their wedding Anna had to face the shock of his epilepsy. He seems not to have told her of it. Suddenly he fell roaring to the floor and at once the family ran away, noses in the air, and left the 'silly girl' to deal with his fits as best she could. After this experience, she guarded her tongue and became the constant watcher for the rest of her life. She saw that the first step must be to free him from his family and that the only way to do this was to get him out of Russia. The relations came round whining, threatening, and defying her at once. They waylaid him to get his money from him and he was too weak to stand out against them. Her master-stroke was to use the money of her own small dowry: even the stepson saw that they could not touch that – and for the four years during which she and her husband were travelling in Europe the family were defeated and the marriage became unshakable.

Despite the dislike of Europe which was – and is still – a religion among Russians and in Dostoevsky's writings particularly, both he and Anna were deeply happy. She was, of course, seeing an entrancing new world for the first time. Dostoevsky was a tireless walker, a firm visitor of art galleries. Anna walked, listened, and marvelled; but also noted down the prices in shops and was overcome when she saw her genius fussing about new underclothes for her at the draper's or choosing hats. From Dresden they went to Wiesbaden and Baden-Baden. But she noticed he was not writing. She had not transcribed *The Gambler* for nothing. She saw the gambler's passion stir when their money began to go. She was sensible enough not to try to stop this obsession from bursting out when it did, though it soon brought them to the pawnshop and to desperate letters to her mother and his friends. She listened to his mad hopes and remorseful sobs: she gave in when he begged again. She even writes:

All of Fyodor Mikhailovich's rationalisations about the possibilities of winning at roulette by using his gambling system were entirely correct. His success might have been complete – but only on condition that this system was applied by some cool-headed Englishman or German and not by such a nervous and impulsive person as my husband, who went to the uttermost limits in everything.

But she adds shrewdly:

In addition to cool-headedness and perseverance, the roulette player must have substantial means in order to be able to hold out through unfavourable turns of the wheel.

He came home in despair after one more ruinous evening, saying that just as he was winning he caught sight precisely of one of those cool-headed Englishmen at the table – this is much better reported in the shorthand notes, of the 1925 edition – and at once lost his nerve and everything he had won. (One sees how visual his disturbed mind was: calamity was a person.) Anna was proud of keeping her own domestic head and of not uttering a word of reproach. The passion did at last burn out and suddenly he began to write.

The return to Russia had its traditional risks that have lasted until today. Knowing that his manuscripts and papers would be taken from him at the frontier and that, as a one-time political prisoner and still under surveillance, he might not get them back, he decided to burn his drafts of *The Idiot* and his notebooks. Anna argued him out of that; her mother had come to stay with them and they got her to smuggle his notebooks in.

Back in Russia Anna took one more bold step. She knew that he was incapable of dealing with money and with publishers, and when *The Devils* was written she decided to get his work printed, published, and distributed by herself. She knew nothing of the trade. She was ignorant of the Balzacian nature of Russian commerce, and that it depended on the promissory note and on dealing in discounted bills. She had the housewife's suspicion of a practice so mystical but soon mastered it.

The bookseller Kozhanchikov came to us with an offer to buy 300 copies on a four-month promissory note. He asked for the regular discount of 30 percent. . . What troubled us was that he would be taking them on Notes. . . I had no idea what a commercial Note was at that time and therefore suggested to my husband that he should chat for a while with the buyer while I would drive over to the printer. . . He assured me that Kozhanchikov's Notes were good and that he would be willing to accept them in payment of our printing debt.

She was amused when buyers came in and did not know the title of the book: 'Sometimes they called it 'the Evil One,' sometimes they would say 'I came for the devils,' and sometimes "Let me have a dozen demons."'

She took over the business of dealing with people who, at several removes, had taken up his own promissory notes: a crowd of widows, landladies, retired officers, and frauds arrived, threatening attachment and prison. Put him in prison and he will earn nothing, she said. That brought them to compromise, and after thirteen years of embittering struggle she paid off the debts which Dostoevsky had taken over from his dead brother and their own: 20,000 roubles. Her only bitterness is that burden. When she looked at the easy lives of Turgenev, Tolstoy, and Goncharov, all of whom had money, she was indignant when critics complained of Dostoevsky's repetitive and clumsy style:

How many times did it happen in the last fourteen years of his life that two or three chapters [of a novel] had already been published in the journal, the fourth was in the process of being set up in type, the fifth was in the mail on its way to the *Russian Messenger*, and the rest had not yet been written down and existed only in his head.

And, as we know from his notebooks, only in a confused and speculative state.

Their holidays in the country were as perilous as their life in St Petersburg. In a country of wooden buildings disastrous fires swept through villages and towns. The Dostoevskys scrambled into the streets with their belongings and then scrambled back when the fire stopped short of their dwelling. The carting about of luggage by road, steamer, or ferry was a nightmare. Landing at Novgorod from Lake Ilmen one night they lost the suitcase containing the manuscript of *A Raw Youth*, for which they were frantic to collect the money next day. Anna guessed it might have been stolen at the docks, a neighbourhood noted for armed thieves and hoodlums, and herself drove there with a scared driver who was afraid a dock gang would seize his cab. They ran off when they saw Anna, who had found the case. It took courage for a woman to go into these slummy neighbourhoods at night. It is characteristic of their life that she left Dostoevsky standing with the children while she herself went off on the search.

The present edition of the *Reminiscences*, revised by the Soviet scholars S. V. Belov and V. A. Tunimanov, was published in 1971 and was based on over thirty notebooks of rough drafts, in confused chronological order. Anna rewrote, duplicated, and had not arrived at a definitive text. There were 800 pages of manuscript and it is now at last in order. Certain things from the shorthand notes in the Leonid Grossman edition have been smoothed away or have vanished: the direct explosive account of the famous quarrel with Turgenev about *Smoke* which Dostoevsky gave when he returned from his row has gone, perhaps because it has been described by other hands or because Anna had come to idealise the past. The only faults she allows her husband are the irritability natural to writers, and his absurd and violent fits of jealousy or terror when he saw her speaking to other men. In a giddy moment she once provoked his jealousy by faking an anonymous letter: he nearly strangled her.

Her shocked refutation of Strakhov's attack on her husband after his death, in which he insinuated that Dostoevsky had seduced a child in a bath house, is printed in full. In an early version of *The Devils*, Stavrogin is said to have done this, and the publisher made Dostoevsky cut it out. But, Anna said, she had learned enough about the artistic imagination to understand that an artist does not need to be a criminal in order to describe a crime. She defends him, too, against the common charge that he was a nasty, suspicious whisperer of malicious things when he was in company: he came into crowded rooms and flopped down 'not in arrogant silence', she says, but because his incurable emphysema left him struggling for breath. The marriage succeeded, she wrote, because neither of them tried to meddle with the other's 'soul'. 'In this way my good husband and I both of us felt free in spirit.' And as Helen Muchnic adds in her feeling introduction to this book, Anna did not pry. He was her idol, she said. Perhaps because, unlike the idols of a young girl's dreams, she saw an idol who worked like a demented slave and was helpless without her.

(1979)

IVAN TURGENEV

Turgenev in Baden

In 1861 Turgenev's great novel *Fathers and Sons* was published in St Petersburg. He was forty-three; the book was his masterpiece but it brought violent abuse upon him in Russia both from the conservatives and the young radicals who considered that they had been caricatured in the portrait of Bazarov, the Nihilist doctor. The abuse was wounding, for until then Turgenev had been able to think of himself as the liberating voice of the young. From this moment his life as an expatriate began: he left Russia in disgust and anger.

The attacks were not the sole cause of his decision to leave. There was an emotional reason of deep importance. Ever since he was thirty, indeed earlier, he had been in love with Pauline Viardot, the famous Spanish opera singer. At one time they were possibly lovers, living out the drama of *A Month in the Country*, but it seems that the feeling was stronger on his side than on hers and that she put her art, her career, her marriage, and her children first and kept Turgenev at a distance.

But in 1861 there was a change: the feeling or the need for Turgenev revived on her side. Her famous voice was failing although she was scarcely forty; she withdrew from the great opera houses of Europe, and she and her husband settled at the immensely fashionable spa and little court of Baden on the Rhine, where she could hold a salon, give concerts, and take a few pupils for enormous fees. Now she beckoned to Turgenev once more. He was rich. He could build a small theatre for her, help her publish her musical albums, and he was an enormous social asset at her salons. The slavery (as he called it) of his old love for her revived, their affections were close. What Russians resented was that from this time until his death his home was Europe and close to the Viardots: to his estate in Russia he certainly went from time to time, but as one whose ties were elsewhere.

It is clear from his letters to his friends in the Baden period that he feared expatriation would injure his talent. More and more, he feared he would drift into mere reminiscence and lose his knowledge of contemporary Russia. He began to defend himself and to ask what was wrong with non-contemporary characters, what was wrong with the past. In 1870 – which turned out to be the end of his Baden period because of the outbreak of the Franco-Prussian war – we find him writing to a correspondent that a 'Russian writer who has settled in Baden by that very fact condemns his writing to an early end. I have no illusions on that score, but since everything else is impossible, there is no point in talking about it. . . But are you really so submerged in what is "contemporary" that you will not tolerate any non-contemporary characters?' Such people, Turgenev says, have lived and have a right to be portrayed. 'I admit no other immortality: and this immortality of human life (in the eyes of art and history) is the basis of my whole world.'

What is one to think of Turgenev's writing in the Baden period? The most important book to come out of it was the novel *Smoke* (1867), and although the Russian critics attacked it violently for political and patriotic reasons, it is a very able book. His occasional visits to Russia had not been wasted: he had another long book in mind – *Virgin Soil* – but he was not ready for it and, after *Smoke*, his Baden period is remarkable for his long short stories in which he rarely failed. He was simply, he said, 'too full of subjects'.

In his early fifties he wrote two reminiscent stories – one of them the horrifying tale 'The Brigadier', based on an incident in the life of his Lutvinov grandmother who had committed murder. A very old and senile brigadier, 'of the age of Catherine', is seen fishing, accompanied by a bullying servant who ridicules him. The brigadier has become a ruined and childish simpleton, reduced to poverty and ostracism because in middle years he had loved and lived with a terrifying young widow who, in a rage, had killed her page. Out of love and in a fit of honour the brigadier assumed guilt for her crime and was tried for it, but his sentence had been short. The widow and (after her death) her sister bleed him of all his money until he is destitute. Yet once a week he visits the widow's grave with adoration. At last he knows he is going to die. He knows because of a dream.

I, as maybe you know, often see Agrippina Ivanov [as he now calls her] in my dreams – heaven's peace be with her – and never can I catch her: I am always running after her but cannot catch her. But last night I dreamed she was standing, as it were, before me, half turned away and laughing. . . I ran up to her at once and caught her . . . and she seemed to turn round quite and said to me 'Well, Vassinka, now you have caught me. . .' It has come to me that we shall be together again.

The tale is told in the old-fashioned way of picking up the story by hearsay in the manner of a folk tale, but in the servant's mockery there is something of the mockery of Shakespeare's cynical comics and Turgenev has made it powerful. The hearsay, the careful reader will notice, is not flat in its convenience but is subtly varied as changes of scene and voice are made to carry it. The theme is, of course, familiar in his writings: a man dominated and enduring abasement and suffering in love. He will give everything to the monster but he lives by his honour, which is a kind of exultation. The dream of death as a woman is also a common theme and so is the myth of bewitchment offered as a psychological fact.

The theme of honour as the real test in love and indeed in all crucial circumstances is of great importance in Turgenev's writing and it must not be taken as a romanticisation of an old-fashioned or picturesque idea common enough in the historical novels of the nineteenth century. If the brigadier's honour is not to be questioned, this is for reasons of Russian history. Turgenev believed that Russia was uncivilised in the Western sense because there had been no experience of an age of chivalry in its culture. And if we look beyond this story to his own life, it would seem that his own Quixote-like concept of love in his feelings for Pauline Viardot is a chivalrous vow which once uttered must never be betrayed; in that sense his love of her was not a weakness or an obsession. It was an anachronism – the lifelong vigil. It was not even romantic, but a spiritual law, an article of the aristocratic faith.

'The Brigadier' is not only an important story, but a very revealing one in another connection. In his own life, Turgenev felt he owed it to himself as a duty of chivalrous principle to give money secretly to revolutionaries like Bakunin and others – the Populist leader, for example – even though he hated violence and terrorism and feared the loss of his property.

The idea of honour abused is at the heart of 'An Unhappy Girl', a story drawn from his student days. The girl is half-Jewish, one of the maltreated 'orphans' handed on: the Jewish aspect of her beauty is ancient, ennobled by race and aristocratic instinct. She is helplessly trapped in a coarse German family. Her tale is remarkable for its scenes of vulgar lower-middle-class life, its gambling episodes, and a drunken funeral meal which follows the funeral of the tormented girl who has been driven to suicide. Unfortunately there is an element of plot: it is suggested that the girl may have been poisoned so that her small inheritance would then pass to the awful Germans if she died unmarried. Plot-making was outside Turgenev's competence. The girl's wretched state is well done but Dostoevsky with his dynamic power of dramatising the inner life of the 'insulted and injured' would have made more of her, for Dostoevsky believed in free will whereas the art of Turgenev, the determinist, is in this sense static: people live under fate. Or rather time flows through them: they do not drive blindly forward through time.

In 'The Story of Lieutenant Erguynov' a young naval officer is stripped of his money by a sly, amusing, fascinating girl who is a decoy used by thieves. Again the plot is awkward but there are some brilliant things in the tale, particularly in the account of Erguynov's state of hallucination when, his drink being doped, he sails out of consciousness to the sound of the balalaika, is robbed, knocked on the head, and dumped with his skull split on the roadside. And we get pleasure from the fact that, in old age, the simple lieutenant loves telling the whole story again and again, and loves to dwell on his hallucination so that the company knows the tale by heart. For what we are shown is an innocent young sailor growing into a knowing old fellow, enlarging himself as he talks. He makes us feel that he is telling us something that is now more completely 'true' than it was when it was scattered in the fragmentary experience of real life.

The point of honour crops up at the end, but comically. The thieves escape and so does the girl, but much later she writes to the sailor begging him to believe she herself was not responsible for the attempt to murder him. She had no idea they would go *that* far, and she would like to see him and convince him that although she did deceive him she is not a criminal. The sailor – an honourable fellow – is rather taken by the idea, but he puts it off and does nothing. The fact that he does nothing makes the story rest delightfully in suspense – which is an aspect of life.

None of these stories approaches the power of 'A Lear of the Steppe'. This is a major work. The Lear is Martin Petrovich Harlov, a hulking, rough, bearlike figure who farms 800 acres and owns serfs but who, though claiming to come of noble Russian stock 'as old as

Vassilievitch the Dark', is a hard-driving peasant farmer, a stern, shouting, but honest man. He lives in what he calls his 'mansion', a ramshackle homestead he has built with his own hands, a small manor with courtyard and a tumbledown thatched lodge. His own room in the house is unplastered. His riding whips, his horse collar hang from nails on the wall. There is a wooden settle with a rug, flies swarm on the ceiling, and the place smells as he himself does, of the forest. In the house live his two daughters: Anna, who is married to the whining and greedy son of a petty official, and Evlampia, who is being courted by a battered and broken major. Both girls are beauties.

The narrator is fifteen when the events begin, the son of a wealthy landowning widow. The story has, but only superficially, the tone of *A Sportsman's Sketches*, but it will go much deeper. The widow has always been Harlov's friend and adviser, so that we see Harlov through the eyes of an awed boy, as it might be Turgenev himself as a boy living with his mother at Spasskoye. If Harlov is a primitive giant he seems all the more gigantic to a boy's wondering eyes. Turgenev is careful to convey the physical force of Harlov's person with metaphors that evoke the man and the working scenes of his life. The voice that came out of a small mouth was strong and resonant:

Its sound recalled the clank of iron bars carried in a cart over a badly paved road; and when Harlov spoke it was as though someone were shouting in a high wind across a wide ravine . . . his shoulders were like millstones . . . his ears were like twists of bread . . . he breathed like a bull but walked without a sound.

It is important to the story that the boy's mother had found a wife for Harlov, a frail girl who lasted only long enough to give him two daughters, and saw to it that they had a superior education. Times are changing: we shall see the result of this kindness. The daughters will eventually turn their father out of his own house and drive him to frenzy and death.

The wonder is that this confident, dominant, and roaring man who frightens everyone – 'the wood demon' as people call him – will bring about his own downfall by an act of Lear-like weakness. He is liable to fits of melancholy during which he shuts himself up in his room and starts to hum 'like a swarm of bees'. The hours of humming end in singing meaningless words. He recovers. It is after one of these fits that he comes to his friend the widow and announces that Death has appeared to him in a dream in the form of a black colt that rushes into the house, dances about, and finally gives him a kick in the arm. He wakes up aching in every bone. It is this terror that has driven him to a bid for power which is exorbitant and, indeed, a sign of folly: he is going to divide his property between his daughters now, willing it to them is not enough for he wants to see their gratitude. He wants to establish his absolute rule after death now and before his eyes. Nothing will persuade him that this is foolish.

The story now expands. We are in the Russia of *A Sportsman's Sketches*. A crowd of characters come in, the lawyers, the police, officials, the grasping son-in-law, and a spiteful jeering figure called Souvenir, an orphan, the brother of Harlov's dead wife who is a hanger-on in the landowner's house. Souvenir has a mawkish laugh that sounds like the rinsing of a bottle, and whenever Harlov calls at the house he goes swaggering after him and saying, 'What made you kill my sister?' Souvenir has a goading diabolical role to play. The deed of gift is signed and Souvenir tells the old man with delight that now his daughters will turn him out.

Turgenev always understands how to insert points of rest in which a story can grow of itself. The boy narrator goes away for the summer. In the autumn he goes out shooting snipe and sees a stranger riding Harlov's horse. It is the first sign of the truth of Souvenir's prophecy. Horse and carriage have been taken from Harlov by Anna and Sletkin, her husband. Harlov is being starved and stripped of everything. The two sisters are at odds. Evlampia has turned the major down and is having an affair with Sletkin – the boy catches them in the woods – and when he hears of this Harlov rushes in a state of madness to the big house. In his bid for power, Harlov has exhausted his great will. He has lost his terrifying force and has become helpless, acquiescent, and meek. This is Souvenir's moment. He mocks the old man for his fall, jeering without pity. Suddenly the old man rises to the taunts, recovers his old violence, and rushes back to his manor, and in a terrible scene climbs to the roof and starts tearing down what he has built with his own hands. The peasants cannot stop him as he rips away the rafters and knocks down chimneys. In a final triumph of strength he wrenches a gable and a crossbeam off and is crushed when he falls with them to the ground.

One does not expect such a scene of violence from Turgenev. It succeeds because it is made to seem likely among the people of the steppe. The two daughters have been skilfully kept in the background where, by one small touch or another, they have aroused our

apprehension. We have seen Anna's cold smile; we have seen
Evlampia, silent as stone, a still, sensual beauty with a store of power
in her. Of Anna, the boy remarks in a disturbing Turgenevian
reflection:

In spite of the negligence of her attire and her irritable humour, she struck me
as before, as attractive and I should have been delighted to kiss the narrow
hand which looked malignant too, as she twice irritably pushed back her
loose tresses.

The tragedy is over and the story is restored little by little to the
norms of peasant life.

In studying the peasants as a group, Turgenev has gone beyond the
scope of *A Sportsman's Sketches*, though the luminous quality of
that early work gives the scene perspective and truth. At first the
peasants stand aloof from Anna, but for Evlampia there was a kind
of sympathy, except from an old man who said: 'You wronged him;
on your soul lies the sin.' At the funeral the faces of the crowd
condemn the family, but the condemnation has become impersonal.
That is the next stage.

It seemed as though all those people felt that the sin into which the Harlov
family had fallen – this great sin – had gone now before the presence of one
righteous Judge and for that reason there was no need now for them to
trouble themselves and be indignant. They prayed devoutly for the soul of
the dead man whom in life they had not especially liked, whom they feared
indeed.

Anna's voice, we remember, was 'very pleasant, resonant and rather
plaintive . . . like the note of a bird of prey,' but she says nothing.
Evlampia, fierce, monumental – 'a free bird of the Cossack breed' –
fierce in the glance of her dark blue eyes, was silent too. Sletkin tries
to get a word out of her, but she treats him as she has treated the
absurd major who wanted to marry her.

In a day or two she has sold her interest to her sister and has
vanished. Years later the narrator sees her again, driving in a smart
pony trap, splendidly dressed. She has become the founder, the
dominant mother of a dissenting Order of Flagellant Sisters who live
without priests. Whether this is a genuine order is uncertain: is her
house a place of rendezvous? For the peasants wink and say the
police captain does well out of the Order. It is she who inherits the
primitive spirit of her father, maybe is honest – but maybe not: the
spirit of an extremist.

Sletkin, Anna's scheming husband, has died – the peasants say, probably untruthfully, that she poisoned him – and she is now an excellent farmer, better than her father was, clever in the legal negotiations that have followed the change in the land laws after the Emancipation. The great landlords and officials respect her judgment.

In other words, after tragedy and indeed crime, a new generation rises and forgets, as Turgenev always likes to show when the present grows out of the past. Human life is short.

There is little of love in this tale, but one notices Turgenev's skill in suggesting there has been an act of sexual love. The boy comes across Sletkin and Evlampia in the woods.

[Sletkin] was lying on his back with both hands under his head and with a smile of contentment gazing upwards at the sky, swinging his left leg which was crossed over his right knee. . . A few yards from him Evlampia was walking up and down the little glade, with downcast eyes. It seemed as though she were looking for something in the grass, mushrooms perhaps: now and then she stretched out her hand. She was singing in a low voice. An old ballad.

> Hither, hither threatening storm cloud
> Slay for me the father-in-law
> Strike for me the mother-in-law
> The young wife I will kill myself.

Louder and louder she sings while Sletkin laughs to himself while she moves round and round him.

'The things that come into some people's heads,' Sletkin said.
'What?' said Evlampia.
'What were those words you were singing?'
'You can't leave the words out of a song,' said Evlampia.

And then they see the boy, cry out, and rush away in opposite directions.

The scene tells us all, even to the fierceness of an act of lust and what hidden fantasies it releases in the mind.

'A Lear of the Steppe' is, no doubt, a drama seen from the outside, but it shows Turgenev's mature power of suggesting the inside of his people and of concealing its documentation. The kind of documentation that obtrudes, say, in Zola's *La Terre*, or indeed in most stories of peasant life done by writers who are not peasants, is mercifully absent. In the manner of the greatest artists, he contrives to make us feel that people should be seen as justifying themselves.

The choice of a growing boy as the narrator, with some character of his own, makes this possible and evades the smoothing-over effect of hearsay.

(1977)

A Viennese

Robert Musil's *The Man Without Qualities* is an immense unfinished novel, which this Czech-Austrian began writing in the Twenties and was still working on when he died an exile in Geneva in 1942. It is a wonderful and prolonged firework display, a well-peopled comedy of ideas, on the one hand; on the other, an infiltration into the base areas of what we call 'the contemporary predicament'. There is the pleasure of a cleverness which is not stupid about life: 'Even mistrust of oneself and one's destiny here assumed the character of profound self-certainty,' Musil wrote – not altogether ironically – of the Austrian character and these words suggest the conflict which keeps the book going at its cracking speed. Of course, Musil's kind of egoism had a long run in the first twenty years of the century and he has been – the translators tell us – written down by the standard German literary histories. Musil's tongue does indeed run away with him; but it is stupid to denigrate him. Proust and Joyce, with whom he has been exaggeratedly compared, approached the self by way of the aesthetic imagination; Musil reconstructs egos intellectually. What ideas do our sensations suggest? What processes are we involved in? If Musil has come to us regrettably late, if he sticks for his subject matter to the old pre-1914 Vienna and has some of that period flavour, he is not stranded there. The revival of Henry James has taught us that writers who live passively within history may be more deeply aware of what is really going on than those who turn up in every spot where the news is breaking.

The nearest parallel to Musil is not Proust but Italo Svevo in *The Confessions of Zeno*. Musil is very much an intellectual of that strain. The two writers represent opposite sides of the same Viennese school. They are restless, headlong psychologists and sceptical talkers, to some extent café writers. Like Zeno, the Ulrich of *The*

Man Without Qualities is a gifted and self-consuming man. He burns up his experience. But whereas Zeno is a hypochondriac, a man of endless self-doubt, the clown of the imagination and the heart, whose great comic effect is obtained by the pursuit of folly with passionate seriousness, Ulrich is a healthy, athletic extroverted and worldly character whose inquiring brain captivates and disturbs men of action. He is a mind before he is a sensibility. He has only to appear for others to behave absurdly; his irony muddles them; his perception alarms. Musil's achievement is to make this formidable character tolerable and engaging. Ulrich is endlessly, perhaps pitilessly patient; he has learned that humility of the intellect which comes of continuous use and which is necessary to those who look into other people for what may be useful to their own imaginative and intellectual search. Like Zeno he can never resist a theory; but whereas Zeno's love for other people is really a kind of remorse for having had so many ideas about himself, the love of Ulrich is a feeling of gratitude to others for suggesting so many ideas that he becomes free of them personally. His attraction and power come from an imagination which transposes. Here is a comment on one of his comic characters, a cabaret singer, a Juno of refinement who has a passion for eating. After a good meal she would feel obliged to repay her lover:

She would stand up and tranquilly, but full throatedly, lift up her voice in song. For her protector such evenings were like pages torn out of an album, animated by all sorts of inspirations and ideas, but mummified, as everything becomes when it is torn out of its context, loaded with the tyrannical spell of all that will now remain eternally the way it is, the thing that is the uncanny fascination of *tableaux vivants* when it is as though life had suddenly been given a sleeping draught; and now there it stands, rigid, perfectly correlated within it itself, clearly outlined in its immense futility against the background of the world.

One can see, after this, why Musil has been compared with Proust – though, if the translation is to be relied upon, he does not write as well – yet, where Proust seeks to crystallise a past, Musil is always pushing through that strange undergrowth to find out, if possible, where he is, where life is tending, and what is the explanation. His book is a crab-wise search for a future, for what has not yet been given the sleeping draught.

In the first half of Part One of the novel the time and scene are the Vienna of the Austrian Empire. The main episodes are Ulrich's love affairs with the guzzling singer and with a rueful nymphomaniac; his friendship with a gifted but unstable girl and with a superb bourgeois lady, notorious for mind, whom he calls Diotima, and who goes in for the True, the Good, the Beautiful on the grand scale. Diotima is a monument, an outsize schoolgirl. But the larger themes are political and social. Before long we have, by brilliant implication, an amusing but moving picture of a complete society whose intentions become nobler the nearer it is to destruction. Nobler and more absurd. For Musil has invented a wonderful farce called the Collateral Campaign. This vague political movement is meant somehow and simultaneously to celebrate the Emperor's birthday, boost Austrian culture – with a meaning glance at the Germans – preserve the stagnant existing order and yet arise spontaneously from the hearts of the common people and bring new spiritual life to the greatest minds desiccated by scepticism, intellectualism, etc. In short it is an all-purpose piece of uplift which is touchingly sincere and hopelessly muddled. It is very fond of the word 'true' – not patriotism but 'true' patriotism, not values but 'true' values. The comic beauty of the Collateral Campaign is that it can never settle on its precise form; it swells into committees, exhausts all the clichés, and turns into its opposite: a movement for chauvinism and rearmament. Really it is a midwife of Fascism. Nothing is more certain of comic reward than Musil's sympathy. It is tender and deadly.

The people of the Collateral Campaign are 'good'. They are responsible. They represent 'the best elements'. They can choose. They choose ridiculously. But what of the bad, the irresponsible who cannot choose – a man like the homicidal maniac Moosbrugger who may or may not be executed? (He wants to be executed because he has an almost pettifogging regard for the law.) The Moosbrugger case puts its shadow on all the characters in the book and one of Musil's feats as a novelist is to show us exactly how Moosbrugger seeps into every mind in some way or other. If society is tending towards progress what is it going to do about this Caliban? Ulrich reflects; 'If mankind could dream collectively it would dream Moosbrugger.' If we do not know by what absolute standards to settle the Moosbrugger case, then a great social catastrophe is inevitable. Writing in the 'twenties Musil could hardly have been more prophetic.

There is an interesting account of Musil's life in the very good introduction to the Wilkins and Kaiser translation of his novel. He came, we are told, of a gifted family. He was educated for the Army, fought in the 1914 war, became a civil engineer, a distinguished inventor, a mathematician, a psychologist, and was about to teach philosophy at Munich before he turned to writing. Musil brought to his writing not only the capacity for seeing but also the habit of hypothesis. Ulrich is, in many ways, Musil translated. In his several attempts to define what he means by 'the man without qualities', he notes,

He will perform actions that mean something different to him from what they mean to others, but is reassured about everything as soon as it can be summed up in an extraordinary idea.

Or again, the translators give us these lines from the page he was adding to the last volume of his novel on the day he died:

Of course it was clear to him that the two kinds of human being . . . could mean nothing else than a man without qualities and, in contrast, the man with all the qualities that anyone could manage to display. And the one might be called a nihilist, dreaming of God's dreams – in contrast to the activist who is, however, with his impatient way of acting, a kind of God's dreamer too, and anything but a realist, who goes about being worldly clear and worldly active.

Consciousness was Musil's real subject, not the 'stream' but the architecture, the process of building, stylising and demolishing that goes on in the mind. How does an idea like the Collateral Campaign grow in various minds? How, sensuously, does it breed? At what point does sensation become idea? How does reality look after that intoxication? These things bring out Musil's alacrity and focusing power as a novelist; for though he never stops talking he always enacts what he sees. He has a poetic yet practical ability for showing an idea coming to someone – a slow-minded and simple aristocrat, a blackamoor servant, a woman beginning to feel indignation and remorse in love, any transition in fact from one state of consciousness to another. He has the merit of loving people for their essence. There is, to take one example, a striking study of that special bourgeois protégé, the failed artist who takes to blaming his failure on the collapse of culture. From a hero he has turned into a petty domestic tyrant and rules his wife, who has ceased to love him, by making her play duets on the piano. Their marriage is sustained by a neurotic frenzy of piano-playing:

The next moment Clarisse and Walter shot away like two railway engines racing side by side. The music that they were playing came flying towards their eyes like the glittering rails, then vanished under the thundering engine

and spread out behind them, as a chiming, resonant, miraculously permanent landscape. . . . Precise to a fraction of a second, gaiety, sadness, anger,
fear, love and hatred, longing and weariness went flying through Walter and
Clarisse. It was a union like in a great panic. But it was not the same
mindless, overwhelming force that life has. . . .

The more music sublimely unites them, the more they are separated
in life, each thinking his way away from the other. Walter, the
rejected husband, fearing failure and impotence, begins to slip into
thoughts comfortably too large for him, and ends by playing Wagner
for erotic reassurance. Here he begins to strike wrong notes. Clarisse's mind jumps from image to image and to questions becoming
more and more savage: does civilised life yearn for brutality? Does
peacefulness call for cruelty? For there is an empty room in Clarisse
where 'something tore at the chains'. At the end of this volume we get
a glimpse of that empty room.

In making raids into Musil's novel one risks either making it sound
thin or melodramatic in the heavy Central European way; a pound of
realism to a ton of essay-writing. He is, on the contrary, subtle, light,
liquid, serious. He is, no doubt, a bit over-fond of himself, perhaps a
bit too tolerant to the 'I' who is never brought up against anything
stronger than itself; a bit too much on the spot, especially in the love
affairs. What the novel does show is that the habit of intellectual
analysis is not stultifying to drama, movement or invention, but
enhances them. It is a delightful insight that a movement like the
Collateral Campaign, which has no distinctive idea, will inevitably
attract all those people in the Austrian Empire who have only one
idea; it is perfect that Ulrich shall be put in charge of sorting out these
cranks. His theories, the whole apparatus of the book, are the
forgiveness of the artist, not the examination papers of the master.
Consciousness is, for him, a pardonable folly. Some critics have
discerned what they believe to be a mythological foundation to this
novel, in the manner of *Ulysses*; the density, suggestiveness and
range could support the view. For it is cunningly engineered. The
second volume of *The Man Without Qualities* sustains the
impression of a major writer of comedy in the Viennese manner, and
of an original imagination.

A French friend of Musil's, M. Bernard Guillemin, suggests that
what Musil meant by 'a man without qualities' (*Mann ohne Eigen-
schaften*) was 'a man completely disengaged and uncommitted or a
man in quest of non-accidental attributes and responsibilities self-

chosen – the German counterpart of Gide's *"homme disponible"* though there is nothing of Gide in Musil's work'. In the later volumes, it is said to have worried Musil himself that a character as disengaged as Ulrich is will eventually become isolated and by-passed by life. The sense of adventure which exhilarates the early volumes becomes paralysed in the later ones, where the intellectually liberated man is not able to take the next step into 'right action'. It is significant that Musil's novel was never finished. He had spun a brilliant web of perceptions round himself and was imprisoned by them.

In this second volume, the absurd Collateral Campaign is still going on in Austria, Diotima, the lofty-minded Egeria, who runs the social side, discovers the 'soul' just as she is getting tired of her husband, a high government official. She has risen out of the middle classes into aristocratic society, and she plants this idea of the soul in an international financier and arms manufacturer, a German called Arnheim. There are Generals who come in because 'the Army must keep an eye on things'; Diotima's social rivals appear to keep an eye on her, and so on. There is a wonderfully complete picture of a society at the edge of the precipice of 1914. The novelist's comic sense of character is speculative, and is strengthened by his pen-etration into the kinds of consciousness current at the time, into how private ideas become public, and public ideas affect the emotions of private life.

In the meantime, the Moosbrugger case – Moosbrugger is the homicidal sex maniac awaiting execution – underlies the social picture and makes its own disturbing footnotes. What about the law's attitude to insanity in murder; what about violence in the state, in personal life? At the most unexpected moments, Moosbrugger – who is merely a name in the papers to most of the characters – raises his idiot head and poses his devastating questions. 'Ordinary life,' Ulrich concludes, 'is an intermediate state made up of all our possible crimes.' So Musil dresses a platitude in epigrammatic form; he becomes rather free with epigrams; but his gift is to enact epigrams imaginatively.

In this volume the analysis of character is done at much greater length than in the introductory volume and so there is more discus-sion and less action. Of the portraits, Arnheim's and the absurd yet subtle General's are the most impressive, but we must not omit the girl Gerda and her lover who are moving towards an early form of

Fascism. Musil's Arnheim is by far the most cogent and exhaustive study of a millionaire magnate's mind that I have ever read. The irony is exact and continuous. Arnheim, for example, had 'the gift of being a paragon':

Through his understanding of this delicate interlocking of all forms of life, which only the blind arrogance of the ideologist can forget, Arnheim came to see the prince of commerce as the synthesis of revolution and permanence, of armed power and bourgeois civilisation, of reasoned audacity and honest to goodness knowledge, but essentially as a symbolic prefiguration of the kind of democracy that was about to come into existence . . . he hoped to meet the new age half-way.

Under the influence of his love for Diotima, Arnheim seeks to bring about the 'fusion of interests between Business and the Soul'. His craving for power leads him to writing books: 'with positively spectral prolixity' his pen began to pour out reflections on 'the need of this fusion' and 'it is equally certain that his ambition to master all there was to be known . . . found in the soul a means of devaluing everything that his intellect could not master'. Arnheim is morally devastated by his love for Diotima, for she is monumentally high-minded; and Musil has the pleasure of showing us a sumptuous, high-minded *femme du monde* reduced to the frantic condition of a woman forced to the bed of a testy, cynical husband, and a magnate paradoxically reverting to his native instincts the more his 'soul' is elevated. All roads leave from the soul, Musil reflects, but none lead back to it: Arnheim is no more than a magnate after all and, once Diotima can be his, he falls back on the old maxim that in love, as in business, one had better spend only the interest, not the capital. Arnheim's character reminds one of Walter Bagehot's dictum that a kind of intellectual twilight, with all its vagueness, is necessary to the man of business and, towards the end of this volume, Musil reveals what Arnheim is really after in the ideological mists of the Collateral Campaign and the higher life of Diotima: he is after control of the Galician oilfields.

Ulrich, the man without qualities, is the natural enemy of Arnheim; his natural foil is the comic General. An air of unworldliness in civilian life is an obligatory mask of the military profession; all 'a poor soldier man' may permit himself to point out is that, if the military have a virtue, it is their sense of order. There is a farcical scene of discussion when this soldier describes his visit to the National Library where he approaches the whole task of improving his mind in the spirit of the strategist. The General is a wit in his way. Even after a carefully worked-out campaign of reading, in which he allows for substantial casualties, he discovers it will still take him 10,000 years to read what is necessary. 'There must be something wrong about that,' he says, raising his glass of brandy.

Musil writes with the heightened sensibility of a man in love; that is to say, under the influence of the unrest of seeking a harmony and completion in things. The Collateral Campaign itself is a kind of communal love affair. In the description of love affairs and especially in the portraits of women in love, Musil is truly original; in managing scenes of physical love, he has not been approached by any writer of the last fifty years. What has been missing, in those accounts, has been Musil's transcendent subject: the sense of the changing architecture of consciousness. He brings the effect of the imagination into the fears and desires of these women, their sense of living out an idea which may indeed well be a love fantasy about quite a different lover from the one in whose bed they lie. He is sensitive to the power of 'erotic distraction'. Of Rachel, the maid who goes to bed with a fellow servant because she has been stirred by the touch of a guest's hand, he writes:

The object of this yearning was actually Ulrich, and Solimon was cast in the role of the man whom one does not love and to whom one will nevertheless abandon oneself – a point on which Rachel was in no sort of doubt whatsoever. For the fact that she was not allowed to be with him, that for some time past they had hardly ever spoken to each other except in a whisper, and that the displeasure of those in authority over them had descended upon them both, had much the effect on her as a night full of uncertainty, uncanny happenings, and sighs has on anyone in love; it all concentrated her smouldering fancies like a burning glass, the beam of which is felt less as an agreeable warmth than as something one will not be able to stand much longer.

The high-minded love affair, the violently neurotic, the absurd one, the desperate affair carried on against the will, the one crossed by other lives; from all these Musil extracts the essence with dignity and gaiety, the comi-tragedy of human loss and incompleteness. The history of love is the history of absence, of arrival and departure. He is able to do what no contemporary ever does: to move from the imaginative and emotional to the physical without change of voice; even the naked fight on the bed or the brazen or terrified undressings are not marred by the worst fault of our erotic realism: its unconscious grotesque. The tenderness, subtlety and disinterestedness of Musil's intelligence enable him to do this; and the almost conversational style. Critics tell us that, whatever the awkwardness of translation may be, he has in German a style that is as lucid as that of Anatole France and less florid than Proust's. One cannot judge this, though the translation of the second volume seems to me an improvement on the first. (The whole difficulty has been to avoid translating German abstractions into the kind of technical or administrative super-jargon which these become in English.) Musil is an addiction. The most irrelevant criticism made of him by some Germans and Austrians is that his kind of café sensibility is out of date. It may certainly be familiar in Schnitzler and Svevo, but Musil's whole scheme prophetically describes the bureaucratic condition of our world, and what can only be called the awful, deadly serious and self-deceptive love affair of one committee for another. And he detects the violence underneath it all. In only one sense is he out of date: he can conceive of a future, of civilised consciousness flowing on and not turning back sick and doomed upon itself.

(1962)

ALESSANDRO MANZONI

I Promessi Sposi

I Promessi Sposi (in English, *The Betrothed*) is often said to be 'the only Italian novel'. It is certainly the only Italian novel that can be compared with the great European novels of the nineteenth century. It was begun in 1821 when Scott dominated European taste and when Balzac had not emerged from the writing of shockers, and it was revised many times before the final edition of 1840. The last rewriting is said to have taken twelve years and the result is that we have a compendious Romantic work in a state of real digestibility which neither Balzac nor Scott troubled to attain. *The Betrothed* was Manzoni's only novel. It contained the fullness of his mind, his sensibility and creative power and (as Mr Colquhoun, a new translator, says in a very informative preface to a new edition) seems to represent the culmination of an experience to which life could add no more. In Italy this novel is a kind of Bible; long passages are known by heart; its reflections are quoted in the political debates that have taken place in Italy since the war. But in England, possibly because the chief translation was done over a hundred years ago – and not very well, by a clergyman who disapproved of its theology – the book has been but mildly regarded. The English had already the novels of Scott, with their energetic romance, their bourgeois valuation of life, their alternating choice of the highly coloured and the domestic. Scott was a Tory and, though a generous man, he drew in his horns before the outcome of the Enlightenment, whereas Manzoni had exposed his mind to it in his youth. Our critical ancestors preferred a safer, unreal Italy and, later on, the libertarian, anti-clerical Italy of the Risorgimento. Among the mass of Victorian readers we must remember those who were drawn towards Manzoni by the Oxford movement; but in matters of piety the critics seem to have preferred their own Protestant vigour and sentiment to Manzoni's obedient, passive, Catholic gravity, and it is a good indication of Victorian feeling that the clergyman who translated Manzoni said that he wished the name of Christ could be substituted for that of the Virgin throughout.

Manzoni's reformed Catholicism – that old desire to do without the Jesuits and the temporal power – is a greater obstacle to Protestants, one often suspects, than the ultramontane. Manzoni's religion is, in tendency, liberal and democratic, but it is also melancholy and pessimistic. In *The Betrothed* our ancestors would miss what they so much admired in the English novel – the high-minded woodenness of the exemplary characters. The chief victims of tyranny and evil in the story – the two peasant lovers who are forcibly separated by the lawless Don Rodrigo – are passive sufferers who do little to help themselves and are, in fact, finally rescued not by their own efforts but through the aid of a remarkable priest and the sudden conversion of the chief villain. There is no Protestant suggestion of an aggressive worth or a self-reliance that depends on direct access to God; on the contrary there is an ironical recognition of the hapless drama of Fate and of the painful need for selfless love. It is true that the wicked are destroyed by the plague which comes to Milan at the end of the book – this is a magnificent episode – and that the good lovers are quietly rewarded; but the lasting impressions are not of righteous success but of inexplicable luck – the luck in catching the mysterious eye of the Almighty. One is reading a benign, spacious and melancholy fable of the most tender moral sensibility, an epic of understatement; whereas the English novelist of the nineteenth century – and the eighteenth century, too – commonly provided his readers with a number of obvious statues to socially estimable Virtue and the reader admired them because he hoped, if only in his own eyes, to become a statue himself.

Changed times and a translation which is closer to our idiom make *The Betrothed* immediately sympathetic to the contemporary reader, once he allows for old-fashioned methods of narration and apostrophe. We turn with recognition to other times of chaos, as Manzoni himself transposed the upheaval of the French revolution into the material of the religious wars of the seventeenth century. Manzoni is the novelist of those who expose themselves but cannot take sides. They belong, where humanity abides, to the spiritual third force. His personal history was of the kind that makes the psychologist, the man whose thought and feeling are finely meshed; an aristocrat, a Voltairian and militant anti-Catholic, he married a

Protestant woman and was reconverted by the Capucines to a profound if ambiguous faith. He writes with the gentleness, the irony, the anxiety and love of one who has passed through a deep personal crisis. His texture is rich, his variety is great; we enter a world of innumerable meanings and contrasts. Beside the account of the plague, which recalls the curious realistic precision of Defoe, must be put very different things, like an abduction to a brigand's castle or a flight to a convent. In contrast again with these, there are comic scenes like the famous one where the peasant lovers try to trick the timid priest into marrying them, which is at the height of Italian buffoonery; the portraits of politicians have the flowering malice of Proust; the historical reflections are wise, subtle and dyed with experience, and in every episode there are psychological perceptions that have the fineness of the French novelists without their often wounding vanity in their own effects. Manzoni was devoid of the intellectual's self-admiration. His grave manner removes the sickliness from piety and restores to it the strength of nature.

I will quote two examples of Manzoni's kind of perception to which the reader of Proust will at once respond.

One is taken from the colloquy between the neurotic and tragic nun and the peasant girl who has found sanctuary with her.

[The peasant] also tried to avoid replying to Gertrude's inquisitive questions about her story before her engagement. But here the reason was not prudence. It was because to the poor innocent girl this story seemed a thornier and more difficult one to describe than anything which she had heard or thought she was likely to hear from the Signora. Those dealt with tyranny, treachery and suffering – ugly, painful things, yet things which could be expressed but hers was pervaded by a feeling, a word, which she felt she could not possibly pronounce, and for which she would never be able to find a substitute that would not seem shameless – the word love.

Put this beside a very different situation, an innkeeper putting his drunken guest to bed. He covers the snoring drunk and

Then, drawn by the kind of attraction that sometimes makes us regard an object of our dislike as attentively as an object of our love, and which is only the desire to know what it is that affects our sensibility so strongly, he paused a moment to gaze at this irksome guest, raising the lamp over his face, and shading it with his hand so that the light fell on him, almost in the attitude in which Psyche was painted as she gazed stealthily at the features of her unknown spouse.

In all the meetings of his characters, in the strong situations and in the neutral, there is this watchful, instinctive, animal awareness of the other person, a seeking of the meaning of their relationship. To compare the innkeeper to a spouse is not grotesque: the drunk man has already involved the innkeeper with the secret police, there is the marriage of two fears. Fear and love are, in fact, Manzoni's subjects.

The story of *The Betrothed* is a strong one. The hired bravoes hold up the cowardly priest. There is murder on the road. There are bread riots in Milan – Manzoni is an excellent narrative writer unencumbered by picturesque baggage – there are flights and pursuits, tremendous confrontations of the tyrannous and the good. The immunity of the priests gives them boldness. There are political intrigue, invasion and looting by foreign armies, the plague. Manzoni is as brilliant as a diplomat in recomplicating the moral issues; the brigand's sudden conversion, for example, frees the girl from her dangers and seems to guarantee her happiness but, perversely and in her terror, she now vows herself to the Virgin! To the obstacle of wickedness is added the obstacle of faith. That delicate tangle of faith and desire and pride has to be undone. The characters are not thrown on in crude, romantic strokes but are put together precisely by a writer who has understood their pattern and the point at which they will behave unexpectedly or feel the insinuations of time, fate and mood. There is not a stock character anywhere; nor can a too gifted author be seen bursting through these figures. The skill in the change of mood or in anticlimax is wonderful.

When Manzoni described how the notion of writing *The Betrothed* came to him – I quote from Mr Colquhoun – he said:

The memoirs of that period [the Counter Reformation] show a very extraordinary state of society; the most arbitrary government combined with feudal and popular anarchy; legislation that is amazing in the way it exposes a profound, ferocious, pretentious ignorance; classes with opposed interests and maxims; some little-known anecdotes, preserved in trustworthy documents; finally a plague which gives full rein to the most consummate and shameful excesses, to the most absurd prejudices, and to the most touching virtues.

With this stuff he did fill his book. The contemporary reader must reflect that this is exactly the kind of material which has, in our time, become degenerate in the novel. The great, even the extensive subjects, have fallen into inferior hands. They have become the fodder of the middlebrow novelist. Is it really true that this kind of material can no longer attract the best minds in the novel? Has it exhausted itself? Clearly Manzoni, like Scott and Balzac, had the excitement of doing something new and they had the tremendous intellectual and emotional force of the Romantic movement behind them. But they were more than capable inventors, copyists, historians or story-tellers who comfortably relied on a commonly accepted language and values. Indeed, although it is generally said that our lack of these common symbols is the central difficulty for contemporary artists, I wonder whether Manzoni's situation was as different from ours as it seems to be. He is a singular example of the artist, who, finding no common basis for himself and a disjointed society, sets laboriously to make one. His religion was uncharacteristic for a man of advanced ideas; as far as its elusive quality can be discerned, it seems to have connected the ideas of Pascal with those of liberalism and this profound change of spirit led him to seek an equally important change of language. He wished to find a language in which all men communicate with one another and to abandon literary language. Problems of belief raise at once problems of style: in both Manzoni was revolutionary. His case somewhat resembles Tolstoy's though, with Manzoni, conversion was not a mutilation of the artist but his fulfilment. He succeeded (where the English Protestant novelists on the whole failed) in creating characters who were positively good yet his 'message' that love above all, self-sacrifice, courage, long-suffering and charity are the only, and not necessarily successful answers to tyranny and injustice, is not introduced as a sort of pious starch into the narrative, but is native to it. One is undermined rather than incited by this teaching, as in one or two of the Russian writers; and the very pessimism of Manzoni, by which he continually moves the rewards of the righteous just a little beyond their fingertips with a gentle scepticism, is like that of Cervantes.

(1951)

LIST OF BOOKS

Books referred to

LAURENCE STERNE
Four Portraits by Peter Quennell.

LORD BYRON
A Heart For Every Fate by Leslie A. Marchand.

GEORGE CRUIKSHANK
Graphic Works of George Cruikshank selected and with an introduction and notes by Richard A. Vogler.

R. S. SURTEES
Horses, Hounds and Humans by Aubrey Noakes.

CHARLES DICKENS
Oliver Twist. Introduction by Graham Greene.

LEWIS CARROLL
Letters selected by Professor Morton N. Cohen.

ANTHONY TROLLOPE
Anthony Trollope by A. O. J. Cockshut.

FORD MADOX FORD
Ford Madox Ford by Richard Cassell.
Ford Madox Ford's Novels by John Meixner.
Novelist of Three Worlds by Paul Wiley.

VIRGINIA WOOLF
The Letters of Virginia Woolf: Vol. V, 1936–41 edited by Nigel Nicolson and Joanne Trautmann.
The Diary of Virginia Woolf: Vol. III, 1925–1930 edited by Anne Oliver Bell and Andrew McNeillie.

MAX BEERBOHM
Max: Sir Max Beerbohm by Lord David Cecil.
A Peep into the Past. Introduction by Rupert Hart-Davis.
The Lies of Art: Max Beerbohm's Parody and Caricature by John Felstiner.

JOSEPH CONRAD
Conrad: A Reassessment by Douglas Hewitt.

CYRIL CONNOLLY
Cyril Connolly: Journal and Memoir by David Pryce-Jones.
The Selected Essays of Cyril Connolly edited by Peter Quennell.
Enemies of Promise by Cyril Connolly.
The Unquiet Grave: A Word Cycle by Palinurus (Cyril Connolly).
The Rock Pool by Cyril Connolly.

HENRY JAMES
Letters edited by Leon Edel.

S. J. PERELMAN
The Most of S. J. Perelman by Dorothy Parker.

GEORGE SAND
George Sand: A Biography by Curtis Cate.
Mauprat. Introduction by Diane Johnson.
Lelia translated and with an introduction by Maria Espinosa.
The Companion of the Tour of France translated by Francis George Shaw.
The Haunted Pool translated by Frank Hunter Potter.

BENJAMIN CONSTANT
Adolphe edited by Gustave Rudler.
Le Cahier Rouge

STENDHAL
A Lion for Love: A Critical Biography of Stendhal by Robert Alter, in collaboration with Carol Cosman.

MARCEL PROUST
Marcel Proust: Selected Letters (1880–1903) edited by Philip Kolb, translated by Ralph Manheim, with an introduction by J. M. Cocking.

ALBERT CAMUS
Camus by Patrick McCarthy.

CAMILLE PISSARRO
A Catalogue of the Drawings in the Ashmolean Museum, Oxford by Richard Brettell and Christopher Lloyd.
Pissarro: His Life and Work by Ralph E. Shikes and Paula Harper.

FRANCISCO JOSÉ DE GOYA
Goya in the Democratic Tradition by Francis Klingender.
Goya: The Origins of the Modern Temper in Art by Fred Licht.

VLADIMIR NABOKOV
Lectures on Don Quixote edited by Fredson Bowers, with a preface by Reynolds Price and an introduction by Guy Davenport.

EÇA DE QUEIROZ
The Mandarin and Other Stories translated by Richard Franko Goldman.
The City and the Mountains translated by Roy Campbell.
The Illustrious House of Ramires translated by Ann Stevens.

MACHADO DE ASSIS
The Psychiatrist translated by William Grossman and Helen Caldwell.
Epitaph for a Small Winner translated by William Grossman.
Dom Casmurro translated by Helen Caldwell.
Esau and Jacob translated by Helen Caldwell.

ALEXANDER PUSHKIN
Pushkin: A Comparative Commentary by John Bayley.
Alexander Pushkin: Complete Prose Fiction edited and translated by Paul Debreczeny.
The Other Pushkin by Paul Debreczeny.

MIKHAIL YUREVICH LERMONTOV
A Hero of Our Time translated by Eden and Cedar Paul.

FYODOR DOSTOEVSKY
Dostoevsky: Reminiscences by Anna Dostoevsky. Translated and edited by Beatrice Stillman, with an introduction by Helen Muchnic.

ALESSANDRO MANZONI
I Promessi Sposi translated and with an introduction by Archibald Colquhoun.